First published in 1989 by
Hansib Publishing Limited,
139/149 Fonthill Road,
London N4 3HF, England.
Tel: 01-281 1191. Fax: 01-263 9656.

Copyright © Hansib Publishing, 1989.

Design: Hansib Publishing Limited
Typesetting and Origination:
Desktop Graphics Ltd. London, England.
Printing: Hazell Watson & Viney Ltd.
Aylesbury, England.

*Pages 1 to 40 and 81 to 120 are unhindered
views of the Commonwealth of Dominica ten
years after Hurricane David.*

ISBN 1-870518-17-9

DOMINICA

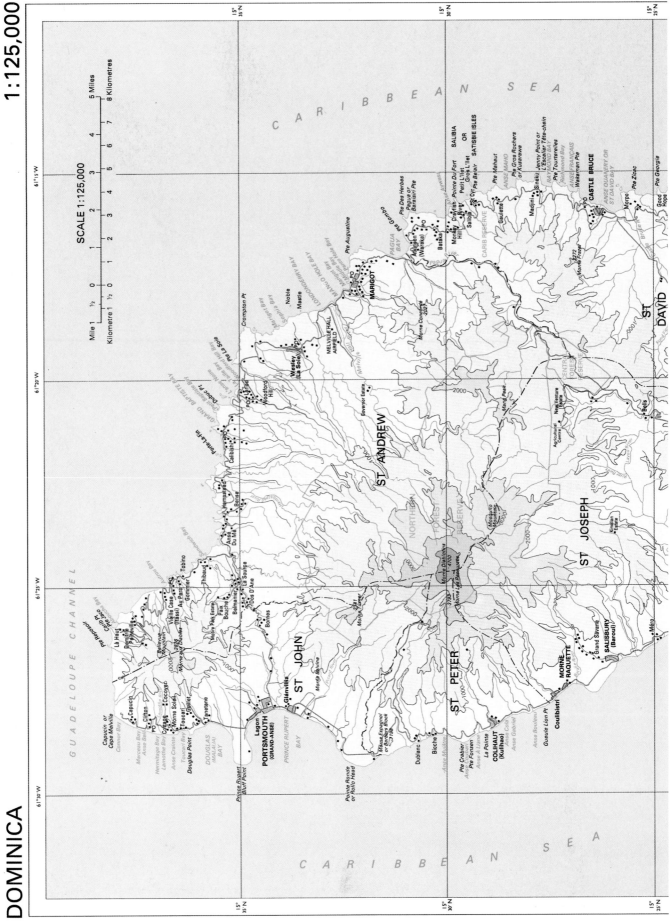

1:125,000

SCALE 1:125,000

Mile 1 ½ 0   1   2   3   4   5 Miles
Kilometre 1 ½ 0 1 2 3 4 5 6 7 8 Kilometres

CARIBBEAN SEA

GUADELOUPE CHANNEL

ST JOHN

ST PETER

ST JOSEPH

ST ANDREW

ST DAVID

Capucin or Cape Melville
Prince Rupert Bluff Point
PORTSMOUTH (GRAND-ANSE)
Glanvilia
MORNE RAQUETTE
SALISBURY (Barouli)
COLIHAUT (Kulihao)
Coulibistri
MARIGOT
MELVILLE HALL AIRFIELD
Wesley (La Soie)
Woodford Hill
CASTLE BRUCE
SALIBIA
SATISBIE ISLES
Portsmouth

CARIBBEAN SEA

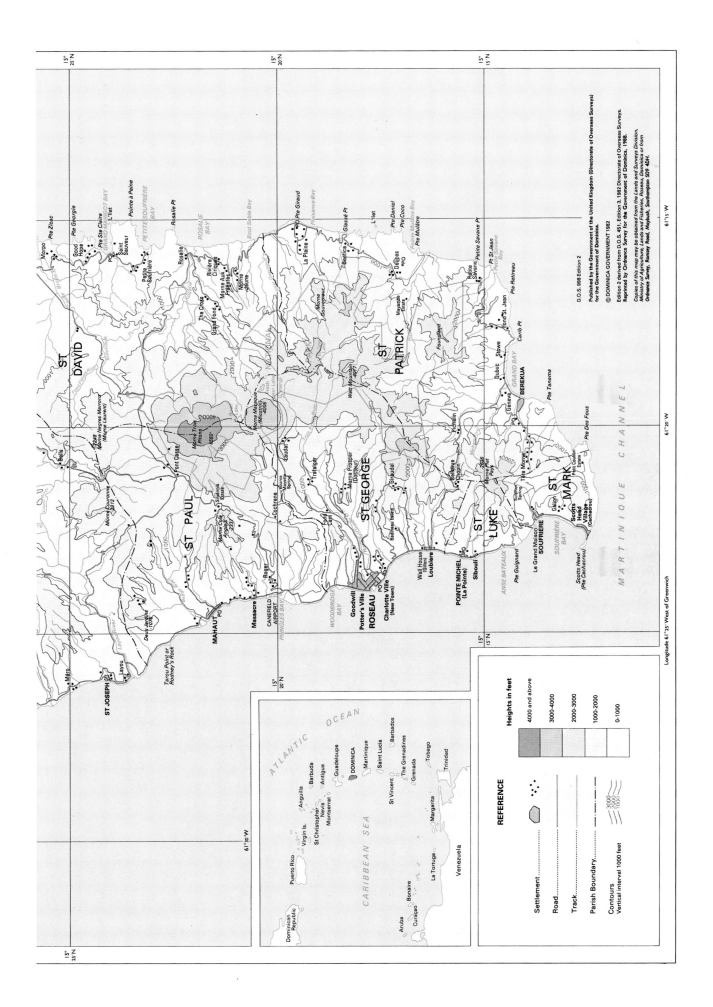

15°
25'N

15°
25'N

15°
20'N

15°
15'N

ST DAVID

ST PAUL

ST JOSEPH

Morpo
Pte Zicac
Pte Georgia
Pte Sta Claire
L'Ilet
Pointe à Paine
GRAND MARIGOT BAY
PETITE SOUFRIÈRE BAY
Good Hope
Saint Sauveur
Petite Soufrière
Rosalie Pt
Rosalie
ROSALIE BAY
Bout Sable Bay

The Cross
Grand Fond
Morne Aux Frégates
Rivière Cyrique
Morne Jaune
La Plaine
Pte Giraud
Puisance Bay
Bagatelle
Glassé Pt
L'Ilet
Petite Soufrière Bay
Pte Daniel
Pte Coco
Pte Mulâtre

2000'
Morne Macaque 4006
Morne Trois Pitons 4550'
4000'
Morne Diablotin (Micotrin) 4097'
Fresh Water Lake

Boeri Lake

Belles
2248 Morne Negres Marront (Morne Laurent)
Morne Couronne 2812
Deux Branch
Pont Cassé

Silvania Estate
Morne Côté Aguilus 2337'
Cochrane
Trafalgar
Laudat
Morne Prosper (Doctout)

Morne Sauveraux

Watt Mountain 4097'

ST PATRICK

Dubuc
Stowe
FondSt Jean
Carib Pt
Pte Retreau
Petite Savane Pt
Petite Savane Bay
Pt St Jean
Petite Savane
Rosalie
Mayabbe Estate

Morne Prosper (Doctout)
Morne Couronne
Girardel
Badineau Estate
Bellevue Chopin
Pichelin
Founapard
Geneva
BEREKUA
GRAND BAY
Pte Tanama
Pte Des Fous

ST GEORGE

ST LUKE

ST MARK

SOUFRIÈRE

MARTINIQUE CHANNEL

2356 Morne Fout Parts
Galion
Scotts Head Village
Sulphur Spring
Petit Coulibri Estate
Le Grand Maison
Pte Guignard
ANSE BATEAUX
SOUFRIÈRE BAY
Scotts Head (Pte Cachacrou)

Morpo
Méro
Lavou
Tarou Point or Rodney's Rock
Layou River
Deux Island 1072'
Layou

MAHAUT PO
Massacre
CANEFIELD AIRPORT
PRINGLES BAY
Rogir
WOODBRIDGE BAY
Goodwill
Potter's Ville
ROSEAU
Charlotte Ville (New Town)
Wall House
Loubiere
POINTE MICHEL (La Pointe)
Sibouli

NATIONAL

1000'
2000'
3000'
1000'

Longitude 61°25' West of Greenwich

61°30'W

61°20'W

61°15'W

15°
20'N

15°
15'N

ATLANTIC OCEAN

Dominican Republic
Puerto Rico
Virgin Is.
Anguilla
St Christopher
Nevis
Montserrat
Barbuda
Antigua
Guadeloupe
DOMINICA
Martinique
Saint Lucia
Barbados
St Vincent
The Grenadines
Tobago
Grenada
Trinidad
Margarita
La Tortuga
Bonaire
Aruba
Curaçao
Venezuela

CARIBBEAN SEA

REFERENCE

Settlement	⋰⋰
Road	
Track	
Parish Boundary	
Contours Vertical interval 1000 feet	3000 2000 1000

Heights in feet

	4000 and above
	3000-4000
	2000-3000
	1000-2000
	0-1000

D.O.S. 998 Edition 2

© DOMINICA GOVERNMENT 1982

Edition 2 derived from D.O.S. 451, Edition 3, 1982 Directorate of Overseas Surveys.
Published by the Government of the United Kingdom (Directorate of Overseas Surveys)
for the Government of Dominica.
Reprinted by Ordnance Survey for the Government of Dominica, 1988.

Copies of this map may be obtained from the Lands and Surveys Division,
Ministry of Agriculture, Lands and Fisheries, Roseau, Dominica or from
Ordnance Survey, Romsey Road, Maybush, Southampton SO9 4DH.

OFFICE OF THE PRIME MINISTER
CABINET SECRETARIAT

GOVERNMENT HEADQUARTERS.
ROSEAU.
COMMONWEALTH OF DOMINICA.
WEST INDIES.

Telegrams: External, Dominica,
Telex 613 EXT. DO
Reference: P.

WELCOME TO OUR NATURE ISLAND

A Message from the Prime Minister

This book on our nature island of the Caribbean is the first of its kind and to lift a little of the veil of secrecy that has hidden our treasures from the outside world. Our Government thought it necessary to promote the realities of our country to an international audience and, accordingly, we commissioned this book. We hope that it will be a source of insight and enlightenment to readers at home and abroad.

Dominica is unique in many ways - our rain-forests are just one example. But our greatest asset is our people, at home and abroad. We are proud of the fact that the Caribs who lived in Dominica when Christopher Columbus first visited are still our citizens today.

We are equally proud of the fact that so many overseas nationals participated in 'Reunion' when we celebrated our tenth anniversary of independence late in 1988. This will no doubt help to heighten awareness of the potential that Dominica holds for tourism - nature loving and otherwise - as well as for investment.

We hope that after having gone through this book many overseas Domincians and foreign nationals might see Dominica as a good place in which to both holiday and invest.

The Government of the Commonwealth of Dominica is always ready to listen to ideas regarding mutual cooperation for the benefit of our nature island.

M Eugenia Charles
Prime Minister of the Commonwealth of Dominica

*The Government of the Commonwealth of Dominica
is grateful for the support of the following,
whose contribution made this book possible.*

A.B.C. Container (DCA) Ltd
Cable and Wireless
Geest Industries (W.I.) Ltd
Seabright Chemicals Ltd
The East Caribbean Group of Companies Ltd
O.A. "Ken" Boyea
Hugo Lodrini
National Commercial Bank of Dominica
National Development Corporation
Barclays Bank PLC
Royal Bank of Canada
Sir Alexander Gibb and Partners
The Bank of Nova Scotia
Banque Francaise Commerciale Antilles – Guyane
Harris Paints Dominica Ltd
Dominica Coconut Products Ltd
Belfast Estate Ltd
Springfield Trading (1959) Ltd
Candle Industries Cooperative
Gloves Dominica Ltd
Paul's (Paul Joseph & Co. Ltd)
Paul's Plastic International
International Garments Ltd

DOMINICA

NATURE ISLAND OF THE CARIBBEAN

DOMINICA

PARADISE FOUND
THE NATURE ISLAND

This book has seen publication for a whole number of reasons but partly, it must be said, it came about by chance or happy coincidence.

Early in 1988, whilst working in Antigua, I met with David Jardine, Marketing Manager of the airline LIAT, who suggested that the Caribbean Times prepare a special feature for the "Reunion '88" programme that was to mark the tenth anniversary of the independence of the Commonwealth of Dominica.

Having arranged to meet the Honourable Charles Maynard, the country's Minister for Agriculture, Trade, Industry and Tourism, I flew to Dominica in the spring of 1988, arriving early in the morning, meeting the Minister and still leaving by 10am! The welcome result of this meeting was that the feature was commissioned, with the government of Dominica promising all necessary facilities - with the notable exception of finance which we then set out to raise from the private sector.

Through the succession of working visits that followed one could not help but fall in love with this island on which nature has so unmistakably left its imprint. This enchanted fascination ranged from the simple pleasure of being able to drink the pure river water to the spectacle of nature at full stretch when our departure was delayed by the storms that heralded the coming of Hurricane Gilbert.

Whilst compiling the 10th independence anniversary special supplement I had occasion to interview Prime Minister Eugenia Charles and at one of our meetings I took, as a gift for the Prime Minister, a copy of "Antigua and Barbuda - A Little Bit of Paradise", a book Hansib had just produced in collaboration with the government of that country. To my great delight the Prime Minister was not only already aware of the book but had acquired a copy at the Antigua Heads of Government Meeting of the Caribbean Community (Caricom).

The idea of producing such a book on the Caribbean's nature island had already germinated but it seemed then that the government already had other arrangements in hand. But just about a week later I was asked to address the cabinet of Dominica on the proposed project and after two such discussions the word went out to start preparing the book that you are now reading.

Inevitably, the production of such a book was a learning process for all concerned. But it was not simply educational - it was also a great pleasure to get to know the government and people of the country and to get such a detailed insight into their history, culture and economy and above all the unique natural attributes of the land that they are blessed to live in.

There are many who will wish to visit Dominica once a few of its secrets start to leak out and become more widely known - a task that this book is attempting to shoulder. All those with an interest in, and a love for, nature will find themselves drawn to Dominica for its quiet tranquillity, its perfect locations for swimming and its tremendous range of beaches and rock formations.

A tiny land of 365 rivers it is possible to lose oneself in the interior, imagining that you are in the deepest jungles of South America rather than on a small Caribbean island.

In matters of conservation there is so much that the rest of the world could learn from Dominica - for example from its every effort to preserve the rainforests that are unique to such a small land area. No doubt this respect has contributed to the fact the descendants of the people living in Dominica or Waitikubuli as it was called when Christopher Columbus stumbled upon the area are still actively contributing to the life of Dominican society having escaped the genocide that tragically overtook them in so many other parts of the region.

It is so good too that consciousness is growing throughout Dominican society so that that most objectionable word and concept - Reservation, as applied to peoples of the Americas, is disappearing from the Dominican vocabulary, thereby safeguarding the dignity of the nation's Carib people.

Prime Minister Eugenia Charles is one of those dynamic political leaders who often comes to personify their country in the eyes of the rest of the world. She is certainly a straight talker and over several meetings one could not but feel and appreciate the depth of her commitment to her country and its people. One can easily believe (and we do not think that Eugenia Charles would deny it herself) that she is not interested in approbation or compliments from overseas. Rather her main, sometimes it seems her only, focal point is Dominica. The Prime Minister may drive her ministers to work hard - they all seem to have the reputation of rising early and starting work in their offices early - but she drives herself just as hard and with the same sense of urgency. Indeed, the close personal attention she paid to every aspect of this book's production is a typical example. To see her enthusiasm, and commitment and energy is to remind oneself of the lines of a famous poem:

The woods are lovely, dark and deep
But I have promises to keep
And miles to go before I sleep
And miles to go before I sleep

Indeed, the Prime Minister still has many tasks that she wishes to accomplish - two of the most important are to build an international airport and to expand the port so that it may accommodate cruise ships. These developments will, of course, greatly enhance tourism but one should not get the impression that the Prime Minister and her government wish to see a mad rush in this or any other area. The emphasis is to be on selection and quality with a gradual expansion in the infrastructure so that each and every visitor may be well looked after.

When thinking about the country's ambitious plans one must keep in mind the fact that Dominica was devastated by hurricanes in 1979 and 1980. The progress made in the last ten years clearly shows the great efforts and sacrifice made by the government and all Dominica's people to restructure, rebuild and develop their country.

In order to help recreate that infrastructure Dominica is offering good incentives for investors who wish to build hotels - big and small - as well as in other areas which the country wants to get moving.

Whether in terms of investment or aid the country takes a responsible attitude. As one overseas aid donor recently commented to us:

"The Dominican government, when they accept aid, draw it down to the country quickly, use it efficiently and account for the money spent to the last cent."

The future trends will undoubtedly be up - Dominica has the ambience of a pleasant country and its people are very friendly and receptive.

For the holidaymaker wanting peace and relaxation this is an ideal paradise. With its unique variety it can offer many types of holiday and Dominicans should not worry about introducing extraneous attractions - there are more than enough people in today's world who will love Dominica for what she is without her having to go down the slippery slope of mass commercialisation. Dominica is fortunate to have a government that has grasped this point.

Dominica may become known for many things but it has one outstanding quality that this book tries to highlight in a number of salient ways - this Paradise Found truly deserves its second name of - Nature Island of the Caribbean.

Arif Ali
Roseau
Dominica April 1989

ACKNOWLEDGEMENTS

The production of a book of this nature would not be possible without the commitment and co-operation of a great number of people.

Firstly our thks must go to Prime Minister Eugenia Charles who enthusiastically backed the project and constantly kept in touch with its progress - even during her overseas travels. We can only hope that the final project will justify the confidence shown by the Prime Minister and her government.

In this connection we also thank the Honourable Charles Maynard, Minister for Agriculture, Trade, Industry and Tourism, who has been a tower of strength throughout. It is with him that we continue to liaise regarding any problems and bottlenecks even as this book goes to press. We are sure that his family will be pleased that the early and late telephone calls from our side will now be coming to an end.

Thanks to the Honourable Alleyne Carbon, Minister of Communications and Works, for invaluable support and to other members of the cabinet for advice and help and for always making themselves available.

Thanks also to Minister Maynard's Permanent Secretary Wolsey Louis, and to Kenny Alleyne, Josie Edwards, Michael Fadelle and others at the National Development Corporation who were also of great assistance, displaying a spirit of absolute co-operation.

With regard to our own team thanks must go to those who worked ridiculous hours and put in so much hard work to transform the project from idea to reality.

A sterling effort was made by John Hughes, our Special Projects Director, who travelled several times to Dominica in the recent period and who co-ordinated the production of this publication.

Thanks, too, to Kash Ali, who also travelled to Dominica - both his and John's ideas and photos are heavily utilised.

Lennox Honychurch has been a great source of information, advice and guidance, both personally and through his "The Dominica Story" and other writings on the culture and various aspects of general life in Dominica. It is all greatly appreciated.

Kevin Menhinick's writing, research and the general trouble he went to proved more than worthwhile as did his lengthy sojourn in the country. We are pleased that he could utilise his valuable ideas and experiences in the completion of this project.

A special thanks to Arlington James and the Forestry Division of the Ministry of Agriculture for use of their publications. ('The Lake District of Dominia', 'Freshwater Swamps and Mangrove Species'. both by Arlington James)

Thanks to Hansib's Political Editor, Keith Bennett, whose continuing support for all our projects helps to keep the wheels turning.

Thanks to Richard Painter for his all-round support, to Ella Barnes whose ideas and proposals amazed and sometimes confounded us - but eventually convinced us, to John St Lewis, Hansib's Marketing Director, to Chris Hill, Tim England and other members of our studio and design department, to Drucilla Daley and other members of our typesetting department, to Jackie Kaiser who continues, against impossible odds, her valiant attempts to keep some sense of sanity in my office, and to all members of the Hansib team who backed us up so admirably when all our attention was absorbed in this project.

Thanks to David Jardine who was instrumental in initiating the project and to his LIAT colleague Katherine Pinder. The LIAT staff in Antigua specialised in making our travel arrangements at short notice and under the most difficult conditions. Thanks also to the British Airways staff in London and Antigua who displayed the same consideration and support.

Thanks to the management and staff of hotels and restaurants in Dominica, including the Continental Inn, Guiyave Restaurant, Papillote Rainforest Restaurant, Vena's Garden Restaurant, Anchorage Hotel, Evergreen Hotel, Excelsoir Hotel, Sisserou Hotel, Reigate Hall Hotel, Castaways Hotel and Castle Comfort.

A special thanks to our tireless driver Etinoff Robertson and to Judith Pemberton for her co-operation.

Thanks to diving instructors Derek Perryman (Dive Dominica) and Felix Armour (Anchorage)

Thanks to Dive Dominica for precise dive site information.

Thanks to the taxi, airport, customs and immigration staff who always treated us with great courtesy and to Marie J. Edwards and Norma Rolle of the Dominica Tourist Board and to government tourism adviser, Dr Kunwar Singh.

Additional thanks for photographs - The Ministry of Agriculture Forestry and Fisheries, Duane Bush, Lennox Honychurch, Gordon Yerry, Dive Dominica, Anita Amholta, Jackie Uhl, Alan Aflak, Mr and Mrs Anquetil, Arlington A James, Ashton Shillingford, Daryl Phillip, Zahid Ali, Charles James (Communications Department) and Dr. Mike Freed (O.A.S.), The National Development Corporation -, The Tourist Board, Linda Harris (Castaways) -.

Thanks to Steve, Ken and Mary of Desktop Graphics.

Thanks to printers Hazell, Watson and Viney , for their help, understanding and support.

Our thanks also go to Felix Gregoire and Mr. Christian, to the Dominica Commissioner of Police E. Pierre, to P.A. Brown (O.A.S.), Jep the guide, Hannah Gordon, Loye and Marshall 'Barney' Barnard, Linda Harris, Janice A. Armour, Gary Airde, Mrs R.E.A. Volny, Lambert V. Lewis, L. Earle Johnson, Susan Watty and Robin Emmanuel Rock; to Wykie of Wykies Bar, H. Shillingford of Shillingford Estate, Mr Scotland of Geest, Hannah Claredon of the Dominica Export and Import Agency (Dexia), Colin Bully, Gaie Mendlesohn,

Special thanks go to Mr. M.A.D. Elwin J.P., Honourary Consul of the Commonwealth of Dominica in London, and the staff of the Dominica High Commission, (London)

Thanks to the Carnival Committee, the Canefield Tourist Office and Debbie Kneeshaw, (London)

Thanks to the ladies in national dress.

Our most heartfelt thanks go to those we have carelessly forgotten to mention and a special thank you goes to all the people of the Commonwealth of Dominica.

Arif Ali
Hansib Publishing

CONTENTS

COVER PICTURE: *Trafalgar Falls.*

FRONT COVER:PANELS: *Sisserou Parrot, Anthurium flower, Indian River, Traditional fisherman, Hummingbird at Heliconia, Hot Springs, Prince Rupert Bay, Underwater Dominica*

BACK COVER: *Roseau Valley.*

School children at Fort Shirley, Cabrits.

DOMINICA

THE BEST KEPT SECRET IN THE CARIBBEAN
By *KEVIN MENHINICK*

Lying quietly between the busy French-controlled Westindian islands of Martinique and Guadeloupe, is a little known, sleepy oasis where time appears to have stood still. The tourists that visit Dominica each year marvel at this unique Windward Island that boasts three roundabouts, one set of traffic lights, and a major town, Roseau, whose inhabitants casually disregard the occasional roaming goat or chicken. Dominica recently celebrated its tenth year of independence from Britain, its former colonial master, but the visitor may still be forgiven for thinking that they are stepping back in time. Quaint wooden balconies look out onto tiny streets with a breathtaking backdrop of beautiful green mountains.

You won't find a profusion of pulsating discotheques here, nor hordes of trendy young people liberally applying sun-tan oil whilst stretched out on a crowded beach. No, Dominica is mainly for the nature lover and for those who enjoy peace and tranquillity in an unspoilt, pollution free environment, with a warm tropical climate; hence Dominica's unchallenged claim to be the 'Nature island of the Caribbean.'

Dominica measures 29 miles long and 16 miles wide, covering some 305 square miles, and has a population of only 84,000. Rugged and mountainous, thick with lush green vegetation, a mass of trees, and intersected by narrow, winding mountain roads, Dominica provides a wonderful opportunity for those who wish to retreat from the pressures of modern day living, and for the adventurer who longs to explore the woodlands and virgin territory of the dense mountain rain forests. For, surprisingly, much of Dominica's interior has yet to be conquered, due to the wild and inaccessible nature of the seemingly impenetrable forests.

Dominica is blessed with 365 rivers, and can lay claim to be one of the few remaining areas in the world where it is safe to drink the river water. Many of these rocky rivers are highlighted by spectacular cascading waterfalls.

The island is also the home of the last remaining community of Carib 'Indians' in the Caribbean. The oldest surviving inhabitants of Dominica (or Waitikubuli as they named their island), number 3,500 and live mainly on the east coast. Although only a relatively small percentage of them are full blooded Caribs, they are, nevertheless, a proud people descended from the Amerindians of South America. Their language has sadly long since disappeared, but their chiefs and leaders regularly attend conferences of indigenous peoples all over the world. They are particularly adept in handicrafts and their hats and baskets are a feature of Dominican life.

The vast majority of Dominicans, except for those living in a small area around Marigot in the north-east of the island, are bilingual. The official language is English, but Creole (or Patois) is also extensively spoken. Creole is a French-based language (a vestige of French colonial rule) with a smattering of English and African words. Until comparatively recently it was purely an oral language.

"Paradise found" is a message emblazoned on local T shirts, and it is a description that Dominica can rightly lay claim to. For, on this Caribbean retreat there are no dangerous animals, no poisonous spiders or snakes and nothing in the rivers or seas to cause alarm. Add to this fresh drinking water, a pollution free environment, an abundance of food from the fertile land, and a climate in which the temperature rarely exceeds 85°F/29°C or drops below 75°F/24°C, then we may have found the reasons.

So, how long will it be before the world suddenly finds out about Dominica? Only time will tell. But, as one United States visitor commented whilst hypnotically gazing into a deep, green, forested valley:"I wonder, when is Hollywood going to discover all this?"

Those who know the island well would, no doubt, like to hang on to their secret just a little bit longer; but we will share with you a little bit of Dominica's beauty.

DOMINICA TODAY

Night falls quickly in Dominica, by 5.30 pm in December and 7.00 pm in July, it is usually dark. However, Caribbean nights are usually warm and beautiful with clear skies and bright stars. Here is an astronomer's delight and the romantic's dream - a moonlit walk to the background accompaniment of frogs, crickets and shooting stars.

In such a fertile environment almost anything will grow, Dominicans particularly enjoy dasheen, tannia, yam, sweet potato, breadfruit and avocado pear, all grown locally. Vegetables are grown all year round, although some difficulties can be experienced in the wet season.Fruit of almost every variety abounds.Most fruits, however, are seasonal, with mangoes available in the summer months, and grapefruit and oranges in the winter. Apples are one of the few fruits that will not grow in the Caribbean, due to the climate not having a cold period which is essential for the apple to germinate.

Looking at the steep slopes where Dominicans plant bananas and other produce, it would appear to the visitor to be almost impossible to harvest the crops. But despite the difficult terrain and the yield is regularly produced, whether it be for local consumption, export or the busy colourful Roseau market.

Dominicans also enjoy a 'drolt' or 'mess', which usually consists of a goat or a cow's head which is cooked either at the beach or the river, and enjoyed with drink, music and friends.

Other local dishes, much enjoyed , include 'souse' (pig trotters in a 'hot' spicy gravy) goat water (soup), crab-back(dressed crab), black pudding (with hot pepper) akra (fried salt fish or 'titiwi wee' in batter with hot pepper) and a broth (soup with dumplings, fish or meat and ground provisions). Agouti, manicou, mountain chicken (frog legs) and cray-fish (king prawns), all found in Dominica's mountains, woods , rivers and seas.

Donkeys and mules were, before the advent of roads, much in evidence in rural areas. They are now to be found only in certain regions in the north and south of the island.

Cable T.V. has played a large part in 'westernising' Dominica. Clothing, hair styles as well as language have been affected, with many people worried that the traditional Dominican culture could be

THE CARIBBEAN

superceeded by that of the United States. However, whilst the world is seemingly getting smaller it is very doubtful that Dominica will lose its special culture, a metamorphosis of Africa, Europe, and other influences.

In addition to traditional jing ping music and quadrille dance, young theatre groups have recently emerged. These include the Karifuna group, from the Carib territory, and Koulirou from La Plaine. Indeed, Koulirou is the Carib name for La Plaine. These talented young people regularly perform plays they have written , portraying historical events, like the La Plaine Tax Uprising, and modern social and political dramas.

Religion is also important in Dominica. Although the majority of Dominicans are Roman Catholic (another vestige of the period of French rule), many other religious beliefs have, over recent years, gained in popularity. Amongst these are the Baptists, the Christian Union Mission, the Pentacostalists, the Seventh Day Adventists and Jehovah's Witnesses. Methodism has a long, if a minority, tradition on the island. The north-east of Dominica, around Marigot, was inhabited long ago by people from the Leeward Islands, particularly Antigua and Montserrat. With these people came Methodism. They even named a village, Wesley, after John Wesley, the inspiration behind the Methodist faith. This is also the only area in Dominica where people do not speak Creole. They do, however, speak their own English-based patois, which is known as Kokoy and cannot be understood by most other Dominicans.

Driving in Dominica is on the left side and can be an experience for the visitor. The mountain roads are narrow and winding. However, fear not, the accident rate is very low, which can only lead one to assume that ability on the roads must be high.

Car hire is readily available, and local 'buses' travel to Roseau daily from all country areas and are a cheap form of transport. The visitor is advised, though, to ensure that their return journey is possible. Hitch hiking is easy in Dominica and is a great way to see the island and meet the people. Sitting in the back of a pick-up gives one a completely undisturbed view of the countryside. Safari tours are available and are recommended. Driving through the interior in the early evening , one

The church at La Plaine.

The church at Portsmouth.

OPPOSITE TOP: *Bananas are planted in all available space.*

OPPOSITE BOTTOM: *Roseau market on a Saturday morning.*

is immediately aware of the sunlight throwing different hues onto the green mountains. The rain begins to gently fall, which in turn leads to a beautiful rainbow.

The drive from Grand Bay to Fond St. Jean, in the south of the island, is equally fascinating. This is a long, curving bay with beautiful views of the rocky coastline. The road is currently little more than a track (although there are plans for a new road) with fords and dykes to cross. Fishermen pass by with their catch and the island of Martinique is visible in the distance, shrouded in a hazy mist. The sea sparkles a silvery blue as the sun catches the waves.

Grammar school.

The Dominican currency is the East Caribbean dollar, but U.S. dollars are generally accepted everywhere.

Dominica's education system is based on the British system. Until recently, Dominican school children sat the same G.C.E. 'O' Levels as British school children (except for history where Westindian history was studied). Now the equivalent, the CXC, which is considered a more thorough examination, has replaced the 'O' Levels. On leaving secondary school, students wishing to sit GCE 'A' Levels attend the sixth form college in Roseau.

A large number of Dominicans have for many years travelled abroad for their university education. The United States and Canada are popular destinations, although many have attended the University of the Westindies' in Jamaica, Barbados and Trinidad, whilst some have gone to England. Dominicans have returned to their native land as doctors, lawyers and business administrators. The island has its own Teachers' Training College, which is situated in Roseau.

Dominica has a two-tiered legal system, with stipendary magistrates and a high court presided over by a judge assisted by a jury.

'Wob Douilette' The national costume.

Although the island does not have an army, there is a small military section of the police force who are trained in armed and unarmed combat.

Dominica also has various charitable organisations including a Rotary Club and a Lions Club.

Although the island's white population is small compared to other Caribbean islands, Dominica does possess areas where European

OPPOSITE TOP: *Truckload of workers.*

OPPOSITE BOTTOM: *Government building, Roseau.*

54

influence is visible. Two villages near La Plaine, La Ronde and Case O' Gowrie, are good examples of this.

During the last century, a whole community of poor white Martiniquans sailed to the east coast of Dominica and established themselves near the village of La Plaine. Eventually the area they inhabited became known as La Ronde, after the largest family there. Inevitably the community inter-bred with the native Dominicans, but the French influence is still strong.

France has had a more recent involvement with Dominica. Agronomists, doctors and dentists have all been sent to the island to assist in its development and French money has helped to build a health centre and an agricultural training centre.

The United States and Britain have offered assistance in the form of Peace Corp volunteers and VSOs (Voluntary Service Overseas). These volunteers have worked in agriculture, schools and industry. Venezuela and Taiwan have also been active in Dominica, assisting in various projects, including free Spanish language lessons.

Other Europeans and North Americans have for many years been attracted to Dominica. There is a small Swedish community in the mountain village of Cochrane and other Europeans are dotted around the island.

Apart from being proud, Dominicans are a happy people who enjoy partying, laughing and having fun. They also have their own special sense of humour. This is reflected in some of the strange nicknames that many seem to have, 'By the Bay' and 'Happy Time', being two examples of people who are known by no other name.

The names of sports teams also have a tongue in cheek air about them. The cricket teams in the Carib territory, for example, seem to depict the Carib's former warrior status - "Missiles", "Battlers", "Avengers" and "Harder They Come".

OPPOSITE: *Many homes in Dominica make great use of flower gardens.*

THE HISTORY

Compiled by *KEVIN MENHINICK*
(using `*THE DOMINICA STORY*`
by *LENNOX HONYCHURCH* as
his main source of reference).

Millions of years ago, when the Eastern Caribbean was merely a range of mountains underneath the sea, a series of volcanic eruptions took place disturbing the ocean floor. Slowly, a chain of islands began to emerge from the sea. At the centre of this volcanic action rose an island of towering mountains. This was the beginning of Dominica.

Situated 15½ degrees north of the equator, surrounded by the Atlantic Ocean to the east and the Caribbean Sea to the west, Dominica lies in the inner arc of the Lesser Antilles. It is also an integral constituent of the Windward Islands, which, along with the Leewards, make up the Eastern Caribbean states of the Westindies.

Although historical evidence is limited, Dominica's first inhabitants are thought to have been a group of Amerindians known as the Ciboney, who are believed to have arrived in Dominica around 1,000 years B.C. However, little is known about these people.

For a study of the first true Dominicans we have to move to Central East Asia and back over 10,000 years B.C. It was here that a group of nomadic tribesmen crossed the ice-capped Bering Strait into Alaska from Siberia. Some settled in North America while others moved further south and were subsequently named 'Eskimos' and 'Red Indians' by the European colonists.

The remainder made their way to Central and South America to become Mayas, Incas, Aztecs and other Amerindian nations. Around 500 years B.C. one group of Amerindians, known as the Arawaks, left their homes on the banks of the Orinoco river in South America, and travelled north by boat to inhabit Dominica and other Caribbean islands. Once settled, they lived peacefully in Dominica for almost 1000 years until they were invaded and conquered by another group of South Americans who became known as the Caribs. Over the years both cultures and languages became fused and their simple lifestyle, centred on fishing and the sea, continued peacefully until the 15th century when a new set of conquerors from Europe discovered the Caribbean.

In 1492 Christopher Columbus, the Italian explorer, sailed into the Caribbean while searching for Asia. Consequently he named the islands he had unwittingly stumbled upon the 'West Indies'. One year

The Carib name for Dominica, Waitikubuli, means "tall is her body", a very appropriate name. However, today the Carib language has practically disappeared. The last Carib speaker died in 1920, although many words are still in existence and the language lives on in the names of Dominica's towns and villages; Calibishie, Mero, Layou, Bataka and Coubilisti, to name a few.

OPPOSITE TOP: *Traditional canoes being made.*

58

later Columbus returned and on November 3, 1493, he discovered an island of rugged green mountains and natural beauty. Being a Sunday, the island was called Dominica (the Latin word for Sunday being Domingo).

However, due to the island's rugged terrain and the resistance of the inhabitants, it was nearly 200 years before the Europeans made a profound impact on the island. Dominica became an important source of water and wood collection, but the ferocity of the Caribs dissuaded the Spanish from attempting full colonisation. On many occasions Spanish sailors and missionaries were beaten back whilst attempting to subjugate the Carib people. Slowly, however, they began to accept the Europeans and traded with the various vessels from France, England and Holland which had started to visit the island. Plantain, cassava, fruit and tobacco were exchanged for beads, knives, glass and tools.

In 1642, a French missionary, Father Raymond Bretan, landed in Dominica and through his self-taught knowledge of the Carib language managed to mix with the people. Four years later the first Christian (Roman Catholic) Mass was celebrated and in 1650 a thatched chapel erected.

Despite having the confidence and friendship of the Caribs, Father Bretan failed to establish the Christian faith in Dominica, and with his death Christianity was quickly forgotten. During this period, many other Carib communities were being destroyed by the Europeans who had also introduced diseases to which the Waitikubulis had little resistance. By the 1650s the Caribs had disappeared from St. Kitts and those Leeward Islands which had become colonised by the English. Martinique and Guadeloupe, Dominica's neighbouring islands, fell into the hands of the French, and are to this day 'departments' of France. Still, Dominica's indigenous population resisted; their resilience proving a thorn in the side of England and France who had by now gained the ascendancy in the region.

In 1664, Indian Warner, the son of a Dominican Carib slave, and the English governor of St. Kitts, Sir Thomas Warner, successfully led 600 Caribs into battle alongside 1,000 Englishmen who together attacked a French settlement in St. Lucia. As a result, and in an attempt to gain

Traditional headwear.

OPPOSITE TOP: *18th CENTURY DRESS a painting by Agostino Brunias who lived and painted in Dominica from about 1770-1796. This shows the origin of the national dress.*

OPPOSITE BOTTOM: *Another painting by the same artist entitled Dominican Dancers.*

Both paintings were photographed by Lennox Honychurch and reproduced with permission from his book 'OUR ISLAND CULTURE'.

control in Dominica, the governor of the "British Possessions in the Caribbean", Lord Willoughby, made Warner deputy governor of Dominica.

In 1674 the Caribs of Dominica raided Antigua. In retaliation, a militia led by Colonel Phillip Warner, Indian Warner's half-brother, attacked and killed eighty Caribs in a west coast area which is still known as Massacre. Indian Warner also perished in the attack. This incident appeared to strengthen the resolve of the Dominican Caribs, who over the next eight years raided and killed colonists in Antigua, Montserrat and Barbuda, reportedly with support from Caribs from St. Vincent.

The French and English authorities were becoming more and more exasperated by the Caribs, and, after an unsuccessful attack by the English on Dominica in 1683, a treaty was agreed between France and England stating that Dominica be declared a neutral island belonging only to the Caribs. This treaty was signed on February 7, 1686. However, the Carib population had been quickly eroded due to battle fatigue and illness, and in less than 100 years their numbers had dwindled from 5,000 to a mere 400 people. This might have been thought to be the death knell of these brave warriors, but remarkably their descendants live peacefully in contemporary Dominica.

The next few decades proved a placid period in Dominica's history. Shortly after the 1686 Treaty, French lumbermen began to settle on the island and by 1727 sixty French families were living peacefully alongside the remaining Caribs with a handful of Spanish, Portuguese and English settlers.

In addition to wood exports, small tobacco and cotton plantations were established. The early settlers endured difficult conditions, their houses being basic timber and thatch constructions. They inhabited the flat coastal areas on the west coast such as Roseau, Pointe Michel and Soufriere. These and other place names, Petit Savanne, Saint Sauveur and Vieille Case, for example, are evidence of early French colonisation.

DOMINICAS FIRST SLAVES

Slowly the population expanded. In 1727 the governor of Martinique, ignoring the 1686 Treaty, appointed a French officer, Le Grand, as Commander of Dominica. With him came Dominica's first African slaves. Poor whites, criminals and freed slaves left other Westindian islands to find refuge in Dominica and by 1750 the remaining Caribs had been forced to withdraw to the east coast of the island.

By 1745, Dominica's population had grown to over 3,000, half of them slaves. Also around this time the governor of Martinique ordered the building of a prison and appointed a judge and five assistant military officers, in addition to a customs officer. Import and export duties were levied on English and Dutch traders, and attempts made to apprehend smugglers and pirates.

As can be seen, the French had strongly imposed their influence on Dominica. Despite this, Dominica's neutrality was officially preserved when the Treaty of Aix-La-Chappelle was signed by England and France in 1748. Religion, brought by French Catholic Jesuit priests, had also begun to make its presence felt. Churches were built and land and estates purchased, particularly on the south coast at Grand Bay.

In 1756 France and Britain became engaged in what was known as the Seven Years War, which was waged in Europe, Canada, India and the Caribbean. Following clashes between French and English ships off the Dominican coast, England decided to invade Dominica.

On June 6, 1761, eight ships carrying 2,000 men attacked Roseau and by noon the following day Dominica was in English hands. The French inhabitants reluctantly accepted British military rule and Dominica officially became a colony of Britain at the peace conference in Paris in 1763. However, the south-east part of Dominica in terms of its language, religion, place-names and surnames was to reflect permanently nearly eighty years of French colonialism.

With the imposition of British rule came an increase in the number of British settlers. Protestantism became the official religion and in 1776 an Anglican church was built in Newtown. However, the British newcomers were not particularly religious and the church soon fell into disrepair. To this day Roman Catholicism remains Dominica's major religion.

The old market place.

The first Spanish slave ship had actually sailed from West Africa as early as 1518 (Africans being considered stronger than the Caribs they had enslaved on other islands) but it was not until the latter half of the 18th Century that Dominica became heavily involved in this trade in human beings due mainly to an absence of the large sugar cane plantations prevalent in islands such as Jamaica and Barbados.

OPPOSITE TOP: *An Egret, more often seen in the swamps.*

Land distribution was considered important and a commission was set up to sell land by public auction in Britain; many of the purchasers being speculators. The Caribs, meanwhile, were still living quietly on the east coast. A small portion of land, 232 acres, was declared their 'reserve' in an attempt by the English authorities to placate Dominica's oldest inhabitants.

British place names were now becoming established. Portsmouth, situated in Prince Rupert Bay, was originally intended as Dominica's capital, but at the time low stagnant water lay around the town, bringing disease. Other examples of British influence are Hampstead, Woodford Hill, Londonderry Bay, Salisbury, Belfast and Castle Bruce. One area of failure, though, was the attempt to rename the Layon River, the Thames.

As with almost every other British colony throughout the world, Dominica adopted the British political, legal and educational systems.

For seventeen years, from 1761 until 1778, Dominica remained peacefully in British hands. But this repose did not last and in 1778, in an attempt to win back lost ground, France registered its intention to oppose Britain in the American War of Independence. On September 7 of that year, 3,000 French troops launched a surprise attack on Dominica and within twenty-four hours the British had surrendered. This signalled the beginning of five years of French rule.

By this time, Dominica's population had swelled to over 16,000, nearly 14,000 being slaves. The rest was made up of 1,500 whites, the majority of whom were French, and over 500 freed slaves and mulattos (free persons of mixed races).

For the British on the island this period proved an unhappy one as restrictions were placed upon them by the French governor, Marquis Duchillean. As a result many abandoned Dominica, never to return. During Duchillean's reign, forts and roads were constructed, with numerous slaves being seconded from the plantations for manual labour. Consequently crops and livestock were neglected, creating hardships for the island's inhabitants.

Disaster struck Dominica a year into French rule when, in 1779, the island was hit by a major hurricane, followed by another one year

Jing Ping band. Jing Ping is the traditional music of Dominica.

OPPOSITE TOP:*A traditional waterwheel.*

OPPOSITE BOTTOM: *School children.*

later. It is interesting to note that exactly 200 years later, history was to repeat itself when Hurricane David devastated Dominica in 1979, followed by the less destructive Hurricane Allen in 1980.

In 1781 there was a third disaster when Roseau was almost totally destroyed by fire, causing £200,000 worth of damage to property - not an inconsiderable amount in those days. This proved the final straw for Duchillean who resigned as governor and returned to France in despair.

In April 1782, a large French fleet, comprising warships and 10,000 men, set off for an attack on the British-controlled island of Jamaica. The British admirals Rodney and Drake, who were patrolling the area, were alerted to the situation and set sail in an effort to apprehend the enemy ships. On April 9 the French fleet was sighted off Dominica's north coast and on April 12 the inevitable battle took place in the Guadeloupe Channel midway between Dominica and a small group of islands known as the Saintes. This became known as the Battle of the Saintes, and the English fleet's victory heralded the return of British rule to Dominica; this was confirmed by the Treaty of Versailles in September 1783.

So once more Dominica was in the hands of Britain and was to remain so until independence in 1978.

Wood turning handcraft.

In July 1784, 600 Americans loyal to the British flag arrived in Dominica following the United States, Declaration of Independence. The British government stipulated that these people should be given preferential treatment and Dominica's new governor, John Orde, acceded to their various demands. These included free transportation of their possessions, food for nine months and no taxes for fifteen years. This inevitably put an extra economic strain on the already struggling island and the situation was exacerbated when problems arose over the granting of land. Living conditions for Dominica's newest arrivals became even more difficult when, three years later, the island suffered yet another serious hurricane. However, most of the Americans were assimilated into the society and were responsible for introducing cotton plantations and the growing of rice.

A more intricate and enduring problem, however, was that of the Maroons. These people (in Patois 'Negres Marron') were runaway

African slaves and had inhabited Dominica before either the British or the French occupation. The early Maroons had escaped from neighbouring islands or, in a few cases, had been captured by Carib raiding parties. The Maroons lived either alongside the Caribs or in their own forest settlements.By 1785 thirteen Maroon camps had been established around the centre of the island. Each camp had its own chief and men were sent to the plantations in order to persuade other slaves to join them

Finally, the planters decided on action and an army was constituted; 500 men consisting of Europeans, mulattos and slaves were enlisted and a camp was set up near the Freshwater Lake - one of the few passable tracks on the island. However, their knowledge of the mountains was limited and they were powerless to prevent a Maroon attack on the east coast estate of Rosalie, where four men, including the plantation manager, were murdered and the estate plundered and burnt.

Embarrassed, the army decided on retaliatory action and, with assistance from private individuals, located and attacked the Maroons who were responsible for the Rosalie assault.

The Maroon men managed to escape, but women and children were captured. At the subsequent trial in February 1786, a Maroon woman divulged important information about various camps, and within months four chiefs had been captured and executed, including Balla, the perpetrator of the Rosalie attack.

The events of the previous few years had taken their toll on Dominica, and by 1790 thirty out of eighty plantations had been abandoned by their British owners. Mulattos and 'free coloureds' from Martinique and Guadeloupe purchased some of the estate land. Meanwhile laws had been passed denying these people a number of basic rights. For example, they were barred from holding legal posts and it was made illegal for them to carry swords - the mark of a gentleman at the time.

From 1789 until 1799 France was embroiled in revolution. French Royalists and Republicans sought refuge in Dominica with an inevitable consequence being the influencing of Dominica's slaves. The island had

OPPOSITE TOP: *There are many species of lizard in Dominica and many change their colours to suit the enviroment in which they are in.*

OPPOSITE BOTTOM: *With the coming of roads and automobiles, the donkey has almost faded away as a working animal.*

become a melting pot of political refugees and nobody seemed certain who was on which side. In 1791 a Martinique mulatto, Jean Louis Paulinaire, was found guilty of inciting a slave revolt in Grand Bay and planning a coup in the south of the island. He was subsequently publicly hanged, drawn and quartered.

In 1793, Governor Orde was replaced by George Hamilton and in the same year France declared war on Britain and Holland. As a consequence many of Dominica's free inhabitants left the island and those who remained could only muster an army of 400. Other able-bodied men set about repairing the forts, particularly the Cabrits. That same year the British captured St. Lucia, Martinique and Guadeloupe, the latter being recaptured by France the following year. In a shrewd move, slavery was temporarily abolished in Guadeloupe and every available man utilised in the defence of his country, or in readiness for attacks on British colonies. In 1795, the jittery British authorities in Dominica declared martial law and forced all the French inhabitants to sign a declaration of loyalty to the British crown. More French refugees arrived in Dominica, many of them spies. The whole scene now was one of confusion. French Republican sympathisers, who lived in the west coast Dominican village of Colihaut, became involved in an invasion plot. These people were coffee planters who had established some form of civilisation with a church, shops, taverns and billiard tables.

On June 4 the attempted invasion was successfully rebuffed at Woodford Hill on the north-east coast. But two days later, on June 6, 200 French soldiers entered Dominica via Hampstead and encountered little resistance. They marched to Hatton Garden where they set up camp in the sugar works. Alerted to the situation, Governor Hamilton sent 200 men to apprehend the invaders and, despite an injection of a further 400 French soldiers, the British were triumphant, capturing and imprisoning over 300 French troops.

Simultaneously, 150 French Republican sympathisers from around the Colihaut area marched across country to support their compatriots. They too were defeated, with 110 being sent to England as prisoners of war, others simply banished, four hanged and three receiving 200 lashes each.

The Green Parrot and Cartwheels Restaurants bay front Roseau.

"He feels that the most significant development made in his ministry during the last 10 years is the road rehabilitation project. Out of an average 100 miles of roads on the island, 80 miles of new roads have been constructed or built. This project also runs simultaneously with the development of farm feeder roads."

The Honourable Alleyne Carbon, Minister of Communications and Works

"There is always a need for your help at home. Any possible assistance will be welcomed. We need it!

Ronan A. David, Minister of Health and Fire Services

OPPOSITE TOP: *The Hot Springs colour the rocks a bright orange and this natural shower is beleived to contain health benefits.*

In 1797, Dominica had another new governor. He was twenty-nine year old Andrew James Cochrane Johnstone, better known as Cochrane, for whom a west island village was named. Cochrane was a corrupt governor who allegedly made substantial profits from the slave trade and from vice. It is also said that he kept a harem on his estate.

Due to battle fatigue and illness - malaria and yellow fever had depleted the troops at the Cabrits around the swampy Portsmouth area - slaves had been enlisted alongside British troops. They became known as the Black Rangers. Eager to reinforce his army, Cochrane bought 200 African slaves and formed the 8th West Indian Regiment. However, Cochrane's treatment of his new black army was, at best, harsh and on April 9, 1802, the 8th West Indian Regiment revolted. Troops from Roseau, including the Royal Scottish Regiment, were sent to the Cabrits to quell the uprising, and after a brief battle the 8th West Indian Regiment were defeated. Many escaped to the surrounding hills to join the Maroons, but thirty-four were hanged following a court martial. Soon afterwards the 8th Regiment was disbanded.

In March 1804, Governor Cochrane was court martialled on four charges and, although cleared, he was forced to resign his commission. He was replaced by Governor George Prevost, whose arrival coincided with renewed French attacks.

In February 1805, French ships flying the Union flag landed in Roseau. The 200 British troops were no match for the 2,000 French soldiers and the capital was easily taken. Governor Prevost was determined not to surrender and, summoning reinforcements, he escaped to Fort Shirley at the Cabrits. The French commander, La Grange, pursued Prevost and demanded a ransom of £20,000. Prevost refused the French demand, and, obviously deterred by the seeming invincibility of the Cabrits fortress, La Grange returned to Roseau. Here he sacked the town and took with him large numbers of slaves before withdrawing from the island. This was to prove the final French attack on Dominica.

In 1810 rewards were offered for the capture of Maroons, and in desperation the new governor, George Robert Ainslie, even offered a

18th century dress.
Photo: Lennox Honychurch.

"One of the most positive aspects of our government is unity among us, honesty and education. We have a leader who knows what she is doing and where she is going. There is no doubt about her, and with that level of leadership and commitment among us we are bound to succeed."
Henry George,
Minister of Education and Sports

Despite the fact that Dominica is a small country, many of its villages have their distinct cultures and Alexander feels that their wider appreciation is helpful to the process of acquiring a proper and integrated national identity.

The Honourable Heskieth Andrew Alexander,
Minister of Community Development

OPPOSITE: *Dominica is rich in nature.*

free pardon to any Maroon who came down from the hills and surrendered. When no response was forthcoming Ainslie sent messengers in an attempt to negotiate with the rebels. Suspicious of the governor's intentions, the Maroons murdered the emissaries. Enraged, Ainslie set about a programme of extermination and sent out local rangers to flush out and kill the insurgents. In 1814 Jacko was shot dead. Shortly afterwards other leaders were killed so that the Maroons were forced to surrender. This action seemed to break their spirit and Maroon numbers soon dwindled.

Times were changing, and Dominica's African community was no doubt aware that six years previously, in 1808, the William Wilberforce-influenced Abolition Act had ended slave trading in Britain and its colonies.

Just when Dominica appeared to have rid itself of two problems, the French threat and the Maroons, the island was struck by three hurricanes - two in 1813 and one in 1817. Widespread damage was caused, resulting in an inevitable shortage of food. When Britain refused aid, Dominica's merchants and planters were understandably aggrieved. Economic problems were aggravated when Britain increased import duties on sugar, and food supplies were hampered due to the United States declaring war on Britain. Dominica's problems were far from over as the island was once again destroyed by two further severe hurricanes in 1825 and 1834.

One can but marvel at the obvious patience of the island's free community. Nonetheless, the threat of invasion, natural disasters, internal strife and economic depression had left Dominica in a state of poverty by the mid 19th century.

In 1815 the French Emperor Napoleon was defeated, and with his political demise the threat of invasion seemed to have abated. However, the abolition of the slave trade had caused great consternation among Dominica's plantation society. Their discontentment was exacerbated in 1831 when the Brown Privilege Bill became law, creating equal political and social rights for the island's non-whites who were not enslaved. The wind of change was blowing and three years later, on August 1, 1834, slavery was finally abolished; 668,000 slaves in the

During the early years of the 1800s Maroon activity increased. It has been estimated that their numbers had risen to over 800 with new camps being established near Woodford Hill, Hampstead, Rosalie and Pointe Mulatre, amongst others. Many of the Maroon leaders had now become household names in Dominica, with the most infamous being Jacko, who by now had been in the forest for over 40 years. It is interesting to note that to this day an area of land near Bells, in the centre of the island, is named after him.

OPPOSITE: *The Antiquity Monument commands a superior view of Roseau and the harbour.*

British Westindies, including 14,175 in Dominica, were set free.

It was a time for rejoicing in Dominica, but instead of the drunkenness anticipated by the planters, many freed slaves instead attended Mass in thanksgiving.

In compensation the planters were awarded £275,547 and were given a stipulation that the freed slaves had to undergo a period of 'apprenticeship', varying from four to six years; only children under six were exempt. Additionally the masters had to provide shelter, clothing, food and medical attention. The apprentices could, however, purchase their freedom.

Methodists and Quakers had long campaigned for the abolition of slavery. During a visit to Dominica, a Quaker group found the conditions of freed slaves on French plantations far superior to that of their counterparts on the British plantations, where the death rate was particularly high. One reason appeared to be that the owners lived on the French estates, whereas the British estates were owned by absentee landlords. They also observed that the 'apprenticeship' system was little improvement on slavery. The British authorities obviously concurred with these sentiments and on August 1, 1838, the apprenticeship system was discontinued.

During the period immediately following Abolition, many British colonies, particularly Jamaica, Trinidad and Guyana, employed indentured labour from India and China to fill the positions vacated by the freed slaves.

However, this was not the case in Dominica, where only small numbers of Portuguese came to work the estates. In Dominica land was plentiful and freed slaves took advantage of easy term loans or 'peppercorn' rent to occupy land for use as smallholdings. Others simply squatted long-term on land and created their own 'gardens' supplying all their needs. This probably explains the strong feeling of independence that still exists in Dominica today.

This situation is unique in the Caribbean with, for example, nearly ninety percent of the population living on the east coast of Dominica, still being self-employed small farmers, late into the 20th century.

OPPOSITE: *Brain coral, found in a cave on a hill near Roseau, which illustrates the island's eruptive beginnings.*

Despite the advantages that the freed slaves now enjoyed, the planters were hardly delighted, and many now faced financial ruin.

Dominica's French-controlled neighbours were also feeling the effects of Abolition. Although Guadeloupe had experienced temporary emancipation in 1793, this had subsequently been reversed, and it was not until 1848 that slavery was finally abolished in the French colonies. As a result many slaves from Martinique and Guadeloupe were to brave treacherous seas to find refuge in Dominica during the intervening years.

Since colonisation, Dominica's mulattos had been an important constituent in the commercial and social life of the island. Dominica was again unique in the Caribbean for the equal social status these people enjoyed with the island's white community; they even owned their own slaves! However, one area in which the mulattos did not experience equity was that of political power, from which they were debarred. The 1831 Brown Privilege Bill presented the mulattos with the opportunity to share power and the following year three 'coloured' members were elected to the House of Assembly.

By 1838 there was a 'coloured' majority, with Charles Gordon Falconer emerging as a leading political figure. Falconer was an ex-school teacher who edited the liberal newspaper *The Dominican*. Directly opposed to this paper was the white-backed conservative journal *The Colonist*. Many political disputes ensued with the whites becoming embittered at the increasing power of the 'coloured', or mulatto, members. Another leading political figure was businessman James Garraway who, in his capacity as President and Senior Council member, became the first man of African blood to achieve high office in the British colonial dependencies.

By 1850, Dominica's population had risen to 25,000 but with only twenty per cent (5,000) being literate. Educational facilities for the freed slaves were very poor and they alone continued to be deprived of political rights.

In 1862, a bill was passed creating a single chamber Parliament. Previously Dominica had been ruled by the British-style two House system. Many whites were now of the opinion that the 'coloured'

continued page 122

CALENDAR OF EVENTS

1493   A ship from Columbus' fleet enters the bay.

1504   Columbus lands here on 4th voyage

1535   The Spanish Council of The Indies declares this bay as a station for its treasure ships.

Sir Francis Drake, Hawkins, Prince Rupert and others use the bay to refresh their ships, trade with Caribs.

1763   Dominica ceded to Britain by Treaty of Paris.

1765   First small battery erected on this site.

1774   Construction of Fort Shirley and Prince Ruperts Garrison begins.

1778   French capture Roseau. The garrison surrenders. French continue building work.

1782   Battle of The Saints fought off the Cabrits.

1783   Dominica returned to Britain by Treaty of Versaille.

1795   French revolutionaries invade north coast but are repelled by troops from Cabrits.

1802   The revolt of the 8th West India Regiment at Fort Shirley.

1805   Garrison refuses to surrender to French forces under General La Grange.

1854   Fort Shirley and Cabrits abandoned by the army. The forest takes over.

1982   Restoration of Fort Shirley begins.

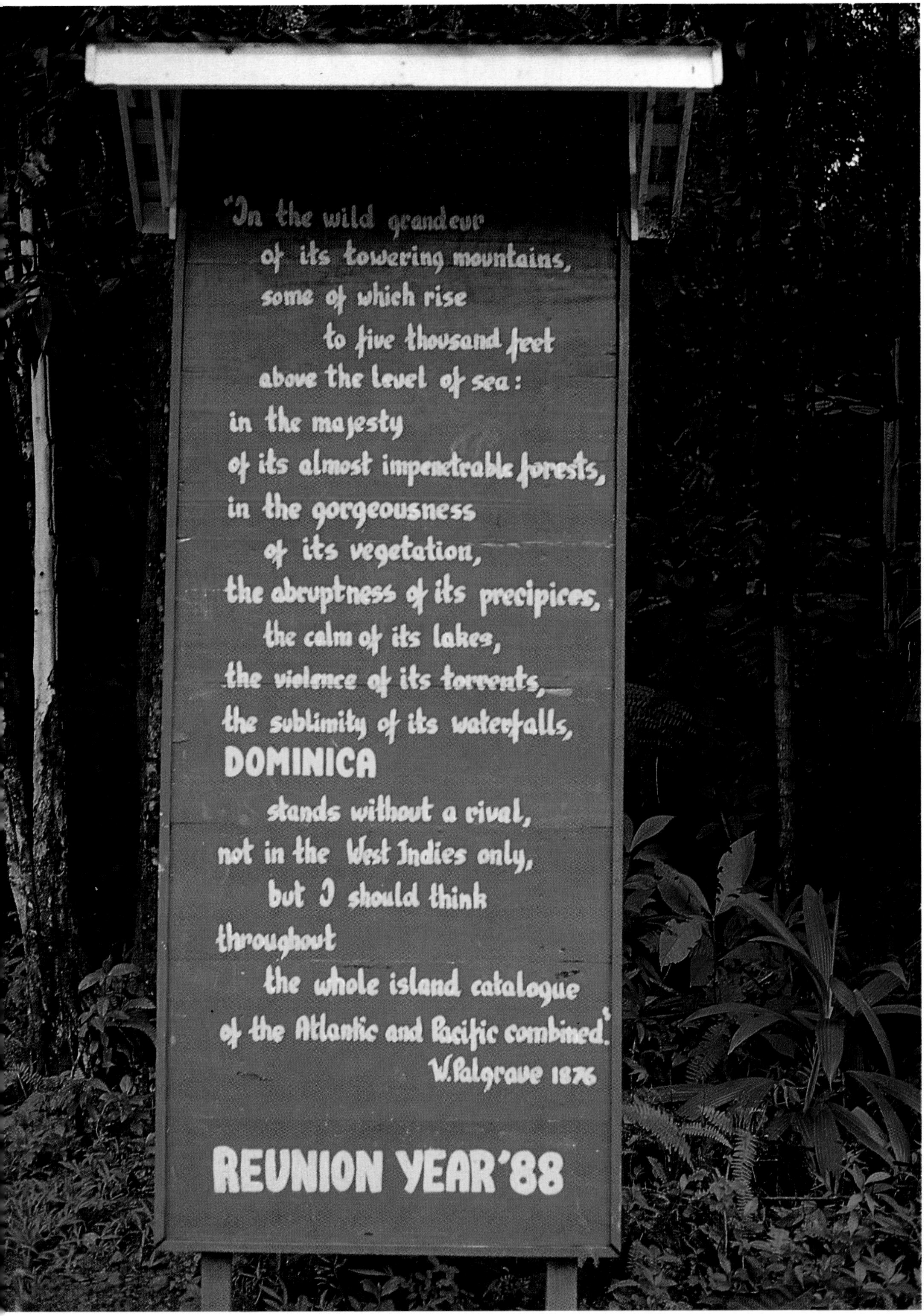

"In the wild grandeur
of its towering mountains,
some of which rise
to five thousand feet
above the level of sea:
in the majesty
of its almost impenetrable forests,
in the gorgeousness
of its vegetation,
the abruptness of its precipices,
the calm of its lakes,
the violence of its torrents,
the sublimity of its waterfalls,
DOMINICA
stands without a rival,
not in the West Indies only,
but I should think
throughout
the whole island catalogue
of the Atlantic and Pacific combined."

W. Palgrave 1876

REUNION YEAR '88

COMMANDANT'S QUARTERS

influence had to be abated and attempts were made to change Dominica's constitution to that of a crown colony. Many political wranglings dominated this period, during which Falconer was awarded £1,000 damages following his wrongful imprisonment after an argument with the Speaker of the House. Such was the financial state of the island that this money had to be paid in instalments until Falconer's death in 1917.

In 1865 a new and reduced constitution was enacted allowing for seven elected members and seven nominees, and by 1871 the writing was on the wall for Dominican elected government when the island was declared a federal colony, under the auspices of the Leeward Islands. Much bitterness was felt following this transfer of power to Antigua. But the final blow came in 1898 when the Crown Colony Bill created a Legislative Council made up of six nominated members.

Elected government had been replaced by naked imperialism, and it was to be many years before this situation was reversed. While these political activities were taking place, social disturbances were also occurring in Dominica. Following the announcement of a proposed government census in June 1844, rumours circulated to the effect that the census was in fact a forerunner to the reintroduction of slavery. The inevitable riots took place with deaths occurring in Canefield, Colihaut and, more particularly, in Grand Bay. Martial law was imposed and one rioter was publicly hanged in Pointe Michel, although others facing the gallows were pardoned. During the Grand Bay riot, soldiers shot one man and stuck his head on a pole as a deterrent to others.

Tension was also running high in the religious communities with rioting between 3000 Roman catholics and Methodists in Roseau in 1847 resulting in many wounded. Later in 1869 rival catholic groups clashed on Boxing Day at Fond Cole.

In January 1856, the owners of the Batalie Estate unsuccessfully attempted to evict squatters from land that bordered their estate. When the police arrived they were similarly rebuffed, only this time in a more violent manner. Finally soldiers were sent and on this occasion the squatters compromised and agreed to terms whereby they occupied the land on a lease and paid a small rent.

In the same year, the Road Act had stipulated that all Dominican citizens either had to pay taxes for road maintenance, or had to work a certain number of man hours without payment. This created great resentment and during the first few months 130 people were imprisoned for defying the Act. In 1881, however, women were exempted from the Act. Probably one of the most famous landmarks in Dominican social unrest occurred in La Plaine in 1893.

In 1886, the island's governor, Viscount Gormanston, had implemented, through the legislature, a tax of half a per cent on the value of land and property. Previously only Roseau and its environs were subject to this tax. A general income tax was also imposed. As a result a 1,000 strong body of landowners and businessmen marched on the governor's house in Roseau to protest. Despite the hostile crowd and the strong opposition to the Act, the governor refused to relent and two years later the land tax was increased to two per cent with surprisingly little objection. Then, in 1893, the first serious confrontation relating to the Land Tax Act erupted. La Plaine, a village on Dominica's east coast, had become one of the island's poorest districts. The sugar industry had been reduced to a virtual standstill and the villagers had to carry arrowroot, cassava and farine across the mountains, by foot, to Roseau. This was an arduous journey via Grand Fond and the Freshwater Lake which could take up to eight hours, depending on the weather. This journey, known as Chimen Letang (Lake Walk), was still taking place in the early 1960s before car-worthy roads were constructed. The sea was an alternative form of transportation, but the rough Atlantic Ocean meant much loss of life as well as merchandise. When the villagers finally arrived in Roseau, their produce was purchased at very low prices.

All this created a virtual money-free society for these country folk. Everyone was community minded and helped each other. There was an abundance of food from the rich fertile land and La Plaine, like other Dominican villages, had become a self-sufficient society. As a consequence, serious repercussions should have been expected with the implementation of the Land Tax Act. On April 6, a certain Pierre Coliare, unable to pay the tax on his house, found himself facing a bailiff and a police inspector. Angry villagers turned on the two men as they attempted to evict Coliare and they were driven off. One week later, on April 13, the Royal Navy Cruiser, HMS Mohawk, landed in Plaisance Bay with twenty-five armed sailors, nine policemen and the island's latest governor, Haynes-Smith. They marched to Colliares' house but he refused to vacate his property. As soon as Coliare had been evicted, the troops were attacked with stones by an angry mob. In retaliation the sailors opened fire killing four men and injuring two women. As a result of these deaths no land tax is paid in Dominica today, although a nominal rate is levied through the village councils.

By the turn of the century the British Empire had grown to its largest in its history, encompassing one quarter of the world's population. But Dominica had been badly neglected and had fallen into a state of disrepair and poverty. The reasons for this were many and varied, including natural disaster, continuous invasion and the impenetrable rugged terrain which discouraged the British authorities from supplying money for development. In 1896 the British government acceded to demands from the Colonial Office minister, Joseph Chamberlain, and granted £30,000 to be spent on road construction and to pay off the colony's debts.

In 1988, 95 years after the uprising, a plaque was unveiled in Case O'Gowrie, La Plaine, (the site of the insurrection) to commerate what has become known as the La Plaine Land Tax Riot.

During this period various British individuals began to make their presence felt in the development of the island. A Scot by the name of Dr John Imray, discovered previously unknown species of plants and was also instrumental in finding natural cures for tropical diseases such as yellow fever and malaria; diseases unknown now in Dominica. Imray was followed by a Londoner, Dr Henry Nicholls, who, amongst other achievements, cultivated tropical crops. He was later knighted for his services to the island, where he died in 1926.

By 1889, the position of Dominica's governor had been elevated to administrative status, and in that same year the island was to experience the beneficial effects of Administrator Henry Hesketh Bell. He quickly assessed Dominica's malaise and set about a vigorous programme of improvement. Many roads were constructed (previously there was only three or four miles of driveable roads), 200 miles of telephone lines were installed and electricity was introduced to the island. It is interesting to note that all of the south-east district of

Dominica did not receive electricity until 1988; Bell's early pioneering took nearly a century to reach that particular area.

Bell also arranged for the Royal Mail to supply a small steamer to service the island and introduced property insurance against hurricanes. In 1905 he encouraged the United States philanthropic millionaire, Andrew Carnegie, to donate £1,500 to build a public library in Roseau. Years later, another rich American philanthropist, the lime producer Andrew Green, donated a large sum of money which was used to improve health care including the establishment of entire water and sewage systems.

One further project which Bell embarked on was the encouragement of new settlers. He wrote articles in British newspapers on the benefits and potential of the island, and also produced a guidebook for those intending to settle. Many did, in fact, arrive, and by 1907 the white population, which had previously declined significantly, had risen to 400.

This was not the first time that an Englishman had attempted to sell the benefits of Dominica to the British. In 1791, the Chief Judge of Dominica, Thomas Atwood, wrote, "Emigrations of English subjects from other settlements, or even Great Britain, might be turned to great advantage to the Island of Dominica; as the lands there, if cleared of the excessive forests of wood, are capable of far greater improvements than the lands of Trinidad, or of any other still unsettled country in the West Indies. There is no doubt that in a few years this Island would be in a very flourishing situation."

In the event, Atwood's projection of Dominica did not materialise. Administrator Bell continued his good work, cutting the central Imperial Road (resurfaced only in 1988) and trying to establish rubber trees, something which was unsuccessful. The island, thanks to Bell, who was greatly admired by the majority of Dominicans, was gradually making an economic recovery. But unfortunately, in 1905, Bell was promoted to the post of Commander-in-Chief in Uganda and left Dominica.

Meanwhile, the sugar and coffee industry had been superceeded by cocoa and limes, with the latter booming. In fact during this period, and after the First World War, Dominica was by far the largest producer

The east coast from the hillside near Point Mulatre.

126

of limes in the world, with the cane mills being turned into lime processing plants. Green limes, raw lime juice and lime oil were all exported in large quantities to the United States and Britain.

The English Quaker chocolate manufacturers, Rowntree of York, owned three large estates in the north of the island, and oranges, coconuts, vanilla and spices all had markets abroad.

Suddenly there was a positive balance of trade, with exports exceeding imports for the first time in many years. But war in Europe was looming, and just as it appeared that economic recovery would be sustained, Germany declared war on Russia.

Two days later, on August 5, 1914, Britain also entered the fray. With the advent of the First World War many of the white families encouraged to settle in Dominica by Hesketh Bell sold up and went home. Most of the island's inhabitants declared their loyalty to Britain and many joined up to fight for the British Empire.

Inevitably there was a reduction in trade, particularly in limes, and prices for imported food and cloth soon increased.

The island's legislative council directed money towards the war effort and money was also raised for the Red Cross.

Although Dominica had been spared active involvement in the war, the natural elements were not in a conciliatory mood, and in August 1916 the island was rocked by a serious hurricane. Destruction was widespread, particularly on the east coast where roads and bridges were swept away.

The lime industry was badly affected with the cocoa crop and livestock also suffering damage.

November 1918 signalled an end to the war. There had been twenty-four Dominican fatalities, their names later engraved on a memorial in Roseau.

Following the 1898 Crown Colony Act, Dominica had lost its franchise During the interim period, much bitterness and resentment had been felt and in 1919 the Representative Government Association was formed. Its aim was to re-establish an elected assembly in Dominica. Pressure was brought to bear and surprisingly the legislature voted in favour of a reintroduction of elected members. The British government,

TOP: *Fruit grows in abundance in Dominica, both wild and cultivated, the future market potential is enormous.*

BOTTOM: *The Botanical Gardens, in Roseau, had been established in 1891 and now tended tropical plants from all over the world, as well as providing agricultural training. It was also regarded as the finest of its' kind in the Westindies of that time.*

realising that feelings were stronger in Dominica than in many other islands, agreed to alter the Constitution, and in 1925 four elected members were once again participating in the government of Dominica.

Since the 1916 hurricane, the island's lime industry had made a significant recovery. But disaster struck in May 1922 when 'Withertip´ disease was discovered on estates in the south. This quickly spread and within months few estates had been spared the trauma. This was shortly followed by 'Red Root' disease and this twin attack left Dominica's lime industry shattered and broken. Exports dropped dramatically and by 1925 lime production had practically ceased on the island. With the lime industry finished, Dominica began to look towards new crops, and coconuts and bananas were quickly introduced.

The 1929 Wall Street crash confirmed the island's economic dejection as it created a world-wide depression. It was to be another twenty years before Dominica's agricultural fortunes were to recover.

In September 1930 trouble erupted when five armed policemen entered the Carib territory to search for smuggled goods. They seized rum and tobacco, at which point a riot broke out with the police being attacked with stones and bottles. In retaliation they fired into the crowd, resulting in two deaths and four injuries. The police then escaped to nearby Marigot. The following day the Royal Navy warship HMS Delhi arrived off the coast and fired warning shots. Marines accompanied police into the territory who made a thorough search of the area. As a result of this incident the Carib chief lost his title. It was not to be reinstated until June 1952.

In 1925 elected members were returned to the legislature. These were professional or business people who were very firmly entrenched in the middle classes. If we look at their names, H.D. Shillingford, C.E.A Rawle, S.L.V Green and A.A. Baron, we can see that some of their descendants are prominent in Dominican business life today.

The newly elected members, however, were experiencing difficulties in influencing the legislature, as they made up a tiny minority.

In 1931, the Constitutional Reform Association was formed with the aim of bringing about greater constitutional freedom. The following

For 150 years the Carib community had been living peacefully and quietly on a small portion of the east coast, around Salibia, which had been designated as their 'reserve' by the British authorities. They rarely mixed with other Dominicans and lived a traditional life of fishing, hunting and growing their own provisions.

In 1902, Hesketh Bell decided that the Carib territory should be extended from 232 to 3,700 acres.
He also declared that the Carib 'chief' should be officially recognised with a £6 annual allowance. Both measures were implemented and the chief was formally invested.

Today the Carib territory is officially administered by the Carib Council, who report directly to the government. The council also owns all the land and is responsible for allocations to its inhabitants for farming and building purposes. The chief is still the figurehead of the community but can only serve for a term of between three and five years.

year, a conference was held in Roseau, attended by seventeen prominent Westindian political leaders. Their aims were to create a Westindian Federation with self-government, which would automatically bring an end to Crown Colony rule, and the implementation of full adult franchise. The chairman of the conference, Dominican barrister and politician C.E.A. Rawle, firmly stated that change must be created peacefully and constitutionally. The British authorities, aware that Dominica had for many years battled for political independence, and impressed with the reasonableness of the island's political leaders, sent a commission to examine possible political reforms. This resulted in a new constitution in 1936, allowing for three ex-officio members, four nominated and seven elected legislature members, as well as a governor. The British authorities were not risking defeat but rather attempting to appease the island's politicians.

On January 1, 1940, the Windward Islands grouping was formed and Dominica officially ceased to be a colony of the Leeward Islands.

In 1926 and 1928, Dominica had suffered two minor hurricanes, but in 1930 the island was hit by a serious hurricane, which wiped out the slowly recovering agricultural industry.

In September 1939 Germany invaded Poland and Britain came to the assistance of her ally. Europe had been thrown into another war.

Once again Dominica made her defensive preparations and many Dominicans left their homes and fought alongside British and Canadian troops. A blackout was ordered at night for streets facing the sea, and, as in the First World War, the defence force, only thirty in number, prepared for action. This time the food shortages were even greater because of the threat of German U boats fisherman were reluctant to go to sea. In 1942, British boats were sunk by submarines in the waters off Trinidad, St. Lucia and Barbados. Naked and half eaten bodies were washed up on Dominica's eastern Atlantic shore, but fortunately the island was spared any military action.

Trade was at a standstill, agricultural production was low and meat was very scarce.

Many Dominicans feared a German invasion as the neighbouring islands of Guadeloupe and Martinique were colonies of France which by then was under German occupation.

In 1942, 5,000 French citizens fleeing the occupation found refuge in Dominica. This was an added strain on the island's resources, but the people felt obliged to offer their support until the French left in August 1943.

Finally, in 1945, peace was declared and Dominica had to pick up the pieces of its flagging economy.

Socially the island had changed little since emancipation, over 100 years ago in 1834. Political life was dominated by the Roseau middle classes and the road network was still very limited. The country areas existed very much independently with little or no assistance. Each village resembled a small, self-sufficient co-operative where man helped his fellow man. Education was still poor and the villagers relied on their knowledge of local herbs and plants for their medical requirements. Agricultural produce still had to be carried to town, often via rough, muddy mountain passes, although the sea was still used as a form of transportation. This was mainly on the calmer Caribbean Sea, on the west coast. However, the intrepid Atlantic sailor was often undeterred by the treacherous eastern coastline.

With the decline of limes, Dominica's farming community decided to concentrate its efforts on three products - bananas, coconuts and vanilla. In 1936 the price of vanilla began to rise, encouraging further production on the island. Three years later the price in the United States increased rapidly due to Far East supplies being restricted. Small farmers throughout the island were now encouraged to get involved, and the industry peaked in 1945, whereupon a collapse ensued following the destruction of 50,000 lbs of cured vanilla in a Roseau fire. The industry limped on until 1959 when it finally disappeared.

Dominica's coconut industry, concentrated in the north-east of the island, had enjoyed a continuous stable growth. The main utilisation had been as copra, which was turned into oils and fats. Until the mid 1960's this copra was exported almost exclusively to Barbados and Trinidad. But with the emergence of the company Dominica Coconut Products, the island's copra was used to produce soap, liquid detergent and cooking oil for export.

OPPOSITE: *The juice processing plant in Roseau handling limes and grapefruit, when in season.*

In 1931, one of Dominica's premier business organisations, A.C Shillingford & Co., began to export bananas to Liverpool thus establishing the long association Dominica has enjoyed with Britain in the banana industry. Three years later, in 1934, the first Banana Growers Association in the Windward Islands was formed in Dominica. Exports increased rapidly over the next few years, but the industry's progress came to an abrupt halt with the outbreak of war.

Production continued at a low level until 1949 when two Englishmen, P.J. Foley and G.B. Band, formed Antilles Products Ltd with its head office in Dominica. They in turn sold out to Geest Industries Ltd of Boston, England in 1954. Geest made special arrangements with the British government and from there Dominica's banana industry began to prosper. Geest, realising the obvious potential, commissioned specially built banana boats, and the island's economic revival had begun. The advantages for Dominica's small farmers were two-fold: an all year round crop and a regular income.

By the 1960s bananas accounted for eighty per cent of the island's exports, Geest and bananas had become synonymous with Dominica and the Windward Islands. In 1978 banana 'Leaf Spot' damaged much of the crop, and a year later, in 1979, Hurricane David flattened every banana tree on the island. Before a recovery was possible, Hurricane Allen, in 1980, completed the destruction of bananas. The crop has provided Dominica with a sustained period of prosperity. This is particularly true in the country areas, where the vast majority of the population relies almost totally on this one crop for their income.

Following the Second World War, grapefruit and oranges became important crops and limes made a minor recovery. In 1951, a fruit packing and processing plant was opened in Roseau, and in 1954 the Co-operative Citrus Growers Association was formed. Both grapefruit and oranges grew to steady export levels, but many believe the full potential has yet to be tapped.

In 1975 L. Rose & Co., the lime producers, who had been heavily involved in production in Dominica for many years, opened a modern lime crushing plant in Roseau. Unfortunately this was not a success and the company sold up and pulled out of the island in 1979. Bay leaf and

OPPOSITE: *The banana crop was virtually wiped out in 1979/80 - Now back on its feet- the banana industry accounts for almost 50% of all exports.*

134

bay oil production had been an important crop in the southeast of the island, some of it used for perfume manufacturing in the United States and Europe. In the mid 1960s, American perfumer Charlie Prestler swapped his Manhattan penthouse suite, for the 600 acre Taberie Estate near La Plaine. For over ten years, his distillery produced large quantities of high quality bay oil. But like many other crops, his bay leaf industry was destroyed in 1979 by Hurricane David.

At the end of the Second World War, a social welfare department was set up in Dominica. This followed the 1940 Colonial Development and Welfare Act, which in turn was the result of a Royal Commission, headed by Lord Moyne, which looked into the social and economic problems of the British Westindies.

Dominica was recognised as needing urgent attention, and over the next eighteen years a programme of social development was instituted. Roads, schools, hospitals, airfields and reservoirs were all built and a literacy programme was established.

Road construction was a particular problem. Because of Dominica's terrain, the engineers had to cut through mountains and they also had the added difficulty of heavy rain and mud to contend with, which often negated much of the day's work.

Many abortive attempts were made to continue the Central Imperial road, but it was not until 1956 that the north-east of the island was finally connected by a motorable highway.

By 1945, the islanders' health, due mainly to a lack of supplies during the war, was in poor condition. Malnutrition was a cause for concern, particularly in the overcrowed areas around Roseau, malaria and yaws were also creating problems. Today, all serious tropical diseases have been eradicated. The World Health Organisation has played a major role in health development and thanks mainly to foreign aid every village now has a health centre and trained nurses and midwives. Infant mortality has dropped dramatically and medicine is also provided free of charge. In 1956 the Princess Margaret Hospital was opened in Goodwill, a suburb of Roseau, providing 240 beds.

In 1925 Dominica had recorded its first air landing when a seaplane touched down off the Roseau bay-front. In 1943 a single engine,

TOP: *A memorial to C.E.A Rawle in Federation Drive: Goodwill with the Princess Margaret Hospital in the background.*

BOTTOM: *The road to Portsmouth via Picard Estate highlights some of the diverse nature of Dominica.*

four-seater plane landed in Portsmouth, but it was not until 1961 that the island's first airport was opened at Melville Hall on the north-east coast. In 1981, a further airstrip was constructed at Canefield, a few miles from Roseau, and there is now talk of an international airport, with Woodford Hill being the most likely site.

The courthouse Roseau bay front.

From the mid-1930s the north-east village of Marigot had begun to show signs of autonomy with the establishment of a village committee. This was Dominica's first foray into local government and in 1939 house rates were imposed. Instrumental in this scheme was English-born Elma Napier, who in 1940 became the first woman in the Caribbean to be elected to Parliament. By 1945 ten village councils, in every area of the island, were operational, with nominal house rates being levied.

In the 1930s and 1940s many former estates remained idle with some being reclaimed by nature - Castle Bruce, Rosalie and Pointe Mulatre being three examples. However, with the introduction of bananas in the 1950s many of these estates were revived. Geest purchased three and local families bought up many of the others available. Smaller estates of fifteen to twenty acres were snapped up by small farmers and areas of Crown land were sold to individuals for agricultural cultivation. This further enhanced the independence of Dominica's small farmer. Today nearly every person involved in farming either owns a number of acres of land or enjoys a low rent, thus creating a society of self-employed farmers; a situation uncommon in the Caribbean.

In January 1945 the Dominica Trade Union was formed. within six months there were twenty-six branches island-wide. Influential in the establishment of Dominica's first Trade Union was E.C. Loblack, who was to play an important role in future Dominican politics. The following year Methodist Minister, A.E. Belboda, formed the Dominican Workers' Association, whose members were based in the north of the island around Portsmouth and Marigot, and in 1949 the Teachers' Union was registered.

In 1951 democracy finally arrived in Dominica. For many decades political activists had fought for complete emancipation and at last the British authorities granted the right to vote to anyone over twenty-one in Dominica and the Windward Islands. Elections took place in that

TOP: *Take a row-boat trip on the river. It's so peaceful and close to nature.*

BOTTOM: *The old mill wood carving is part of the cultural centre.*

138

year but there were still no political parties.

Two years later, in 1953, Phyliss Shand Allfrey returned to Dominica from England where she had been living. Mrs Allfrey was the grandaughter of Dr. Sir Henry Nicholls, and had been an active member of the British Labour Party.

With Loblack she formed the island's first political party - the Dominica Labour Party (D.L.P.) which was launched on May 24 1955. Two years later Edward LeBlanc joined the party and he soon became a leading spokesman.

In the 1957 elections four Labour Party members were returned and, in an effort to create a majority, the remaining independent members joined forces to form the Dominica United People's Party, (D.U.P.P.) under the leadership of F.A. Baron who later went on to become the island's first chief minister in 1960.

LeBlanc continued building his power base and in 1961 he led the Labour Party to victory in the elections. In the same year Phyliis Allfrey was expelled from the party for publicly criticising it in the local newspaper.' *The Herald*'. Another attempt at reviving the Federation, this time with the remaining eight small islands of the East Caribbean, failed. Instead Dominica decided to push ahead for independence and finally on November 3 1967 achieved Associated Statehood. This was the first stage to full independence which was accomplished eleven years later in 1978. As an Associate State, Dominica was responsible for its internal affairs whilst Britain retained control over external affairs and defence.

The previous year, 1966, had seen a landslide victory for LeBlanc's D.L.P. with eleven seats secured against only one for the D.U.P.P. LeBlanc was a man of the people with powerful grassroots support in the country areas.

Following statehood Sir Louis Cools Lartique became the first Dominican born governor, thus confirming the new independent spirit in the country.

Since the 1932 Conference for Westindian Federation was held in Roseau, Caribbean politicians had been campaigning for a United Westindies. In 1947, a further conference took place in Jamaica. This meeting appeared to be the catalyst, and finally in 1958 elections were held in all ten member islands of the Westindian Federation. Following these elections, LeBlanc and Allfrey were convincingly elected to represent Dominica. But the Federation was to be shortlived when, within four years, the larger islands Jamaica and Trinidad and Tobago, withdrew and the Federation collapsed.

With the D.U.P.P. broken and powerless, the only opposition to the D.L.P. came from the media in the form of 'The Herald ', The Star' and 'The Chronicle.' Following various criticisms of LeBlanc and the D.L.P. in the press, LeBlanc sought to control these outbursts and the Seditious and Undesirable Publications Act was presented to Parliament, in July 1968.

This attempt to restrict freedom of speech was met with a vociferous response, with D.L.P. founders, Loblack and Allfrey, leading the protests. A petition was signed and meetings and marches were held. Undeterred, LeBlanc rushed the bill through and this signalled the start of a new political force in Dominica.

Anthony Moise, former D.U.P.P. Member of Parliament, and one of the originators of the short lived National Democratic Party, now joined forces with Loblack, Allfrey, newspaper editor Edward Scobie and barrister Mary Eugenia Charles, amongst others, to form the Dominica Freedom Party (D.F.P.). This was to be the beginning of a new period in Dominican politics. Meanwhile, economic and social development had been continuing in the island.

Since 1905 a small electricity plant had been servicing Roseau and its environs. In the mid 1950's a hydropowered plant was constructed at Trafalgar supplying electricity from Dominica's most natural and abundant source - water.

During the 1960's, Dominica's ailing telephone system had, to all intents and purposes, collapsed. The old system had to be replaced and the British company Cable & Wireless were invited to install a new system. This was successfully accomplished by 1978, with every village on the island supplied with at least one public telephone. Unfortunately Hurricane David completely destroyed the system, but Cable & Wireless worked hard at restoring it to international standards.

Roads continued to be built and in 1965 the east coast, after hundreds of years of isolation, at last had a motorable link with the rest of the island. Feeder roads for farmers were also constructed and the flow of agricultural produce to Roseau rapidly increased - meaning in turn greater prosperity .

Prior to 1965, only a handful of four wheel drive jeeps were able

Speaking of 1992 and the creation of the Single European Market.

"We have to be stronger and speak as one voice because they will be speaking as one. We want to be strong and really make our point in order to reap the benifits we feel we can get through the Lomê Convention."

Prime Minister Eugenia Charles.

In February 1987 Dominica became the first country in the world to operate a fully digital national telephone system.

to use the coastal tracks. Each appearance was greeted with flag waving and cheering from the local children.

In 1968 a new water system was implemented to service Roseau and the south-west; other areas also began to receive piped water. Previously villagers in country areas had to walk to the nearest river for their supplies. Fortunately Dominica has a surplus of water and since the late 1970s has exported it to St. Martin and other riverless Caribbean islands. Spring water is also bottled for export purposes, with the Emerald Corporation producing Eau Erte.

New housing schemes, mainly to relieve the overcrowded Roseau area, have grown up since the early 1950s when rural High Schools also began to emerge. Previously secondary schooling was restricted to Roseau, at educational establishments such as the Catholic-run St. Mary's Academy and the Dominica Grammar School.

Much of this development was funded by the British and Canadian governments. In more recent years, France, the United States and Venezuela have also provided much needed aid.

The trade union movement also developed in the post-war period.

Following an attempt to evict 1,000 tenant farmers from their homes, the Dominica Trade Union (D.T.U.) took legal action against one of the landlords. This resulted in the 1953 Agricultural Small Tenants Act which gave protection to all tenant farmers. In 1960 the Dominica Banana Employees Association was formed, later evolving into a general union, the Dominica Amalgamated Workers Union (D.A.W.U.). In 1965 the port workers broke away from the D.T.U. to create the Seamen and Waterfront Workers' Union, later to become the Waterfront and Allied Workers' Union under the leadership of General Secretary Patrick John. The Civil Service Association (C.S.A.) also came into existence, and in the 1970s the Dominica Farmers Union was created. In 1977 there was a split in the D.A.W.U, resulting in the formation of the National Workers' Union.

Strikes have been few and far between. However, in 1976 the whole island came to a standstill for seven weeks when the Civil Service Association became embroiled in a dispute with the ruling Labour

TOP: *Container ships unloading at Woodbridge Harbour.*

BOTTOM: *All schools have their own uniform colours.*

Party. Hospitals ran on a skeleton staff, there was no movement at the port and no flights in or out of the island. The dispute was eventually settled when the government agreed to pay monies owed in back pay.

There is little doubt, though, that, since its inception, the Dominica Trades Union Movement has protected its members and has been of benefit to the island as a whole.

In 1949 Miss Eugenia Charles returned to Dominica. She had attended University in Canada, before being called to the Bar in England. By 1968 she had become one of the island's leading lawyers, and she then found herself being thrown into the political arena as leader of the new Dominica Freedom Party (D.F.P.).

The D.F.P. spontaneously found themselves at odds with the D.L.P. To begin with they were predominantly a Roseau-based middle-class group of professional people who did not have the country roots of the D.L.P. However, they took their ideology into the rural areas in an effort to win over support.

In September 1970 a split appeared in the D.L.P. when three ministers attempted to expel LeBlanc from the party. In retaliation LeBlanc sacked them from their cabinet positions. LeBlanc's popularity was still high and the D.L.P. were convincingly returned to power in the elections later that year.

Miss Charles' first foray into electoral politics was not successful; she lost the Roseau North constituency to another newcomer, Patrick John, who was immediately given ministerial responsibility whilst Miss Charles entered the House of Assembly as a nominated member.

In 1971, Dominica, along with other Caribbean states, signed an accord which became known as the Grenada Declaration. This was a declaration of unity, to which the D.F.P. was vehemently opposed. Later that same year, following the D.F.P.'s success in the Roseau Town Council elections, the ruling D.L.P. introduced the Roseau Town Council Bill, which effectively dissolved the Council.

Both these political acts caused great resentment in the ranks of the D.F.P. Demonstrations and protest meetings ensued with support from the unions, the business sector and the Council of Churches. The dispute came to a head when the House of Assembly was occupied by

TOP:*The Karbet meeting house in the Carib area.*

BOTTOM: *A colourful and traditional shop in downtown Roseau.*

those in conflict with the government of the day. The Bill was subsequently withdrawn, but many demonstrators faced charges.

In July 1974, after thirteen years in power, LeBlanc resigned and Patrick John succeeded him as Premier. During LeBlanc's period of leadership Dominica had experienced many changes and improvements to its infrastructure and social welfare. In 1972, the new Roseau to Portsmouth road was constructed, as well as the Hatton Garden to Castle Bruce road which intersected the Carib territory. These isolated people had become shy and retiring, rarely associating with the outside world. Now a highway was running directly through their territory and they responded in a positive fashion. Hats, baskets and other forms of handicrafts, which were previously mainly for internal use, were now displayed outside traditionally constructed thatched huts. Tourists came and left with merchandise as a permanent reminder of their visit. Today the Caribs are almost fully integrated into Dominican society with the majority involved in farming. However, the entrepreneurial spirit is still alive; as well as handicrafts, a few small guest houses now offer accommodation in their area.

In 1974, work started on a deepwater harbour at Woodbridge Bay, near Roseau. Large ships, including the Geest banana boats, utilise the harbour but yachts and schooners are more likely to be found at Portsmouth, in Prince Rupert Bay.

Following Patrick John's accession to power, former D.L.P. politician, Ronald Armour, founded the Progressive Labour Party. Armour, a prominent businessman, had recently been expelled from the D.L.P. But just then Patrick John had more immediate problems to contend with. During the late 1960s and early 1970s Dominica felt, along with other islands in the Caribbean, the reverberations of the Black Power movement which found its highest expression in the United States. Many in the Rastafarian community, known as 'Dreads', were influenced by this movement and this contributed to a period of social unrest and uncertainty for the country. A number of violent incidents led Prime Minister John to authorise offensive operations by the police and volunteer defence force.

Prime Minister John's first political move was to present to

OPPOSITE: *The post office on the bay front, Roseau.*

Parliament the Prohibited and Unlawful Societies and Associations Act, commonly known as the "Dread Act". This was denounced by many, including the
Movement for a New Dominica (M.N.D.) as an infringement on the rights of assembly. However, it was to remain on the statute books until 1981.

Following the death of a volunteer defence force member after a skirmish in the mountains around Belles, a full-time defence force was established with Prime Minister John as Colonel. In 1975 an amnesty was declared with many 'Dreads' returning to mainstream society. The numbers involved, however, had been exaggerated and from this period onwards their activities were very limited.

On March 24, 1975, a new round of elections took place. The number of constituencies had been increased to twenty-one, with four political parties contesting the seats: D.L.P, D.F.P, the Progressive Labour Party and the Caribbean Federal Party. John, like his predecessor LeBlanc, was a popular leader. From humble beginings in Roseau he had elevated himself to schoolteacher, Trade Union leader, Mayor of Roseau and finally leader of his country. His popularity was reflected in the polls with sixteen out of the twenty-one seats going to the D.L.P. The D.F.P. won only three seats, but Eugenia Charles was elected to Parliament for the first time, winning the Roseau Central seat. The position of leader of the opposition went to the experienced politician, Anthony Moise.

This period in Dominica's history was also marked by a natural disaster when the south coast village of Bagatelle was submerged under a landslide following days of torrential rain. Remarkably only eight people died. The police, the defence force and volunteers all worked tirelessly to locate the survivors, and the local community rallied round to offer assistance to the homeless.

In 1976, after nine years of Associated Statehood, the government of Dominica requested to end links with Britain. The opposition Freedom Party (D.F.P.) demanded a referendum, but following a sixteen to three vote in favour of the D.L.P. the matter was officially referred to the British government. In May 1977 a constitutional conference took place

TOP: *Rainbows can be a source of fascination in Dominica, appearing and disappearing, high and low.*

BOTTOM: *A peaceful home near La Plaine district.*

at Marlborough House in London, with both D.F.P. and D.L.P. now in favour of independence. Differences were debated at length both in London and back in Dominica and finally the new Dominican constitution was agreed upon. The government would consist of a president and a single chamber House of Assembly, with the addition of nominated senators.

During July 1978, the Dominican House of Assembly and both British Houses of Parliament agreed to terminate Dominica's association with Britain.

Children in the national costume during the tenth anniversary of independence

On November 3, 1978, 485 years after Columbus first sighted the island, Dominica gained full independence. The Queen was represented by Princess Margaret and the new flag of Dominica was raised. To avoid confusion with the Spanish speaking Caribbean state of the Dominican Republic, Dominica officially assumed the title of the Commonwealth of Dominica. The island's last governor, Sir Louis Cools-Lartique, was appointed Interim President, to be succeeded by Fred Degazon on December 22.

Dominica had finally attained independence from more than 200 years of colonisation. But the following year, 1979, was to prove one of the most traumatic in its history.

P.M. Patrick John had stated that his policy would be based on "New Socialism", encompassing the public, private and co-operative sectors. The Movement for a New Dominica (M.N.D.) had evolved into the Dominica Liberation Movement Alliance (D.L.MA.). They denounced the existing political parties as representing "old farcical politics". The D.L.M.A. was one of a number of so called left-wing organisations which were then emerging throughout the Caribbean. They were largely foreign educated, intellectual idealists who were returning to the countries of their birth in the hope of gaining political power and creating new societies with greater equity. P.M. Patrick John was a charismatic but ambiguous leader, who had perhaps forgot the adage that ultimate power often corrupts. Furthermore his political ideology seemed to have become somewhat confused. He supported the Dominica-Cuba Friendship League and strengthened links with Guyana. On the other hand, ministers, including future D.L.P. leader

Michael Douglas, were dismissed for allegedly having 'communist tendencies' Prime Minister John was additionally responsible for Dominica's membership of the United Nations and the International Monetary Fund, and he also became involved in elaborate deals to sell off or lease parts of the island.

The former Prime Minister seemed to have a predilection for such schemes and in February 1979 he signed a deal with a Texan businessman Don Pierson which would have effectively leased forty-five square miles of Dominica's north coast. Their intention was to establish a Free Port Zone on a low cost ninety-nine year lease. Accusations of 'selling-out' the island were heard, and after vociferous opposition from the D.F.P, farmers' unions and other political and interest groups, the plan was dropped.

Quadrille dancers in national costume.

`Simultaneously, an alleged agreement was made between a Dominican government minister and the racist South African regime relating to petro-chemical products.

None of these deals came to fruition, and whether Patrick John was acting out of naive belief that these actions would improve Dominica, or for self-betterment, it is open to question.

He was also facing problems from the Civil Service Association. The C.S.A. had posted their intentions to strike on June 1, 1979. On May 29 the Industrial Relations (Amendment) Act was to be introduced in an effort to limit strike action by civil servants and workers in essential services. The Libel and Slander Act was also to be amended to prevent editors from withholding the names of people who wrote 'inflammatory' articles in newspapers.

On the morning of May 29, 10,000 demonstrators marched on the House of Assembly at the government headquarters to register their opposition to these bills. It began peacefully, but eventually the defence force saw fit to fire tear gas into the crowd. Tensions mounted and the defence force were attacked with stones. Who actually gave the order to open fire is, to this day, a controversial question, but minutes later shots rang out and one youth was fatally injured. Ten others suffered bullet wounds, four being critically injured.

As a result all trade unions and businesses went on indefinite strike, vowing not to return to work until the government had resigned.

Oliver Seraphin, who later went on to form the Democratic Labour Party of Dominica, was the first minister to resign. President Degazon fled the island on June 11 and former governor Sir Louis Cool Lartique agreed to take over; only to resign himself twenty-four hours later after his house and shop were looted. Road blocks were set up and many ministers resigned. Prime Minister John, however, refused to follow suit, despite widespread calls for him to do so.

It is an amazing fact, and probably an example of Dominica's dislike of violence, that neither a bloody coup, nor any other forceful action occurred during this period. Instead, a Committee for National Salvation (CNS) was created, embracing all political parties, the churches, trade unions, the business sector and farmers.

For the next twenty days the C.N.S. argued and debated and finally on June 21 Judge Winzy Bruno swore in Barrister Jenner Armour as acting president. Armour's first political act was to appoint Oliver Seraphin as Prime Minister, thus ending Patrick John's period in power following the loss of his parliamentary majority.

Dominica then embarked on a period of Interim Government by coalition made up of the 12 elected cross-party members who supported Prime Minister Seraphin, plus three new senators - these being nominated by the Interim Government. All this was taking place a mere seven months following independence.

TOP: *The public library and gardens in Roseau.*

BOTTOM: *Peaceful downtown Roseau.*

HURRICANE DAVID

On August 29, 1979, the island was hit by one of the most severe hurricanes in living memory: Hurricane David.

The day had begun like any other Wednesday morning. Caribbean metereologists had been charting Hurricane David's course and had expected it to strike Barbados. However, fortunately for Barbados, it took a northerly turn and by 9.00 o'clock in the morning it was battering the east coast of Dominica. There was very little radio warning and no disaster preparation. For six hours the hurricane sat over the island destroying almost everything in its path. Winds of 150 m.p.h. stripped trees from the mountains, demolished churches and houses and swept away bridges and roads. Sheets of galvanised tin roofs flew through the air like missiles and stationery cars were found the next day in new parking places.

When the winds finally abated thirty-seven people had died and 5,000 were injured, many needing limb amputation. Three quarters of Dominica's population of 75,000 were left homeless and many months later many were still living with friends or family.

The economy was, needless to say, crippled with only citrus trees and coconuts in the north of the island being spared. There was no electricity and the telephone system had been totally destroyed, leaving amateur radio as the only form of contact with the outside world. There was no piped water and the previously clean rivers were dirty and clogged with the rotting bodies of dead animals.

The next day the British Royal Navy ship, H.M.S. Fife, arrived to give assistance, essentially in terms of repairs to the hospital and by clearing the streets of debris. The whole scene resembled a battlefield.

Dominica had suddenly become the centre of world-wide attention and very soon medical supplies, food, clothing and tents had been gratefully received. Aid came in primarily from Britain, the USA, Canada and other Caribbean islands. Appeals and relief committees were set up by Dominican communities in Britain and North America, and nearby Caribbean islands gave temporary refuge to many.

Money began to pour in. The USA pledged US $37 million, in addition to assistance from the IMF and the Red Cross and other relief organisations.

TOP: *An aerial view of Roseau ten years after Hurricane David had devastated the town.*

BOTTOM: *Ever ready emergency vehicles.*

So once more, and not for the first time in her history, Dominica had to start life all over again.

By the end of the year the Interim Government had practically disintegrated. Ministers had resigned and the need for new elections was pressing.

In February 1980, the President, Jenny Armour, resigned and Aurelius Marie was appointed in his place.

The elections were finally called in July with four parties contesting the D.L.P, D.F.P, the Democratic Labour party and the Dominican Liberation Movement Alliance. Eighty per cent of the electorate turned out, resulting in a comprehensive victory for the Freedom Party which secured seventeen seats. The Democratic Labour Party won two seats but the Dominica Labour Party who had held power for nearly twenty years lost all their seats, including that of former Prime Minister Patrick John. The overwhelming victory for the D.F.P. gave Eugenia Charles a positive mandate to implement her policies. The Caribbean's first woman Prime Minister embarked on an extensive rebuilding programme. During the years that were to follow much has been achieved.

However, in 1980, just as the island appeared to be making a recovery, Hurricane Allen struck, destroying the new crops. Fortunately Hurricane Allen was not as powerful as Hurricane David but it still represented a serious economic blow.

One of Prime Minister Eugenia Charles' first decisions was to disband the defence force, which she thought was politically aligned to former Prime Minister John and the D.L.P.

In 1981, Miss Charles set about a programme of resurfacing the island's roads, which had fallen badly into disrepair. Feeder roads for the farming communities and bridges were also constructed and Dominica can today boast some of the best roads in the Caribbean.

Electricity was also a major priority, and apart from some isolated areas, electric power is now island-wide.

In 1981 an alleged attempted coup took place. American and Canadian mercenaries, some of whom were members of the Ku Klux Klan, were apprehended by police in New Orleans as they were about

TOP LEFT: *Packing coconut meal, a by-product of cocunut oil production.*

TOP RIGHT: *Benjashoe Plastic Co. produces plastic shoes for the home and regional markets.*

BOTTOM LEFT: *Bottling passion fruit syrup at P.W. Bellot & Co.*

BOTTOM RIGHT: *Domestic soap production at Dominica Coconut Products.*

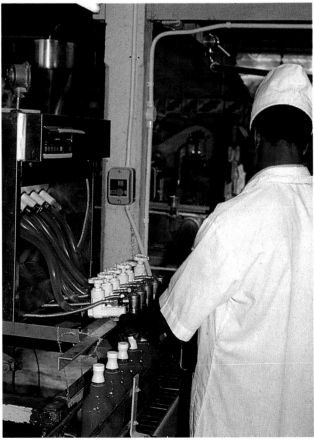
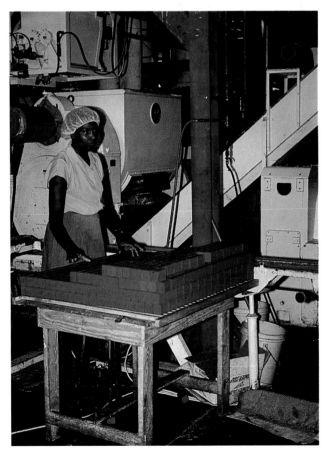

to set sail for Dominica. Police found arms and ammunition and information pertaining to the planned coup. They had planned to use the island as a centre for drug trafficking and international fraud and Patrick John was to be installed as Prime Minister. As a result John was charged and subsequently found guilty of conspiracy to overthrow the Government of Dominica by force of arms. He was sentenced to twelve years imprisonment.

In 1983, Prime Minister Eugenia Charles shot to international prominence when she vocally backed the American-led intervention in Grenada after the murder of that country's popular Prime Minister Maurice Bishop. In her capacity as chair of the OECS (Organisation of East Caribbean States) she stood alongside US President Ronald Reagan and briefed the international media. Miss Charles has subsequently become known as the 'Iron Lady' of the Caribbean.

It cannot be denied that Dominica has seen many improvements in health and education, as well as in infrastructure, since 1980. Funding for the various schemes has continued to come from foreign governments such as those of Venezuela, Canada, Britain , Taiwan and France, and also from organisations such as UNESCO and the World Health Organisation (WHO).

Since 1980 the Democratic Labour Party and the Dominica Liberation Movement Alliance have both disappeared, but in 1988 the United Workers' Party was created. With its roots in agriculture this new party is politically 'middle of the road' with some of its leaders being former D.L.P. members.

Dominica has come a long way in a short space of time in terms of development but the island has still retained much of its natural beauty; or as one Dominican lady returning from abroad observed: "If Christopher Columbus could come back to Dominica he'd be sure to recognise the island as it still looks the same !"

OPPOSITE: *Taking a five minute break at the Bay Oil Distillery, at La Plaine.*

SPORT

BY KEVIN MENHINICK

Frank Bruno

Dominicans, in common with many other Westindians, are naturally gifted sportsmen and women. Cricket is still the island's national game (Dominica regularly wins the Windward Islands trophy), but basketball and soccer have both gained greatly in popularity over recent years. Athletics, volleyball, netball, rounders, table-tennis and, to a lesser extent, squash and tennis, are all popular participation sports. In addition body-building, karate and boxing all have their followers.

Dominica is not, unfortunately, lucky enough to enjoy extensive first-class facilities. However, plans are being formulated to improve conditions for the country's sportsmen, and in particular to encourage the many talented youngsters.

Despite the limited facilities many impromptu games of cricket, football and basketball are regularly in evidence up and down the island. This is particularly true within the Carib community where many young boys can be seen with bat and ball imitating their heroes; Viv Richards, Malcolm Marshall and Gordon Greenidge.

Phillip De Freitas

Not that Dominica does not have its own heroes. Grayson and Irving Shillingford were the first Dominican cricketers to represent the Westindies, in the 1960s and 1970s. They were followed by Norbert Phillip who played nine times in the late 1970s and who also distinguished himself on the English County circuit with Essex. During his stay with the county, Phillip was an integral part of a successful side that won many trophies, including the county championship on three occasions. Phillip was also instrumental in embarrassing Surrey in a county championship match, when in a devastating spell of bowling he returned the remarkable figures of six wickets for four runs to scuttle out the Surrey side for a record low score of fourteen!

Phillip DeFreitas, the England opening bowler, is another famous Dominican cricketer. DeFreitas was born in Scotts Head, but moved to north west London with his family when he was ten years of age. Following a spell on the Lords cricket ground staff, he was offered professional contracts with three counties, including Middlesex. He eventually decided on Leicestershire, considering his opportunities for regular first team cricket and a future place in the England side to be

Vince Hilaire

better there. He was proved correct, as within two years he was playing for England, having taken ninety-four first class wickets and scoring a maiden century in his first full season with the county.

Martin Jean-Jacques, who hails from Soufriere, also played English county cricket, being plucked from relative obscurity, representing the minor county of Buckinghamshire, to open the bowling for Derbyshire. Batting at No.11 in his first county match, he hit seventy-three runs, thus underlying the all round natural talent of Dominican cricketers. Many, in fact, perform regularly in the various English leagues throughout the summer.

Other famous sporting sons include Vince Hilaire, whose parents are Dominican, and who represented England in football at various levels including the under twenty-three's; Francis Joseph, who played for many top English rugby league clubs and Joe Cooks who, in a professional soccer career, played for Bradford City and Oxford United amongst others. The most celebrated Dominican connection in the world-wide sporting arena, however, is Former European Heavyweight Boxing Champion, Frank Bruno. Frank has a Jamaican mother, but his father hailed from the west coast village of Massacre.

Former European Heavyweight Boxing Champion Frank Bruno.

Although not an internationally known fact, Dominica does boast a world champion. He is Roland Peltier, currently resident in Sweden, who is World Middleweight Champion in tae-kwon-do, the Korean martial art. In addition there is the OECS (Organisation of East Caribbean States) Middleweight Body-building Champion, Bertrand Bruney. Both may be minority sports, but both men prove what is possible given natural talent.

Whether dominoes can be classified as a sport is open to question, but it is undoubtedly Dominica's most popular pastime. All hours of the day and night the clatter of dominoes on tables can be heard in bars and rum shops up and down the island.

Bridge also has its advocates and Dominican bridge teams regularly partake in tournaments all over the Caribbean and in South America.

Another minority sport, cycling, has recently gained in popularity. The relatively small number of participants need a tremendous level of

OPPOSITE TOP: *Cricket match in the Botanical Gardens.*

OPPOSITE BOTTOM: *Dominos at La Plaine.*

fitness as they tackle Dominca's hill climbs. However, a number of organised events have taken place over the last few years adding a new dimension to Dominican sport.

No village would be complete without it's rounders team. The ladies keenly enjoy this sporting outlet with many people turning up to watch the games.

Lack of height precludes Dominica's growing band of basketball players from competing at international level. However, the level of speed and skill is high and Dominica always performs well at OECS competitions. The leagues, both for basketball and netball, are well organised and highly competitive.

However, many Dominican's, in recent years, have won scholarships to the USA for basketball and athletics.

Tennis and squash are also available on the island, squash at the Anchorage Hotel and tennis at the Castaways Hotel, the Reigate Hall Hotel and the Dominica Club in Roseau. Water sports is a growth area for Dominica. Scuba diving is available at the Anchorage Hotel, Castaways Hotel and Dive Dominica at Castle Comfort Guest House. Because Dominica's cliffs fall directly into the sea, a series of 'drop-offs' exist which, in turn, provide access to a wonderful underwater world of caverns and caves . Visibility for both scuba diving and snorkelling is good and marine life of all varieties and colours are much in evidence. This is real virgin territory which will be appreciated by the beginner and the serious diver alike. In fact diving in Dominica is acknowledged by experts as being rated fifth in the world and, just like the rain forests, untouched and unspoilt.

Water skiing and windsurfing are available at the Anchorage and the Shipwreck at Canefield, the latter also providing boating trips.

The Atlantic Ocean on Dominica's east coast is a natural area for surfing with large exciting regular waves.

Although the numbers of Dominican surfers are few, the transitory European workers, particularly the French, enjoy many hours of surfing fun.

TOURISM

BY KEVIN MENHINICK

Tourism has never had a high profile in the economic development of Dominica.There are many reasons for this:
the rough, often in accessible terrain has in the past created difficulties in travel; the roads, until relativly recently. were basic and, in some cases, non existent; the visitor to Dominica in previous years has been the explorer and the nature lover.

Today, nearly all of Dominica is accessible by road, and still country areas have lost none of their natural beauty.

Another important reason for the small number of tourists is that, unlike many other Caribbean islands, Dominica has no direct 'jet link' with the United States and Europe. Travellers fly in on the smaller planes from those islands with international 'jet links' such a Barbados and Antigua.

Dominica is a volcanic rather than a coral island resulting in a rocky coastline interspersed by beaches. These are found in the north of the island and are outstanding for being quiet, peaceful and deserted. There are also exceptional black sand beaches.

Hampstead Beach and Pointe Baptiste are situated near the northern village of Calibishie, a coral area and one of the most pleasant villages on the island. Here you will find white sand beaches. Pointe Baptiste, incidentally, can boast two beaches, one black sand, the other white.

Travelling west from Hampstead there are beaches at Anse-de-Me and Sandwich Bay at Thibaud. Travelling east from Pointe Baptiste, there are a series of small beaches, as well as Woodford Hill Beach and Londonderry Bay. Further down, the east coast are Pagua Bay (at Hatton Garden), St. Davids Bay (at Castle Bruce) and Rosalie Bay and Bout Sable (near la Plaine). All are good beaches with black sand and they are ideal for surfing.

Few locals swim here due to the rough sea and strong currents. Care must be taken and it is unadvisable to go out of your depth.

The west coast of Dominica is the best area for swimming. Here the Caribbean Sea is often like a lake with just a ripple to disturb the tranquillity. The most favoured and spacious beaches are found around Portsmouth with beach bars and sun beds; Coconut Beach and

Canefiel airport

OPPOSITE TOP: *New tennis facilities in Roseau.*

OPPOSITE BOTTOM: *Anchorage Hotel.*

FAR LEFT: *Shopping mall Roseau.*

LEFT AND OPPOSITE: *Castaways.*

BOTTOM: *Anchorage complex.*

OPPOSITE BOTTOM: *Castle Comfort Guest House (Dive Dominica).*

LEFT: *Cuba Road Disco open for drinks during week days.*

BOTTOM: *The tourist information office at the market place downtown, Roseau.*

OPPOSITE TOP: *Sisserou Hotel.*

OPPOSITE BOTTOM: *Coconut Beach Hotel.*

Purple Turtle Beach are popular with the locals and tourists alike. Further north the beaches at Toucari Bay and Douglas Bay are quieter but equally pleasant. Mid-way between Portsmouth and Roseau is Mero Beach where the Castaways Hotel is situated. Further south is the small beach at Layou, and for those who do not wish to venture far from Roseau, then there is Donkey Beach at Canefield. From Roseau to Scotts Head sand is very scarce, but it is possible to swim anywhere, in or around the rocks or shingle, due to the calm nature of the Caribbean Sea. Scotts Head provides a small stretch of sand and here it is possible to dive from the rocks. Diving is also practised at Rodney's Rock between Mahout and Layou.

The south coast is bereft of sand, but swimming is feasible at Stowe Bay which is near Grand Bay.

There are also other smaller beaches on the island, barely known and rarely visited because of difficult access - a veritable challenge for the true explorer.

Beaches are not the only place where it is possible to swim. River swimming is a unique feature of the island. The Layou River is best for extended swimming, but it is possible to have fun in the rock pools of practically all of the island's rivers. The vast majority, apart from some industrial areas around Roseau, are pure, clean and free from pollution or disease. It is also safe to drink the water from most of these rivers and there are no dangerous fish lurking at the bottom to worry about. A refreshing river bath is an experience every visitor to the island should include on their agenda as it is said that many of the rivers, particularly the 'White River' at Pointe Mulatre near Delices in the south east, have beneficial effects for both health and skin care.

Dominica's rivers are highlighted by spectacular waterfalls; the most celebrated being the popular tourist attraction Trafalgar Falls with its hot and cold springs. There are lesser known, but equally enchanting, falls such as Sari-Sari, near La Plaine, and Middleham Falls at Laudat. Titou Gorge is a popular spot where snorkelling in the caves is practised by the enthusiastic diving fraternity.

Dominica is also proud to be able to boast the second largest boiling lake in the world. Situated in the interior and rising to a height

Inside Fort Young Hotel.

OPPOSITE TOP: *The remote Layoo VALLEY INN.*

OPPOSITE BOTTOM: *Reigate Hall Hotel.*

LEFT: *Castaways Hotel.*

BOTTOM: *Springfield Guest House.*

OPPOSITE TOP: *Evergreen Hotel and Restaurant.*

OPPOSITE BOTTOM: *Excelsior Hotel.*

of 3,000 feet, the Boiling Lake is accessible via a three-and-a-half hour hike each way, which takes the walker over the mountains and through the mysterious Valley of Desolation. A reasonable standard of fitness and strong walking shoes are required to undertake this walk, however all age groups can partake of it. A guide, or people already experienced in this walk, are essential.

The Freshwater Lake is accessible by road. From here it is possible to view both sides of the island - a wonderful sight. Another lake, the Boeri Lake, is a further forty-five minutes walk from the Freshwater Lake.

For the less energetic the Emerald Pool is worth a visit. This is a nice gentle walk with good viewing points on the road to Castle Bruce. Morne Diablotin is Dominica's highest mountain, peaking at 4,750 feet. Once again, one's state of fitness would determine the possibility of reaching to the top, but the end justifies the means!

There are still a few areas of Dominica's coastline that do not have roads. For the visitor this adds to the charm of the island and is often seen as a challenge. One track, in the south-east, traverses the mountains from Pointe Mulatre (near Delices) to Petit Savanne. Here 'Country Rum' or 'Zied' is distilled in the local distilleries. Another track, further north on the east coast, runs from the Rosalie estate to Petite Soufriere, and a third crosses the northern coastline from Capucin to La Haut. All three walks are enjoyable, with some outstanding views and many colourful flowers. The route from Pointe Mulatre is difficult to find without guidance, but the other two tracks are reasonably easy to follow.

Chimen Letang (Lake Walk) retraces the steps of Dominicans from the south-east who, through necessity, had to walk from the east cost to Roseau, via the mountains, in order to sell their produce in the markets. Today, many hikers walk Chimen Letang purely for the challenge, Starting at Grand Fond the route is fairly well defined but a cutlass should be carried to clear the undergrowth. The walking time from Grand Fond to Roseau is approximately five hours. Food and drink should always be taken on any hiking expedition, and for those with a fair skin a hat and suntan lotion should be carried at all times.

Information Office in the Carib territory.

The Post Office at La Plaine.

OPPOSITE: *The Botanical Garden and Department of Forestry Offices including the Vetinary Centre.*

LEFT: *Carnival Queen contest.*
BOTTOM: *Sunshine Village.*
OPPOSITE: *Roseau market.*

There are, of course, many other fascinating walks on the island, but the fun of Dominica is often to discover them for oneself.

Other popular attractions are the Botanical Gardens in Roseau and the Cabrits near Portsmouth. Here you will find remnants of Fort Shirley where the French and British engaged in battles. Scotts Head, situated on the most southerly tip of the island, is worth visiting, to observe a remarkable peninsula only twenty yards wide, with the Caribbean Sea on one side and the Atlantic Ocean on the other, made more fascinating by the prevailing weather conditions.

Additional tourist attractions include boating trips up the Indian River, visiting the Sulphur Springs at Soufriere, bird-watching, or, for the real adventurer, riding down the rapids on the fast flowing Layou River on large rubber rings; or maybe a retreat into the rainforests and trying to spot the Sisserou or Red-necked parrot, both now recognised as endangered species.

Whatever it is that may attract you to this unique, largely undiscovered Caribbean island, you may be sure that you will find a peaceful retreat into a world of difference.

OPPOSITE: *Botanical Gardens*

HOTELS, RESTAURANTS AND BARS

Dominica has a number of small, pleasant hotels and guest houses. They are found from deep within the interior to the west coast beach hotels.

Visitors to the island will not find any multi-storied concrete monstrosities. All the hotels are tastefully designed to compliment the natural surroundings.

CASTAWAYS BEACH HOTEL was the island's first purpose-built hotel. Prior to which, a few converted guest houses in Roseau offered limited accommodation. Originally opened as the Nomandie Beach Hotel in 1961, Castaways is one of the island's friendliest and most relaxing hotels. Castaways offers twenty-seven rooms, all facing the sea, as well as sailing, windsurfing, diving, snorkelling and tennis. The food is good with regular beach bar-b-que's available. There are two bars, one beach bar and one situated within the hotel - a perfect place to watch the sun go down with a rum punch in your hand.

REIGATE HALL HOTEL is one of Dominica's newest hotels. Situated high above Roseau, with panoramic views of the town, the hotel is built of stone and wood and offers sixteen air-conditioned rooms, a swimming pool and a tennis court. The food is good and television, a sauna, a gymnasium and a games room are also provided.

ANCHORAGE HOTEL is situated two miles from Roseau and is one of Dominica's busiest hotels. thirty-six rooms are available, most with air-conditioning. Situated overlooking the Caribbean Sea, this is a good place for an evening meal watching the twinkling lights of Roseau in the distance. The Anchorage also offers squash, television and a swimming pool. Conferences are regularly held here and it is also an excellent centre for island tours and water sports, including scuba diving, windsurfing, boating and snorkeling.

THE PORTSMOUTH BEACH HOTEL with ninety-seven rooms and ten beach cottages, offers island tours. Situated one mile south of Portsmouth, in Prince Rupert Bay , the Portsmouth Beach Hotel can boast the largest swimming pool on the island plus all the usual water sports.

Also situated in Prince Rupert Bay, near Portsmouth, is COCONUT BEACH HOTEL. The beach bar and restaurant are the attraction here,

PREVIOUS PAGES:

LEFT: *Frontline Shop.*

TOP RIGHT: *Boat making using local timber and skills.*

BOTTOM RIGHT: *A colourful house in the Carib Territory.*

OPPOSITE TOP: *A boat-trip up the Indian River at Portsmouth.*

OPPOSITE BOTTOM: *Anchorage at the Anchorage.*

seafood being a speciality.

Adjacent to the Cabrits, just north of Portsmouth, is the small bungalow beach complex, SUNSHINE VILLAGE. This quiet hotel offers six chalets, a bar, restaurant and water sports. All rooms have a sea view and complete facilities.

The SISSEROU HOTEL is situated about two miles from Roseau and offers nineteen air-conditioned rooms, this hotel is well known for Pearl's Cuisine, a restaurant noted for it's high standard of food. The hotel has television, a swimming pool, plus regular entertainment, and bar-b-ques.

National dress`the Wob Douilette`

Nearby is the quaint EVERGREEN HOTEL AND RESTAURANT. Here you will find a relaxed family atmosphere with good food and a lovely peaceful garden. Scuba diving and island tours are available and there are ten tastefully appointed rooms with air-conditioning. Both the Sisserou and the Evergreen overlook the Caribbean Sea.

The EXCELSIOR HOTEL built in 1987 is only minutes from Canefield airport. It offers ten rooms with television and private porch. It is particularly suitable for travelling businessmen and long or short stay visitors. Bar, lounge, TV and conference facilities.

The CONTINENTAL INN is situated in the heart of Roseau. Offering twelve rooms this hotel is also suitable for the businessman or the Roseau-based tourist.

The FORT YOUNG HOTEL, in Roseau, was one of Dominica's most popular hotels until destroyed by Hurricane David in 1979. This stone built former Fort has recently been refurbished and now offers more than forty rooms. Retaining much of it's original charm, including the cannons, Fort Young Hotel offers full conference, reception and entertainment facilities.

The LAYOU RIVER HOTEL. Situated inland on the Layou River, it offers forty-six rooms, a bar, restaurant and swimming pool and there are conference and reception facilities (about 8 miles from Roseau).

So far we have mainly described most of Dominica's town or coastal hotels. But, of course, being the 'Nature Island of the Caribbean', Dominica has a number of nature oriented retreat hotels.

The PAPILLOTE WILDERNESS RETREAT is a typical example.

OPPOSITE TOP: *Three young ladies in national dress*

Situated beneath a mountain, amidst tropical plant life and a five minute walk from the beautiful Trafalgar Falls, it offers nine rooms, a restaurant, bar and a hot water mineral pool.

Even more secluded is the small LAYOU VALLEY INN. Situated in the heart of the island, this five bedroomed mountain inn, at a height of 1,500 feet, epitomises the peace and tranquillity of Dominica. Offering panoramic views and a restaurant/bar overlooking the rain forests. The cuisine is French and of excellent quality.

Childrens Parade in National dress

The SPRINGFIELD GUEST HOUSE, found on the inland Imperial Road, is a former estate house, offering seven rooms, a restaurant and bar. The hotel is frequented by retiring couples and honeymooners alike and is a fascinating example of the old style colonial wooden houses.

Dominica's most remote hotel the RIVIERE LA CROIX has also been closed since the 1979 hurricane, mainly due to the access roads being destroyed. They have now been repaired and there are plans to reopen this beautiful, tranquil retreat that really does make the visitor feel at one with nature.

Roseau and its environs also offer a number of guest houses, including Castle Comfort, home of Dive Dominica, Cherry Lodge, Vena's and Wykies.

Although Dominica cannot boast a plethora of top class restaurants and bars, it does have some extremely agreeable places to eat and relax.

LA ROBE CREOLE is probably one of the island's best restaurants. Well furnished and with air-conditioning, La Robe provides good food and good wine. The visitor will normally get a wide choice of food with local dishes such as octopus, mountain chicken and agouti often available.

The ORCHARD RESTAURANT is well-appointed and popular. Fresh fish and roti are two of the popular dishes available.(There is also a snackette here)

The GUIYAVE is popular with locals and tourists alike and the food is reasonably priced and of good quality. Juices are a speciality.

The WORLD OF FOOD is a charming garden restaurant in the heart of Roseau. Shaded with trees it is a quiet refuge from the hot

OPPOSITE BOTTOM: *The Church at Point Michel*

streets. They have a large menu.

The PIZZA PALACE has the best burgers in town plus a whole range of snacks (and, pizza of course).

The GREEN PARROT, on Roseau's bay front has become a lunch time meeting place for Dominicans and tourists alike and is a friendly cafe providing traditional Dominican food.

Next door the CARTWHEEL CAFE.is slightly more upmarket, , this is a pleasant place to while away the odd hour.

The SAMAN TREE is Dominica's latest restaurant. With a bar and plenty of space. There are lots of 'specials' on offer.

WYKIE'S bar and restaurant has a cult following of 'ex-pat's' and local Dominican businessmen. A small intimate bar with bamboo on the inside walls, Wykie's attracts many of the local characters. Fish and chips, chicken and steak are normally available, plus snacks. A dartboard is also provided to make the visitor feel at home.

For students or travellers on a low budget, the HOPE RESTAURANT provides food prepared in a way that ordinary Dominicans appreciate, at reasonable prices. This is normally eaten to the accompaniment of local music and the clatter of dominoes.

The restaurants and bars mentioned so far are all found in or near Roseau. Popular Portsmouth venues are the PORTSMOUTH BEACH BAR and the PURPLE TURTLE BEACH CLUB. Food at the latter is good value and they mix an excellent Pina Colada!

Further down the west coast at Coulibistin, LENTI'S BAR is definitely worth a visit and at Tarou, the SEAVIEW provides snacks and bar-b-que chicken.

GOOD TIMES, at Checkall, between Massacre and Canefield, provides snacks and is situated next to the WAREHOUSE which is Dominica's most popular discotheque. The AQUA CADE club and the SHIPWRECK bar at Canefield are both worthy of a visit. Situated on the nearby beach, is the venue for James' Water World where many water sports, as well as boating trips can be undertaken.

The ETIENNE GARDEN CLUB, is situated near the Layou River. The north coast village of Calibishie is picturesque and construction of a new beach bar/restaurant is underway.

OPPOSITE: The big cannon strategically located to defend the city of Roseau,

MANO'S at Pont Casse has become a cross-roads for travellers, with fried chicken being the main attraction.

Apart from the bars, Dominica has many rum shops. These are mainly small wooden structures, with a few wooden seats and a table for dominoes. Cask rum has for centuries been the most popular drink and the visitor really should experience this at least once. Country rum or 'zied' is much in evidence and very cheap in the south of the island. In other areas of Dominica plants are added to the rum to give it flavour. these include 'Nanny', 'Pwev' 'Jine' and 'Lapsent', with the former tasting of aniseed and regarded by some Dominicans as having aphrodisiac powers. Cask or country rum should, however, be drunk with care as it is very powerful!

ROXY'S MOUNTIAN LODGE is situated at the gateway to the Boiling Lake in Laudet (Lake City). A mountainous location at 2000 feet above sea level, just 7.5 km from Roseau. The lodge has six bedrooms, a bar and diner and everything is informal and friendly. It's a great place to spend on the night before and after a long trip to the Boiling Lake. The air is crisp and the views and sunset spectacular.

OPPOSITE: *The memorial at the Carib Church.*

INDUSTRY AND COMMERCE

Agriculture is Dominica's major economic activity and its main source of survival. At present bananas are of prime importance. Other agricultural products are cultivated for internal use and for export, dasheen, yam, ginger, passion fruit, pineapples and plantain being a few examples.

SEDPA (South-East District Plantain Association) is a recently formed organisation designed to promote the cultivation of plantain and related produce, and to secure markets abroad. Dominica currently exports to Antigua and Barbuda and to other members of CARICOM (the Caribbean Common Market) Hucksters have for many decades played an important role in moving Dominican agricultural products throughout the Caribbean. These are essentially groups of women who negotiate with local farmers and then sell the produce in neighbouring islands.

Following Hurricane David, forty per cent of Dominica's coconuts were severely damaged. Since then 5,836 acres of coconuts have been planted throughout the island, producing 2,500 tons in 1988. The bulk of this is used for copra which is utilised by Dominica Coconut Products (DCP) in the production of soap, oil and perfumes. DCP is one of Dominica's most successful companies with export markets throughout the Caribbean.

Coffee and hot pepper are two potential growth areas, with 200 acres of coffee presently under cultivation. Cafe Dominique is recognised as a high quality coffee and is used both for internal consumption and for export to the French-speaking countries.

Dominica is also rich in flora, with cut flowers being exported to the United States and other Caribbean islands.

Crop diversification has become a key concern in Dominican agricultural circles recently. Hundreds of acres of fruits including ruby red grapefruit, avocado pears and mangoes, have all been planted, thus confirming the island's desire not to be totally dependent upon bananas, which currently account for forty-four per cent of all exports.

There is also the Windward Island Aloe Company based near Soufriere with eighty acres of Aloe which is used in the manufacture of soaps and cosmetics, particularly skin lotions.

OPPOSITE: *Farmer with a machete.*

FOLLOWING PAGES: *Roseau market place.*

Other 'Agro industries' include P.W Bellot & Co. Ltd, who produce Bello Hot Pepper Sauce, syrups, juices and Bay rum; the Corona Passion Fruit processing plant; the Soya Processing Centre and the Dominican Agro Industries Company who export dried sorrell and grapefruit.

Although Dominica does not have any heavy industry, light industry has contributed to the country's development. Harris Paints was established in 1978 and is the sole paint manufacturers on the island. This successful company is now looking towards expansion and diversification in Dominica and within the wider Caribbean.Paul Joseph Products currently produce pasta and oats. The Benjashoe Company began manufacturing plastic shoes in 1986, a product that is both popular and practical in Dominica and the Caribbean. The Leather Goods Co-operative is another successful organisation producing hand made leather goods and the Candle Industries Co-operative has, since 1982, been one of the leading candle producers in the eastern Caribbean.

In addition there are various furniture makers, including Raffouls, and Ogheden Industries high in the mountains at Cochrane, basket makers, and the Agape Craft Co-operative at Delices who produce decorative handmade quilts.

Building construction has expanded in recent years, P.H Williams produces sand, aggregate and building blocks, whilst Murraybloc concentrates on blocks and wood. Other companies offering building and hardware supplies include J.Astaphan, E.H Charles and Antilles Cement.

Dominica has two major rum manufacturers - Belfast Estates Ltd, and Shillingford Estates Ltd,. The J.A.S Garraway Tobacco factory, now run by the Rolle family, has long been established in Roseau.

Foreign businesses are also beginning to recognise Dominica's potential and a Puerto Rican-backed project has recently built a new factory and is currently producing banana boxes. There have also been various Taiwanese projects, including king size prawn farming.

Dominica's two major supermarkets, H.H.V Whitchurch and A.C Shillingford, are both old established businesses. Whitchurch , an Englishman, and J.O. Aird, a Scot, together formed H.H.V. Whitchurch

OPPOSITE:

TOP LEFT: *Harris paints factory & warehouse.*

BOTTOM LEFT: *Garment production is a growing industry.*

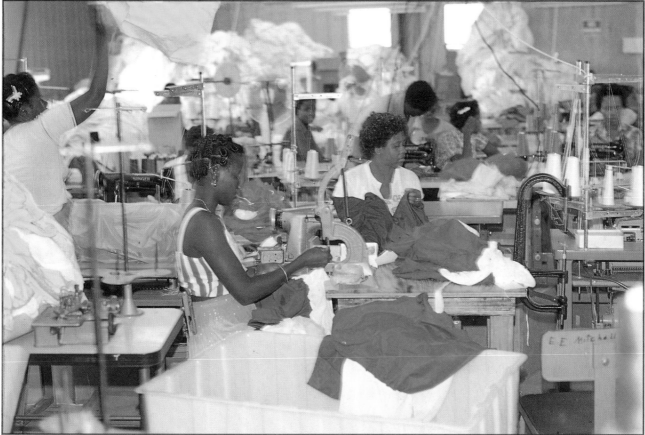

TOP: *Basket making and light industrial work-shop.*
OPPOSITE TOP: *Roseau market.*

OPPOSITE BOTTOM: *One of the diesel electiricty generators which supplements the nations electricity which is mostly hydro -power.*

& Co. around the turn of the century. In 1870, Charles Shillingford, a travelling salesman from Scotland arrived and eventually settled in Dominica and today the name Shillingford is to be found in nearly every area of Dominica.

In 1910 the Arab connection with Dominica began, when Mr. Ayoub Dib arrived from Lebanon. Today the names of Astaphan, Nassief, Raffoul, Issa Gabriel and Karam are synonymous with business life in Dominica. The interests they represent are as diverse as hotels, automobile agencies, departmental stores, importing, manufacturing, and baking. Today's descendants of these Lebanese and Syrian businessmen settlers are very much Dominican in attitude and lifestyle. Other important business families includes the Dupigny's, the Green's and the Brisbanes.

In 1941, Mr. J.B Charles, the father of Dominica's present Prime Minister, Eugenia Charles, opened the Co-operative Bank, which became popularly known as the "Penny Bank". The Colonial Bank, Barclays Bank and the Royal Bank of Canada were already established on the island. The "Penny Bank" provided loans for small house building to those who were not so financially well off. In 1978 the National Commercial and Development Bank was opened. Since then the Banque Francaise Commerciale, the Agriculture and IndustrialDevelopment Bank (AID) and, in 1988, the Bank of Nova Scotia have all set up branches in Dominica.

Dominica's thriving co-operatives were partly initiated by a Roman Catholic Nun, Sister Alicia, who formed the Credit Union League. which now plays an integral part in village financial life.

FOLLOWING PAGES:

TOP LEFT: *Local handcraft shop in the market place.*

BOTTOM LEFT: *Leathercraft Workers Co-operative.*

RIGHT: *The National Commercial and Development Bank of Dominica.*

OPPOSITE TOP: *Dominica Coconut Products Ltd.*

OPPOSITE BOTTOM: *Candle Co-operative supplying the home and regional markets.*

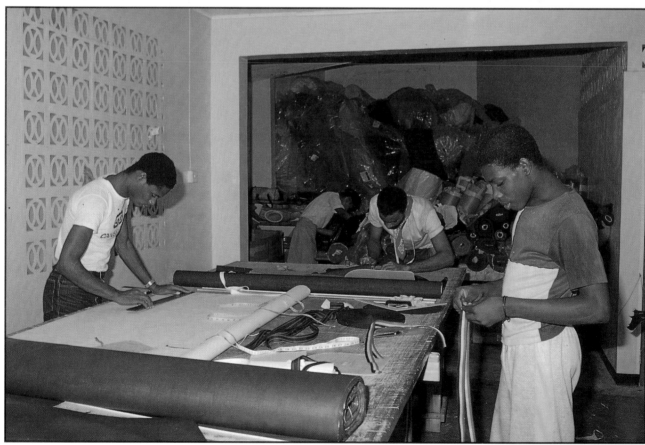

TOP LEFT TO BOTTOM RIGHT:

Solar heating units. Tropicrafts workshop and store. Light manafacturing. Harris Paints. Leathercrafts. Aggregate plant. Traditional basket. Furniture for local market.

OPPOSITE TOP: *Aerial view of Layou River Valley.*

OPPOSITE BOTTOM: *Barclays Bank, Roseau.*

FOLLOWING PAGES:

LEFT: *A shingle maker.*

RIGHT TOP: *A selection of local handcrafted products.*

RIGHT BOTTOM: *A pack shot of Dominican products by P.W.Bellot.*

TIMBER

With the advent of the chain-saw the Dominica timber industry has gone forward in leaps and bounds. for nearly two centuries Dominicans had used the pit-sawing method. This involved a large double handled saw wielded by two men. It was extremely labour intensive and time consuming. Today, however, there are more than a handful of companies, notably North Eastern Timbers and Dominican Timbers, exclusively involved in the manufacture of timber for house construction, furniture making and wood carving. Prefabricated wooden houses are also available for purchase, however the authorities are vigilant about the replenishment of trees - Dominica is determined not to endanger one of its greatest natural resources.

TOP: Home furniture and prefabricated house using local timber and labour.

BOTTOM LEFT: A sawmill.

OPPOSITE TOP: Botanical gardens.

FISHING

Fishing has, since the early Arawak and Carib days, been an important part of Dominican life. In fact Dominica still celebrates special religious feasts in recognition of the island's fishermen.

With the introduction of Fishing Co-operatives, the industry has gradually been developing, and modern equipment such as tuna longlines and echo sounders are now being used.

The co-operative movement has secured financial viability for many of Dominica's fishermen. Instead of having to hawk the day's catch around from village to village, fishermen are now able to sell their catch directly to the co-operatives who store it in freezers. This is possible only in the large co-operatives like those of Fond St. Jean and Newtown. However the island's other co-operatives will soon follow suit. These are to be found island-wide - Coulibistre, Vielle Case, Calibishie, Marigot and Saint Sauveur.

Some of the fishing villages, Saint Sauveur for example, are examples of traditional fishing communities, with all the traumas of loss of life and dependence on the sea.

The boats are mainly twelve foot long are made out of local gommier wood. They have an outboard engine - sail has not been widely used since 1978. Today's fishermen are well schooled in their chosen profession, some having attended courses in South America and the Far East.

There are basically two kinds of fish, Pelagics and Dermesals. Pelagics are found within a twelve mile limit and are caught with nets, and line and hook. Examples of this type include tuna, king-fish and sword-fish. These are mid-water and surface fish. dermesals live at the bottom of the ocean floor or in rocks. They include snappers, parrot fish, coney and trigger fish. Pots and nets are normally used, but many fishermen still use the traditional 'Kali', which is used to hook the fish out of the water. Spear fishing is also practised and lobster pots are much in evidence.

Dominica's fishermen are a hardy bunch of men who still brave rough seas in order to make a living.

FOLLOWING PAGES:

TOP LEFT: *Coast guard.*

BOTTOM LEFT: *Black Sand Beach.*

TOP RIGHT: *Fond St. Jean village.*

BOTTOM RIGHT: *Mending a fishing net.*

ABOVE: *A costume contestant in the run-up to Carnival.* FOLLOWING PAGES: *Carnival celebrations in Dominica are very special. Many villages have their own MINI CARNIVALS, however, the BIG EVENT is in Roseau, where the Prime Minister Eugenia Charles attended and enjoyed Carnival.*

DOMINICA

Dominica lush green beautiful
Land of the Caribs
Gushing waterfalls fresh water
I swam drank and bathed in your cool rocky waters
Surfed on your Atlantic shore
Lay on your Caribbean sand
Sat in your warm evening December sun
Listened to the echoing tunes of your nightbirds frogs and crickets
Felt the breeze strong on my face
Then heard the rain like an orchestra
A crescendo of noise accentuated by the tin roof warm and safe inside
Dominica palm trees swaying gently in the wind
Coconuts oranges and grapefruits the size of small footballs
The ubiquitous bottle of rum on the table of the small wooden house
Old men with weather beaten chiselled faces skin the texture of leather
Smiling courteous old women tend the ever boiling cooking pot
I watched your large bright yellow moon appear in your crystal clear
sky
Millions of small stars twinkling in the still of the night
A dog barks somewhere in the distance breaking the spell of your warm
tranquillity
Dominica Nature Island
Home of tall green mountains and rain forests
Remnants of volcanic action
A History of Spanish French and British imperialism
Stay in your time warp
Cocooned in your vacuum
Untainted and untouched
Cast your magic spell
Repel the march of advancement
And drift quietly peacefully into a long timeless sleep.

FOLLOWING PAGES: *Two coastal scenes where the first shows the costal forest shaped permanently by the winds and the second photograph taken off-shore in the calmer Atlantic south off Scotts Head. This is only a hundred metres or so from where the Caribbean Sea meets the Atlantic Ocean.*

OPPOSITE BOTTOM: *The Prime Minister Eugenia Charles attending Carnival and showing her support.*

OPPOSITE PAGE: *Some local dishes.*

LEFT: *Downtown Roseau at the end of the day.*

241

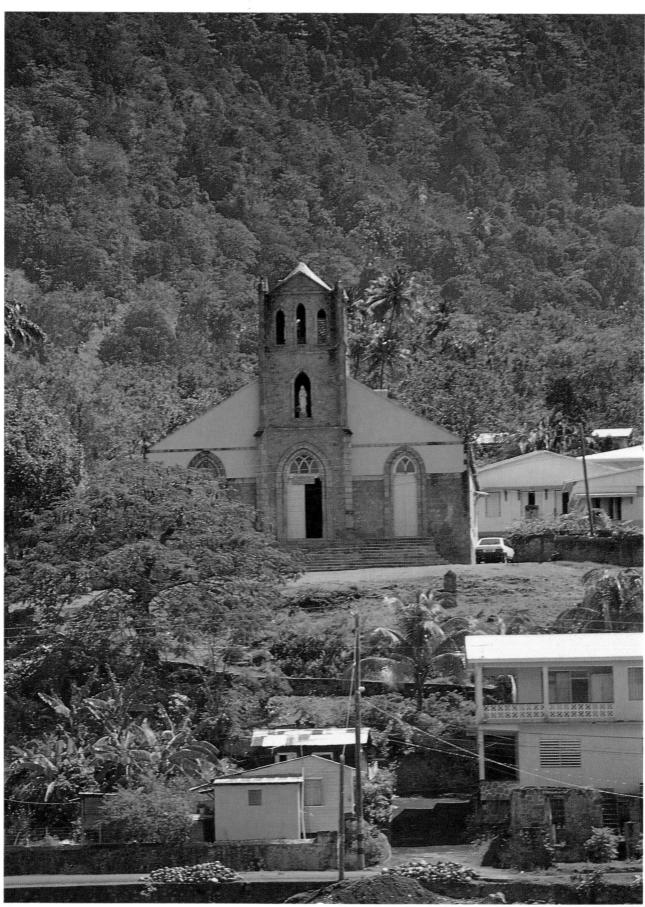

TOP: *The church at Soufriere.*

OPPOSITE TOP: *The Grand Savanne behind St. Joseph's village.*

TOP: *Staff at La Robe Creole Restaurant.*
BOTTOM LEFT: *Local crafts.*
BOTTOM RIGHT: *Downtown Roseau.*
OPPOSITE: *Valley of Desolation.*

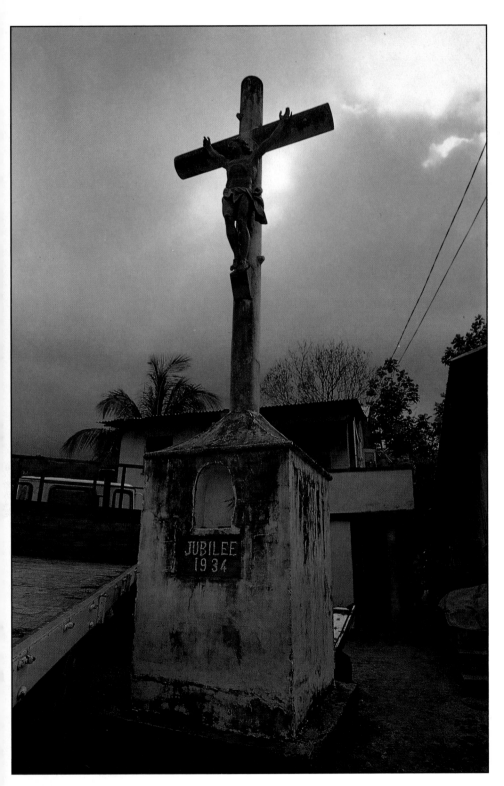

ABOVE: *The Carib chapel which has a canoe for an alter and some beautiful wall paintings.*

LEFT: *La Plaine village.*

OPPOSITE: *The Boiling Lake.*

FOLLOWING PAGES:

RE-UNION 88

TOP RIGHT: *Workers at the new power house.*
Artist and his handiwork.
Royal Bank of Canada.

Mountain path. Typical of those put down for safety and comfort. Leading to most national sights.

Timber removal.

251

" The key to developing the tourist industry, it seems, is to identify and attract a new and different clientele".

"Today, we have a different perspective. We have a product that the people want. People are looking for different destinations and for unspoilt places to which they have never been before.
"They want to visit a place where there is variety - and Dominica has it all!
"There is a new type of visitor who is looking for adventure tourism. So we have something that is in demand."
"Between 1982 and 1987, we have increased agricultural production by at least 50 per cent. The rewards to the economy have been dramatic."
"Our emphasis has been on the idea of pushing trade within Caricom. There are also plans for regular trade missions to various countries in order to market our products. Trade promotion is one of our priorities.
"We are encouraging Dominicans overseas to come back home and invest because of the political stability in the country. A reputation is not something you earn overnight.
"The national development strategy of Dominica incorporates the development of its industrial, tourism and trade sections within the framework of efficient landuse, protection of the environment and the development of its human resources to enhance the quality of life of its people. **"**

The Honourable Charles Maynard,
Minister for Agriculture, Trade, Industry and Tourism.

TOP: School children learning about agriculture.

Lake water flowing from Freshwater Lake to the hydro station at Trafalgar. An average of three million gallons per day is supplied.

Capucin Pte is accessible by dirt feeder road. Martinique is visible most days.

LEFT: *Cactus plant.*

RIGHT: *The Sisserou parrot.*

HERBACEOUS SWAMPS

Herbaceous swamps are those dominated by non-woody species and develop on sites where the water table reaches to the level of the soil. There is little or no drainage in these soils, and as a result, they are highly acidic due to the build up of acids formed during the decomposition of the dead vegetation which, due to the inadequacy of gaseous exchange, occurs at a very slow rate. The vegetation developing on these sites are typical hydrophytes - water plants - and are well suited for this type of environment.

The largest tract of swamp land in Dominica is approximately 35 hectares in extent, and is located just east of the historic Cabrits near the town of Portsmouth. This swamp, which is predominantly herbaceous, can be seen when driving along the road going towards Tane Tane from Portsmouth. Another large area of this type of swamp is located close to the Indian River near Glanvillia; this area is also close to Portsmouth. However, the swamp near the Cabrits is by far the more spectacular and interesting of the two.

There are a few woody species scattered on the drier areas of the Cabrits swamp. These include cachiman marron, white mangrove or mang lamer and bois mang which are all swamp dwellers. A few white cedar and campeche trees also live under similar conditions.

People living near herbaceous swamps often complain of being pestered by the mosquitoes which they claim, breed in the swamps. While this may be true, one should also stress the ecological importance of these wet lands, as the larvae of the mosquitoes form a source of food that constitute part of the diet of many species of local and migratory birds which visit these swamps. Some of these birds are hunted, and so provide a source of protein which is so vital to the human diet.

Clouds gently flowing over Morne Trois Piton, viewed from the Layou Valley Inn.

WETLANDS IN DOMINICA

Dominica, a 289 square mile volcanic island in the Caribbean, has been described by many as the greenest and most beautiful in the region. Hurricane David, which struck the island on August 29th, 1979, did no justice to the vegetation, causing some persons to refer to the remaining trees as 'dead sticks'. As a tropical island, however, the conditions here are suited for the development of many different vegetation types, and so a rich and varied flora can be found here. From the wind and salt-affected littoral woodlands on the east coast, one moves up to the wet rainforests in the mountains, and then across to the dry scub woodlands and savannah types on the dry west coast. Patches of wetlands exist on some of the coastal flats as well as at elevations of over 600 m (2000 ft).

Two of the conditions which determine the vegetation type which develops on a particular site are the amount of soil moisture and the regularity of the supply. While some of the islands in the Caribbean do not have any rainforests, they may possess extensive tracts of swamps along their coasts in the form of mangroves or marshes.

The general ruggedness of the coastline of Dominica has resulted in the absence of true mangroves here. However, three other major forms of swamp formations have developed on sites influenced by the presence of fresh water. At the higher elevations, where the rainforests and montane formations merge, one may sometimes find a unique swamp formation. On the lowlands one may sometimes find freshwater swamp forest bordered by herbaceous swamps or marshes, and vice versa.

THE WETLANDS

The East Cabrits is flanked to the east by an area whose vegetation is influenced by a seasonal supply of fresh water. The area may be classified as a wetland, and contains small patches of swamp and an extensive marshy area. This wetland is about 35 hectares (89 acres) in extent, and is one of two large wetlands in the Portsmouth area.

A wetland may be described as an area where the soil is periodically or constantly saturated by saline or fresh water. Such saturation must be frequent and short enough in order to allow for the survival of a type of vegetation which is typically adapted to life in water-logged and acidic soil conditions.

A swamp is described as a wetland which is dominated by woody plants, and a marsh is usually dominated by herbaceous species.

The wetlands at the Cabrits Peninsula is supplied with water from direct rainfall and from the run-off coming from the eastern side of East Cabrits and from the lands to the immediate east of the peninsula. The water is mostly fresh and there is no direct influx of saline water from the sea to the north or south of the wetland.

Dominica's rugged coastline.

ASSOCIATED MARSH COMMUNITIES

In a few instances the stands of freshwater swamp forest merges with bordering marsh communities. Four areas where this occurs can easily be identified in Dominica; the Cabrits flats, the Lagon swamp, Anse Soldat near the Torite River, and the Indian River flats near Glanvillia. These areas are flooded for the greater part of the year, and so more waterlogged than the swamp forest. The dominant species in these herbaceous swamps are fougere swamp which grows in tussocks, and the sedge known locally as "joun". The latter species is used in cottage industries by the villagers living in areas close to these marshes. The dried stems of these sedges are used for making mats, bags and hats, and also for filling mattresses. cachiman marron, though not a herbaceous plant, sometimes grow among the patches of "joun" and fougere swamp.

THE DRY FOREST

The dry forest, which covers both the East and West Cabrits, is composed of a number of deciduous species which shed their leaves during the official dry season. Old maps of the Cabrits seem to indicate that at some during the 18th and 19th centuries most if not all of the original vegetation was cleared. However, after a number of years following the abandonment of the military complex the vegetation began to return, re-establishing itself in the area. Today the vegetation is so dense that the dry forest must be cut back in order to expose the magnificent ruins scattered in the valley and on the hills.

The trees in this forest type usually attain a height of about fifty - sixty feet, are generally unbuttressed, and support few epiphytes. These trees form a fairly regular canopy, allowing only a minimum amount of sunlight to reach the forest floor, except during the dry season. As such, the ground beneath this closed forest is usually bare of young seedlings or other low level plants.

THORNY PLANTS

One of the characteristics of the dry forest is the presence of thorny species. At the Cabrits peninsula thorns exist on the barks and even leaves of a few trees and shrub species.

The Cabrits.

FRESHWATER LAKE

Although the Freshwater Lake supports colonies of floating and emergent vegetation, there are no apparent changes in the levels of this lake, even with the changes from the rainy to the dry season and vice versa. Measurements taken of the water levels at the outlet indicate a difference of less than one foot, in spite of the seasonal changes in the weather.

Before 1976, the main sources of water for the Freshwater Lake were direct precipitation (rainfall) and underground springs. However in November that year, the local electricity company diverted water from the three streams which flowed down the north-eastern side of Morne Macaque into the Lake. That water would normally have drained into one of the tributaries of the Rosalie River. Today, this diversion supplies approximately one and a half million gallons (6.8 million litres) of water to the Freshwater Lake every day or 550 million gallons per year. The lake has a single outlet, through which an average of 3 million gallons (13.6 million litres) of water flow daily. Water is also lost from the lake through processes of evaporation and transpiration, Most of the lake's surface is exposed, and water is lost via the surface of evaporation. The higher the temperature of the water at the surface, the longer the shape of the lake, and the steadier and stronger the wind, the more water is lost through evaporation.

MAMMALS

Dominica does not have any large wild game animals. Two of the mammalian species which can be considered as game outside of the Morne Trois Pitons National Park may be found in the Boeri Lake-Freshwater Lake area. The opossum or mannikou and the agouti are two mammalian species which were introduced to the island and have now become an integral part of Dominica's wild fauna.

The opossum or mannikou, as it is known locally, is a native of north and Central America. Following its introduction to Dominica the animal quickly adapted to the new environment and has become one of the most widely hunted wild mammals on the island.

EPIPHYTES

One of the common features of the montane forest and elfin woodlands is the abundance of epiphytes on the other plants. Epiphytes are sometimes known as "air plants", and must not be confused with parasitic plants. Both types of plants take physical support on their 'host' plant, but in the case of the parasite the latter is sometimes entirely dependent upon the host for its nutritional requirements. Epiphytes, on the other hand, only take physical support from their hosts. They obtain their water and minerals from the rain and also from debris that collects on the supporting plants. Epiphytes contain chlorophyll and always manufacture their own food. Chlorophyll is a plant pigment which makes leaves etc. appear green, and is necessary for plants to synthesise their food through the process of photosynthesis.

Freshwater Lake.

WILDLIFE OF THE FRESHWATER SWAMP FOREST

The stands of freshwater swamp forest, with the occasional bordering marsh communities often serve as sanctuaries for certain species of wildlife. Some of these animals tolerate a certain degree of interference by man and so frequent the stands of this forest type which are located close to actively cultivated lands.

BIRDS

It has been reported that in the sixties, when the parrot populations were several times the present figures, the Red-Necked or Jaco Parrot, (*Amazona arausiaca*) came all the way down to the "mangroves" to feed on the fruits of bois mang. These parrots could be seen feeding on the trees during their normal nesting season which, commencing from around February, goes up to July/August. These parrots are very intelligent birds and would avoid isolated bois mang trees which are located in some areas. If, however, a few of these trees were scattered among other species as the almond, for example, as can still be found in the Blenheim-Anse Soldat area, these birds would chance coming down to feed.

The increase in human population in the area - and in Dominica as a whole - brought with it an increase in agricultural activity. This in turn resulted in an increase in the noise levels from the chainsaws, vehicles, sprayers etc, and the loss of bois mang trees. As a result, the birds no longer come so low down to feed.

Three common birds which inhabit the swamp forest and marsh community are the green heron, known locally as "calali" (*butorides virescens*), the great blue heron (*ardea herodias*) and the white egret or "cwabier blanc" (*egreta alba*). Small flocks of white egrets have been seen in the swamp at the back of Glanvillia. This birds form an integral part of the food chain of these swamps, feeding on the smaller life forms which they come across. According to the villagers of Glanvillia and Lagon, various species of migratory birds, including wild ducks or "canard sauvage", have been seen at the Cabrits flats, at Lagon and at the back of Glanvillia.

INDIAN RIVER TOUR

One of the tourist attractions for the north of the island is a "boat ride up the Indian River" which is promoted as a sight seeing tour of one of our larger and more interesting rivers in Dominica. The first time visitor going on such a tour is treated to breathtaking views of the giant old age bois mang trees lining the quiet flowing Indian River. Depending on the time of year when the tour is made, the masses of soft yellow pea shaped petals floating on the surface of the water add to the spectacle. The red and yellow flowers of the mahoe doux, which belongs to the hibiscus family, add some more colour to the scene, However, the peace and quiet of this setting is sometimes conveniently disturbed by the splash of a fish in the water, leaving behind only expanding ripples, or by the characteristic "kior" sound of a green heron gliding over the surface of the water.

Indian River.

FRESHWATER SWAMP FOREST

The freshwater swamp forest in Dominica is dominated by a single species, (*Pterocarpus officinalis*) or bois mang. This may be compared with the swamp formation found in the wet rainforest/montane transition zones at the higher elevations; this is dominated by carapite and mangle blanc. In most cases the freshwater swamp forest is two-storied, comprising of the canopy layer which may reach up to 30 metres (100 ft), and the young regeneration on the forest floor. Saplings and pole-sized trees are markedly absent from this forest type in a large number of areas.

Optimum development of this forest type seem to occur on sites which are not constantly flooded, as can be seen at Glanvillia, Picard and Anse de Mai. A stand of this forest type at Woodford Hill contains some dense patches of saplings and pole-sized trees in areas where, it is believed, the water table is persistently at or near the surface of the soil. Some specimens of bois mang growing on the edge of the mud flats near Glanvillia were observed to be fruiting, yet only 2m (7 ft) tall in January 1979.

In some areas the presence of epiphytes is quite noticeable, and these grow on the branches and stems of the supporting bois mang trees. Stranglers may be seen in a few areas, tightening their grasp - with their roots - around the stems of mature bois mang trees. These stranglers are not as widely distributed as are true the epiphytes.

FERNS

The ferns are quite common in the Morne Trois Pitons National Park, and are well represented in the rain forest, montane forest and elfin woodland. Several species may be found in the Freshwater Lake-Boeri Lake area, and these include the tree ferns which attain a height of about twenty feet. One may also find filmy ferns which are only one-cell thick, growing on the tree stems in the elfin woodland and montane forest. Some ferns are used as ornamentals.

Up to 199 species of ferns may be found in Dominica. Some species grow as epiphytes, while others grow as independent terrestrial plants.

SNAKES

There are about 2,600 species of snakes in the world, five of which exist on Dominica. Of these, three species may be found at the Cabrits - the boa constrictor or "tetchyen" (*constrictor constrictor crophias*), the "kouwes nwe or grove snake (*alsophis lucomelas sibonius*), and the checkered "kouwes jenga",(*dromicus juliae juliae*).

There are no poisonous snakes in Dominica.

RAINFALL

Certain parts of Dominica have been described a some of the wettest places on the face of the earth. Yet, despite this excessive rainfall some other areas, particularly on the west coast, are affected by the annual dry season which often creates conditions for bush fires.

In Dominica, rainfall varies from about 50 inches along parts of the west coast, to over 300 inches in the interior. The rainfall is seasonal, with a marked dry season between January and May, and peaking between July and October. It is estimated that Dominica receives up to 10 times more rainfall than is observed for the general region.

The Boeri Lake-Freshwater Lake area is one of the wettest areas on Dominica. Rainfall recorded over a 5-year period near the Freshwater Lake averaged about 340 inches (8500 millimetres) a year. However, even in such a high rainfall area, a "dry season" is also apparent, and was quite evident in 1987, when the level of the Boeri Lake dropped by an estimated thirty feet below its high water mark. Epiphytes on larger plants near the Freshwater Lake wilted during the dry spell.

ELFIN WOODLAND

The elfin woodland is one of the montane formations in Dominica, and is sometimes referred to as "cloud forest" or "dwarf forest". All three names describe the general character of this vegetation type, as the elfin woodland is often bathed in clouds for much of the time. The trees here are shorter than those in the other forest types on the island, and one can sometimes stand above the top of the vegetation in the elfin woodland.

The elfin woodland has also been described as "an impenetrable thicket-like forest, the leaves, branches and trunks covered with moss, epiphytes and decaying plant matter, and the top-most surface solid enough to walk on." The ground is often covered by herbaceous plants which normally occur as epiphytes in the lower forest types. The trees of the elfin woodlands are subject to steady and strong winds which prune the branches, and the tree crowns give the impression that the trees are leaning landward.

Elfin woodland is the highest of the montane formations, and the highest forest type in Dominica. It occurs at the summits and upper slopes of the major peaks and ridges from about 3000 ft above sea level, and is exposed to severe winds and cool temperatures. Trees in the elfin woodland reach heights of only 10 to 20 ft, and this forest type develops on very shallow soils. Here the leaves are often thick and leathery, indicating the occurence of occasional physiological drought, despite the constant rainfall.

The principal species of the elfin woodland is a species of kaklen.

CLIMATES

The local climates of Dominica are closely related to the topography of the island. In general, rainfall increases and temperature falls with increasing elevation, but the distributions are not symetrical about a line joining the highest points on the island. On the leeward or western side of the island rainfall is generally lower and temperatures probably higher than at the same elevation on the windward side. Temperatures are generally lower in the interior of the island than on the coasts.

LAKES

Two of Dominica's fresh water lakes are located within the Morne Trois Pitons National Park, and are major attractions in the area. These are both crater lakes, having been formed within the crater of an old volcano, millions of years ago. A distance of only one mile separates these two magnificent bodies of fresh water.

The two lakes are physically separated by the towering Morne Macaque. Freshwater Lake is located to the east of this mountain, and Boeri Lake to the north. Boeri Lake is also located at the southern foothills of Morne Trois Pitons. Three large natural ponds, almost like mini-lakes can be found to the west and south-west of Boeri Lake, and may be seen from the northern slopes of Morne Macaque.

Freshwater Lake, commonly known to the villagers from Grand Fond and Laudat as "Letan" is located about 2500 ft. above sea level. This is the largest lake on Dominica, with a surface area of nine acres, and a depth of between fifty-five and sixty-five feet. in 1987.

The Boeri Lake, known in the local creole as "Letan Bwewi", is located approximately three hundred feet above the level of the Freshwater Lake. This is the lake with the highest elevation in Dominica, and when full, has a maximum area of about 4.5. acres and a depth of at least 117 ft. (36 m).

BOERI LAKE

The Boeri Lake is located approximately 2850 ft (869 m) above sea level, and covers a maximum surface area of approximately 4.5 acres.

The behaviour of the Boeri Lake is in sharp contrast with that of the Freshwater Lake. Although actual measurements of the levels of the Boeri Lake have not been taken, it is estimated that in a prolonged dry season (e.g. in 1987), preceded by a relatively dry December, the level of Boeri Lake may drop in excess of 25 ft. (7.6 m) below the high water mark (line of vegetation).

However, when it rains occasionally during the official dry season, as occurred in 1986, the drop in levels is usually much smaller and may be only ten feet (3 m). It was observed towards the end of 1986, over a period of four days the level had dropped 18 inches, at a rate of 4.5. inches (11.4 cm) per day. During the dry season and well into the rainy season, one can clearly observe a well-defined water mark of variable width above the edge of the lake to one side, and a bouldery shore line on the southern side of the lake.

Boeri Lake..

278

OPPOSITE: *Trafalgar Falls.*

TOP LEFT: *The Diablotin bird only recently seen in Dominica after an absence of some years no breeding has been discovered.*

PREVIOUS LEFT: *The World of Food Restaurant, Roseau.*

PREVIOUS RIGHT: *L'Escalier Tete Chien The Snake Walk is a massive lava rock which spewed into the sea like a wall. It goes down to a depth of 800 feet. There is a footpath from the main road and the thirty minute walk is through pleasant countryside.*

OPPOSITE TOP: *Woodbridge Deepwater Harbour.*

MIDDLE LEFT: *Aloe Plants.*

BOTTOM LEFT: *A male and female 'Zandoli'.*

PREVIOUS PAGES: *Wall mural monument depicts the tragic events of 1979.*

BOTTOM RIGHT: *The Caribs celebrate carnival in a style of their own.*

OPPOSITE TOP: *Melville Hall the country's first airport.*

OPPOSITE BOTTOM: *Looking across Prince Rupert Bay*

TOP LEFT: *A heron.*

BOTTOM LEFT: *A bannaquit on a paw-paw tree.*

PREVIOUS TOP LEFT: *St Pauls and St Anns Church Massacre.*

BOTTOM LEFT: *The Cultural Centre at Canefield.*

RIGHT: *The ruins of a long abandoned sugar mill tower..*

OPPOSITE: *Government Headquarters Roseau.*

TOP : *Prime Minister Eugenia Charles during the Reunion 88 celebrations marking the 10th anniversary of Dominica's independence.*

PREVIOUS: *Gommier tree, Sari Sari Falls, Memorial to those who lost their lives in the 1914–1918 and 1939–1945 World Wars.*

Roman Catholic Church at Soufriere

BOTTOM: *Village of Massacre.*

OPPOSITE TOP: *Banana boat loading for England.*

BOTTOM: *A cruiser in Woodbridge Harbour.*

PREVIOUS PAGES LEFT: *Valley of Desolation.*

RIGHT: *Shoreline at Mahaut Village.*

TOP: *Local craftwork, heading bananas, modern wooden house, Coconut Beach Hotel.*

BOTTOM: *Roxys Mountain Lodge.*

OPPOSITE TOP: *Canefield Airport.*

BOTTOM: *Sorting out the catch.*

UNDERWATER DOMINICA

Underwater Dominica is as spectacular as above. This breathtaking seascape lives up to the reputation "NATURE ISLAND OF THE CARIBBEAN".

Shallow ledges lead out to dramatic drop-offs and sheer walls. This world class diving being on the Leeward Coast along with windowpane visibility offers adventure to both the experienced and novice diver and snorkeler. Diving this virgin paradise with its unspoiled abundance of marine life is truly an experience.

Dominica's rugged terrain continues into the sea. The sheer underwater granite walls are one of its diving highlights. There are also sheer pinnacles reaching out of the depths nearly touching the surface, arches, caves, wrecks, and deep reefs running off from the shore. There is also a marine sub-aquatic hot (freshwater) spring for divers who want to experience nature's sauna.

Most of the diving is on the west or leeward coast, where there is less wind and choppy seas; and very little current. The average visibility is 100 ft and sometimes more. A ground swell from the west is more of a hindrance to visibility than run-offs from the hills and rivers. But the black volcanic sand being heavy quickly settles once the swell has abated. Freshwater run-offs only restricts the visibility at the surface; freshwater being lighter than sea water. Also there are no rivers beyond the village of Loubiere on the south-west coast; where the majority of the fine dive sites are located.

The marine life certainly lives up to the reputation of the "Nature Island." The walls, pinacles and reefs are granite, and are carpeted with soft and hard corals. There are a wide range of sponges from iridescent tube to huge barrel sponges. The abundance of black coral, some "trees" as shallow as 50 feet, enhances this Garden of Eden. There is a wide selection of invertebrates and tropical fish, each dive site offering its own speciality night and day.

Dominica underwater will amaze and entertain most divers, especially the macro-photographer. Virgin walls, reefs, and wrecks are waiting to be explored.

The average temperature is 30° C/86° F.

DIVE SITES

DES FOUS: 30 min. from Dive Shop
Large rock off sheer cliff, good coral growth, interwoven
with crevices and valleys. This massive "condominium"
rests on a sandy bottom.
- Depth from 10ft to 140ft on sandy bottom.
- Current and sea conditions generally heavy. Definitely a
dive for experienced divers; with best days during the
summer.
- Larger fish: snapper, grouper, barracuda, and other
pelagic fish.

MOUNTAIN TOP: 20 min. from Dive Shop.
- A peak rising out of the channel, forming a small
plateau and dropping off into the deep, standard
Dominica fashion.
- Top of plateau starts at 70ft.
- Current and sea conditions heavy. For experienced
divers; best days during the summer .
- Abundant large fish and lobster.

THE PINNICLE (Scotts Head): 15 min. from Dive
Shop.
- A Pinnacle rising up west of Scotts Head, with
drop-offs to the east, north and south, and sloping
down to the west. Interwoven with ledges, walls,
arches, caves and plateaus. Depths from 15 to
hundreds of feet.
- Current and sea conditions moderate to heavy. A
dive for the more experienced diver, or for a novice
at the end of a dive package (conditions permitting).
- Extensive fish life: barracuda, sting rays, yellowtail
snapper, mackerel, king-fish, midnight blue parrot-
fish; corals and sponges.

SCOTTS HEAD DROP-OFF: 15 min. from Dive
SHop.
- A shallow ledge with a sharp drop-off running
along the north to western tip of Scotts Head.
- Depth from 5ft to 140ft going.
- Current and sea conditions light to moderate. A
dive area for all divers, including snorkelers.
- Extensive coral growth on drop-off, large barrel and
tube sponges, black coral, tropical reef fish, and
sometimes
ocean-fish feeding on the edge.

SOUFRIERE PINNICLE: 10 min. from Dive Shop.
- Small Pinnacle rising out of the Soufriere Bay, with
sheer drops (and walls) to the east, south, west, with
small sloping ridge on the north running to shore.
- Depth from 5ft to.150ft descending.
- Current and sea conditions light. A dive for all
levels of divers.
- Soft corals, sponges, black corals on wall faces and
tropical reef fish.

LA BIM: "The Wall": 10 min. from the Dive shop-
Extensive wall running offshore to the west.
Interwoven with small pinnacles and valleys sloping
down to the west. Southern face is a very deep wall.
- Depth 25ft to 800ft plus
- Current and sea conditions light. For all levels of
divers and snorkelers.
- Extensive coral growth, sponges, black corals
nudibrachs, and tropical reef fish.

DANGLEBEN`S REEF: 10 min from Dive Shop.
- Deep reef running offshore to the west. Interwoven
with small pinnacles and valleys sloping down to the
west. Southern face is a very deep wall.
- Depth 40ft to 120ft.
- Current and sea conditions light. For all levels of
divers.
- Extensive coral growth, large barrel sponges, tube
sponges, black coral, good selection of bigger tropical
reef fish.

POINT GUINARD CAVES: 10 min. from Dive Shop.
- The point drops off quite sharply to a sandy bottom
with good coral growth between 50ft and 80ft. Caves
at 50ft, one of which can be penetrated about 30ft .
Depth from 15
ft to 90ft.
- Current and sea conditions light. For all levels of
divers. Good snorkeling and night dives.
- Corals, sponges and black coral, lobster, tropical
reef fish, sea horses.
At night the cave is full of sleeping trumpet-fish.
Also blood stars, octopuses and crabs are seen at
night.

TOP LEFT: *Diver and the soldier fish.*

BOTTOM LEFT: *Feather duster worms,*

HOT SPRING: 10 min. from Dive Shop.
- Hot sub-aquatic freshwater spring in shallow water, very near shore, and very close to a reef. Area of approximately 300 sq ft, 10ft deep with small hot vents and hundreds of tiny bubbles rising to the surface like drops of liquid crystal.
- Reef starts at surface and drops to a sandy bottom to the west. Good night dive.
- Depth from the surface to 80ft.
- Excellent sea conditions for all divers and snorkelers.
- Drab-brown weed and growth in the spring area gives sharp contrast to `crystal` bubbles rising to the surface. A hang-out for schools of tiny sprats.
- The reef has corals, sponges, tropical reef fish and lobster at its deeper points.

TOP LEFT: *Soldier fish.*

TOP RIGHT: *A juvenile French angel fish.*

BOTTOM: *A green turtle.*

DIVE SITES

SOLOMAN: 5 min. from Dive Shop.
- Wreck, overturned barge lying on a sandy bottom, running east/west.
- Patches of shallow reef south of barge.
- Depth from 5ft to 40ft.
- Good current and sea conditions. A good dive for all divers and snorkelers.
- Basket-stars, anemones, hydroids, stone-fish, snappers, small tropical reef fish.

CANEFIELD BARGE: 10 min from Dive Shop.
- Wreck, overturned barge lying on a sndy bottom, running east/west.
- Patches of shallow reef south of barge.
- Depth from 5ft to 40ft.
- Good current and sea conditions. A good dive for all divers and snorkelers.
- Basket-stars, anemones, hydroids, stone-fish, snappers, small tropical reef fish.

CABRITS: Diving around entire bluff, 5ft to 100ft plus. Rock bottom to south, granite to the west, staghorn and plate coral to the north.

CANEFIELD TUG: 10 min. from Dive Shop.
- Wreck, tug lying upright on sandy bottom. Boat is complete and about 60ft long. It is offshore at a river-mouth, so visibility is sometimes very restricted in the shallower water, but increases with depth.
- Depth 55ft to 90ft.
- Sea conditions good, sometimes moderate to strong current. Good dive for experienced divers, and on certain days for novices.
- Lots of hydroids, anemones, snappers, the odd barracuda, schools of squirrel fish, soldier fish and sargent-majors.

RODNEYS ROCK: 20 min. from Dive Shop
- Rock extended to the west on a sandy bottom with a fissure running north/south right through, giving a cave dive effect.
- Depth from surface to 60ft.
- Good current and sea conditions.
- A bit of coral growth and marine fish life, black coral.

MARINE PARK: Shallow reef 159ft from shore. Good for snorkelling from shore.

CASTAWAYS REEF: About half a mile offshore, running north/shore.
- Depth 60ft.
- Good sea and current conditions. Can be dived by all levels of divers.
- Corals, sea-fans, sponges, tropical reef fish.

GRANDE SAVANNE: Coral formation from shore running west. Depth increases to the west. Coral broken by patches of sand. quite a large area. Sometimes heavy currents.

TI BAYE: Tiny, sandy cove with good diving at either end. Good for all levels of divers and snorkelers. A few sea-hares.

PRINCE RUPERT BAY SOUTH: Coral reef at 50-90ft offshore, south of Prince Rupert Bay. Corals, sponges, sea-fans, gorgonians, good selection of tropical reef fish.

TOUCARIE BAY: Drop-offs and coral formations with cave. Large iron hull sail ship to the north of the bay, broken up and spread over large area. Chain lockers and anchor distinctly visible. Average depth 40ft, some parts to 90ft. Suitable for all levels of divers.

WRECK: Capuchin Point with 2 distinctive sets of wreckage. A World War I gun-boat seemed to have run right up against the cliffs. Engine, anchor, chain, bottles, brass and copper fittings and pipes very distinctive. Also pieces of aluminium from an aircraft, estimated time in water 20 years.
- Depth 20ft to 80ft.
- Sea and current conditions heavy. A dive for experienced divers.
The average visibility is about 100ft, sometimes restricted by heavy rains (run-off) or ground swell. There is diving right off the Dive Shop.

*Dive site information was supplied byDIVE DOMINICA LTD a professional Scuba operation that arranges diving holidays, boat charters, ground transportation, and island tours.

BOTTOM : *Trunk Fish. This fish is in acomplete shellexcept for holes for the fins tail, eyes and mouth. (It's also known as Shellfish)*

TOP LEFT: *A spiny sea-urchin during a nite dive.*

BOTTOM LEFT: *Coral dwelling fish*

NATIONAL PARKS

MORNE TROIS PITONS NATIONAL PARK

The National Park and Protected Areas Act was passed by the Government in July, 1975, as a result 17,000 acres of land has been designated as the Morne Trois Pitons National Park. This park is located in the south central interior of the island.

The Morne Trois Pitons National Park has been named after a mountain which rises up to 4600 ft above sea level. It is a mountain of three peaks.

The establishment of the Morne Trois Pitons National Park sought to achieve the following:-
1. Protect some of the natural resources and ecology of the park.
2. Provide the local people with appropriate natural setting for inspirational and recreational purposes.
3. To serve as a natural laboratory for education and research.
4. To stimulate industries capable of boosting up the islands economy, specifically the tourism industry.

Dominica is promoting its natural resources to "would-be" visitors. The objective is not to attract mass tourism which is specialized. Dominica will therefore not appeal to persons seeking sun, sand and sea alone but the more adventurous and discerning visitor who is interested in nature and who prefers to avoid routine tourism.

ATTRACTIONS

The park contains some of the islands most outstanding physical features. Of the nine volcanic cones which make up the island, four are located within the National Park. Morne Trois Piton 4550 ft (1383m), Morne Macaque (Micotrim) 4006 ft (1120m), Morne Watt 4017 ft (1205m) and Morne Anglais 3683 ft (1218m).

The water resources are an important component of the park system because of its function of providing protection to watershed areas and thus ensuring preservation of water and hydro-electric resources.

VOLCANISM

Dramatic examples of active volcanism are evident in the park. The Boiling Lake which is the second largest in the world is located in the heart of the park. The lake is seventy yards (63m) across with an unknown depth and with temperatures ranging from 180 - 197°F (82°C - 91.5°C) along the edges. The Valley of Desolation below the Boiling Lake contains numerous fumaroles and hot springs and a unique fumarolic type of vegetation. However access to the Boiling Lake is extremely arduous via a 7-mile stop trail (round-trip).

WATERFALLS

Three waterfalls occur in the park. The Middleham Falls 150 - 200 ft (46-61m) in height, the Sari Sari Falls 200 - 220 ft and Trafalgar Triple Falls,120-150 ft (35-40 m). Numerous cascades also dissect the eastern and southern areas of the park.

INLAND BASINS

Of the estimated four or five inland basins found in Dominica, two are located in the National Park. The Freshwater Lake and the Boeri Lake are the largest on the island. They are two crater lakes which have been formed in the space between the volcanic dome of Morne Micotrim and its partially buried crater. The Freshwater Lake lies at 2500 ft (760m) elevation and is approximately 46,366 sq.yds and 45 ft at its greatest depth. The Boeri Lake, lies at an elevation of 2800 ft, has a maximum surface area of four acres and may be at least 117 ft deep.

However, the rich tropical vegetation is without doubt, one of

the biggest attractions of Dominica. All four types of vegetation zones can be found within the park. Rain forest dominated by dacryocles - sloanea association; montane forest, and the elfin woodland or cloud forest are found in undisturbed tracks. In addition, there are lower montane forest, palm break forest - (disturbed forest) and swamp forest. For the botanist or ecologist, its a natural laboratory.

ACCESSIBILITY

The location of the park allows for accessibility from numerous points. From the capital city Roseau, there are major areas of accessibility - Laudat. Trafalgar Falls and Wotten Waven.

Its northern boundary has two major areas. On the Rosalie road to south-east or from the Roseau Airport road in the north. However, the areas allow for many access points.

A system of trails have been developed within the park in addition to picnic shelters. Funding for this was provided by the Canadian International Development Agency (CIDA). However, with the 1979 cyclone every bit of infrastructure developed within the park had been destroyed. As such access to the park had been a major constraint to visitors and the local population. More recently, funds have been made available to the Ministry of Tourism through the European Development Fund for site upgrading of attractions within the park. The funds will allow for trail construction, picnic and toilet facilities and erection of directional signs.

The Forestry and Parks Services, under whose aegis the park falls, does not have the budget for the overall maintenance of the park. The topography makes maintenance quite difficult. In addition, the vegetation grows extremely quickly and requires continued maintenance of the trail. The high rainfall in the areas also takes its toll on the trails.

CABRITS HISTORICAL PARK

The Cabrits Historical Park was recently designated a park through an act of Parliament in 1987. The total concept included Cabrits Historical Monument and Marine Park. However to date, the National Park Act has not been amended to make allowances for the protection of marine areas within our territorial waters.

The area designated consists of four major zones. (a) Cabrits Peninsula (b) the Swamps (c) the Beach Front and (d) the Marine Areas and associated coral community. All four components provide unique features important for historical, recreational or scientific purposes.

ATTRACTIONS

The Cabrits Peninsular contains the historical ruins of Port Shirley and Fort George 18th and early 19th century forts which are being restored. There is also a museum at Fort Shirley.

Additionally the dry scrub woodland covering the twin peaks of the Cabrits is one of the best preserved in the Caribbean.

The swamp is important for the ecological balance of the area and the diversity of plant life. It is the largest swamp in Dominica and provides an important nesting area for local and migratory birds.

The beach front of Douglas Bay and Toucari Bay represent two of the most extensive beaches in Dominica with large grey sand beaches excellent for recreationists and beach lovers.

The marine area and associated coral reefs are two of the best coral reef areas around Dominica. Their preservation is very important

for development of the fishing industry but also provide an excellent area for snorkellers and for organising glass bottom boat trips.

ACCESSIBILITY

The Cabrits National Park is located approximately one mile north from the second town of Portsmouth and twenty miles from the capital city, Roseau.It is accessible by trail or by a motorable road up to forty feet from the gate.

At present, restoration work is being done. Proper development of this area requires a considerable amount of financial resources and expertise. This area, however is already a focal point for tourism, historical education through the establishment of a small museum and for outdoor recreation.

FOREST RESERVES

There are two forest reserves, the Central Forest Reserve consisting of 410 ha, and the Northern Forest Reserve consisting of 8,814 ha.

The habitat of the Sisserou and Red - Necked Parrots is restricted to the Northern Forest Reserve. Within the forest reserve controlled logging ia allowed. However with recent logging practices and recommendations to convert certain acreages for agriculture, a threat is being posed to these already endangered species.

The Northern Forest Reserve and the Central Forest Reserve contains trails of virgin tropical rain forest and provide protective functions to wildlife, water catchments and at the same time provide opportunities for hiking and educational activities.

THE SISSEROU PARROT

The Sisserou parrot (*amazonz imperialis*) is a shy but very attractive native of the tropical forest of Dominica. It is probably the oldest species of Amazon parrot in the world and is found only in Dominica. Sisserou parrots have lived on the island for several hundred thousand years. Sisserou parrots can live to be very old (over 70 years) and in captivity some have outlived their captors. In the wild, however, their life may be shorter.

The Sisserou parrot is the largest of the two parrots of Dominica. It is heavy-bodied bird as big as a fowl. A Sisserou is a well proportioned, beautifully streamlined bird with the coloured feather and curved back characteristic of all parrots.

The upper parts and back are mostly green, the front is mauve coloured, the head is greenish blue and the eyes are red. The tail and upper parts range from purple to violet and there is a red streak on the wing tip.

An adult is 18 to 19 inches (450 - 480 mm) long, 8 inches (200 mm) wide and weighs 2 pounds (0.9 kg). When the wings are spread out the distance from tip to tip is 30 inches (0.76 m).

Each foot has 4 toes, two pointing back and two pointing forward. This arrangement enables the bird to crawl up vertical surfaces without using its wings.

Males cannot be distinguished from females except by behaviour but generally the males tend to be very slightly larger with bigger heads. The colour of the feathers is not a good indication of sex.

HABITAT PREFERENCES

The Sisserou parrot is a bird of the deep forest and is seldom seen close to civilisation. It will not go anywhere near cultivated areas. They are found mainly in rain forests of the gommier/chataignier association.

Although there is a small population in the south of the island, the heaviest concentration is on and around the foothills of Morne Diablotin in the north.

Parrots can live at very high altitudes (over 4, 700ft.). In Dominica they generally do not inhabit such high elevation because at these elevations, gommier, carapite and other dominant species of our forest, which provide food for the birds, are not abundant.

FOOD AND FEEDING HABITS

In the wild, the Sisserou feeds on the flowers, fruit and seeds of the gommier, carapite, mauricif, and almost every tree in the forest. In captivity, however, it will eat peanuts, bananas, boiled rice, coconut, greens and mangoes if offered.

The parrot can fly great distances in search of food. In this regard, it may cover over 10 sq. miles (2,589 ha) in one day.

When feeding, the bird stands on one foot and use the other to hold food to its beak. The foot is very strong and can lift relatively heavy weights (over half a pound).

NESTS

Sisserou parrots do not build nets as other birds. Rather, they inhabit cavities and hollows in branches in the tree tops. These cavities or crops are sometimes in complete darkness. This is advantageous because

1) The chicks are very clumsy and have no balance. If they are exposed in ordinary nests they could easily fall off.

2) The chicks are very noisy. This noise is muffled by the depth of their "homes" and does not carry to predators such as the chicken hawk.

Sisserou parrots are very clean and never allow their nests to become dirty or smelly. They dispose of filth (from their chicks) by eating it and regurgitating it some distance away.

SOCIAL BEHAVIOUR

The birds are very social and can usually be seen feeding together in flocks of four to six birds. They are able to converse with each other and have distinct calls for different purposes. For instance, their feeding call is different from their mating call or the sound they make when in flight.

The parrots pair for life. (i.e. the same pair will remain together for life) and are very faithful to each other. A parrot will only seek another mate when its mate dies, and even then, if it is old it may simply grieve rather than find a new mate.

MOVEMENT AND ESCAPE

Like all birds the Sisserou is light in relation to its size and this, coupled with its large wings, enables it to cover great distance. When climbing vertical surfaces, the parrot uses its beak and feet. It can therefore literally walk up a tree trunk.

When frightened the bird immediately flies away but never goes far. It may fly out of sight, wait a while, then come back. It does so quickly, and may sit silently in a tree for hours while the danger moves away.

SOUNDS

Parrots can make a variety of sounds ranging from loud excited chattering to soft cooing noises. At Syndicate, five miles north-east of Dublanc, two Sisserou parrots were observed chattering back and forth to each other in the same manner that humans keep a conversation. This "conversation" lasted for twenty minutes before the birds flew off.

When trained properly, parrots can be made to sing, talk, or whistle like human beings. They have very good memories and have been classed by some as the most intelligent bird in the world.

Parrots love to bathe and they chatter excitedly whenever it is about to rain. In fact it is still a great mystery how these birds can predict so accurately, the coming of a heavy shower. When it rains, rather than seek shelter, the birds roll over on their backs, stretch their legs, and allow the water to wet their throat and under-parts.

BREEDING HABITS

Mating in the Sisserou is never aggressive or violent. This is understandable since the birds live together, feed together, and move together, throughout their lies. Parrots, however, do not tolerate rivals and even in captivity, two males or two females will not remain in the same aviary without fighting.

In the breeding season, the female will cuddle to the male and beg to be fed. They stroke each other frequently and make loving sounds to each other before and after mating.

The breeding season starts in February and eggs are laid from March to mid-June. The eggs are white and are the size of a very small fowl's egg. Every year two eggs are laid but, usually, only one hatches.

This may be because the risks are so great and the chicks need so much food and attention, that the adult can only take care of one chick at a time.

It takes 70 days from the time the egg hatches to when the chick can attempt to fly. When the chicks are very small their stomachs cannot hold food and consequently they are not fed regularly. As they grow, however, they need more and more food and may be fed up to four times in one day. The chicks remain with the parents and learn what to eat, where to roost etc. until they are able to fend for themselves. Sisserou parrots become mature sexually at six years of age.

Sisserou parrots generally nest and breed in Chataignier trees while the Jacquot nests and breeds in Gommier trees.

CLIMATIC FACTOR

In Dominica, rainfall is the climatic factor with the greatest influence on the Sisserou. If the rains come early so that there is a short dry season, then a lot of the flowers drop off the trees before they become mature. This results in a drop in the food supply.

The period mid-February to late May is the dry season or careme. This is the time when the Sisserou chicks are hatched, and are most vulnerable. Heavy rains during this period may flood the roosts and drown the chicks.

WATER AND FOOD

The Sisserou parrot very rarely comes near the ground. Its water supply, therefore, is not obtained from stream or rivers but rather, from that stored in giant bromeliads and other epiphytes which grow in the tree crowns.

The food source of the Sisserou parrot is very wide and at that moment the bird faces no danger from that angle. However, if we continue to cut down our prime forests at the rate that we are doing today, it will not be long before the birds are cleaned completely from the island. Protection of our forests is the key to the conservation of the Sisserou. To date no diseases have been recorded on the parrots.

PREDATORS

The Sisserou is most vulnerable when young and it faces the most danger while still in chick stage. It then faces danger from two species of birds (malfini and grive), snakes and the opossum.

The grive or pearly-eyed thrasher (*margarops fucatus*) sometimes competes with the parrots for nesting space, and also preys on parrots' eggs.

The chicken hawk or malfini (*buteo platypterus*) is probably the greatest natural enemy of the Sisserou. Chicken hawk also have the ability to crawl up vertical surfaces and so they are able to invade the parrots' nests and eat the chicks. Chicken hawks in times of extreme hunger, have also been known to attack adult parrots.

The manicou or opossum (*didelphys marsupialis insularis*) and the boa constrictor (*constrictor constrictor*), because of their ability to climb, also prey on young Sisserou parrots.

MAN

The Sisserou parrot has, through evolution, adapted itself to various natural changes in its environment but it has not been able to adapt to the influence of man. Man through deforestation and his many poaching activities has, over the years, become the Sisserou's greatest enemy. The steadily decreasing population is proof enough of the destructive powers of woodcutters and hunters.

The Forestry and Wildlife Act, which was passed in 1976, give maximum protection to these very beautiful birds by making it illegal to hunt (it and the Jacquot) at any time. Also, persons wishing to keep these birds in captivity as pets, are required by law, to obtain a permit.

The Sisserou parrot is a protected bird. It is the national bird of Dominica and adorns our coat of arms.

THE JACQUOT OR RED-NECKED PARROT

The Jacquot or Red-Necked parrot (*amaxona arausiaca*) also liveså in the mountain forest of Dominica but for the most part, at lower elevations than the Sisserou. This bird is also native to Dominica, but it is a much younger bird. Like the Sisserou parrot it is also a protected species.

DESCRIPTION

The Jacqout is the smaller of the parrots and is very brightly coloured. It is predominantly a medium shade of green with a blue face. The wings are blue, the tail is dark blue to black with a lime-green tip. There is a bright red patch around the neck.

An adult Jacquot is 16 inches (400 mm) long, 7 inches (180 mm) wide and weighs one and a quarter pounds. When the wings are spread out , the distance from tip to tip is 24 ins. (600 mm).

Like the Sisserou, each foot has 4 toes, two pointing forward and two pointing back, so that it has the ability to climb.

HABITAT PREFERENCES

The Jacquot, though a native of the deep forest, is not as shy as the Sisserou and nests at much lower elevations. In fact in the past, these birds have been known to feed on grapefruit, bananas, and other agricultural crops, causing great damage.

In 1950 they covered most of the island, but today their range is much smaller. It circles that of the Sisserou in the north, includes the wet area in the central part of the island, and around Morne Anglais in the south. Like the Sisserou, the heaviest concentration is in the northern part of the island, where the forest are more or less undisturbed.

MISCELLANEOUS

Apart from the difference in size, colour and range, the Jacquot is similar to the Sisserou in ever respect. Everything else described for the Sisserou also applies to the Jacquot.

SIFFLEUR MONTAGNE

The Siffleur Montagne (*myadestes genibarbis*) can be heard whistling its one or two syllable notes throughout the mountains above 1,500 ft. (450 m) elevation. The tunes are very melodious and this has prompted a local chorale (The Siffleur Montagne Chorale) to adopt its name. It is not shy and in fact frequently comes out of curiosity as one proceeds through the forest. It is the most abundant bird in the elfin woodlands near the tops of the mountains.

TO RECAPTURE A FORTRESS

By *LENNOX HONYCHURCH*

The ramparts of Fort Shirley rise above the forested coastline of Dominica like a huge natural outcrop of rock. Perched upon one of those thick walls, high above the sequinned cobalt of the placid Caribbean, a young stonemason is carefully replacing new coral lime mortar between the ragged joints of weathered clay bricks. He is one of a small team of masons, woodcutters and technical personnel who are working to recapture this 18th century fortress from the clutches of the jungle and turn it into the focal point of the National Historic Park being developed as an educational centre and visitor attraction for Dominica: a sort of open-air museum, offering a variety of exhibits and activities highlighting the historic and natural features of the area.

During the last thirty years of the 18th century the British constructed a garrison on this headland in the north of Dominica so as to defend the magnificent Prince Rupert Bay where ships of the Royal Navy anchored to collect fresh water, wood and fruit, and to rest their crews.

Work on the garrison was sporadic; surging ahead at times when conflict threatened and lulling after peace treaties were signed, only to be revived with even greater intensity when there were renewed signs of war. French engineers took over operations from 1778-1783 during the French occupation of the island in the hope that they would hold it permanently. But the Treaty of Versailles, influenced by the British victory at the Battle of the Saints, returned Dominica to Britain.

Eventually the British, employing rented slaves, white artisans, soldiers and engineers covered the 200 acres with one fort, seven batteries, seven cisterns, powder magazines, ordnance store-houses, barracks and officers' quarters to house and provide for 500 men and a company of artillery with officers, as well as accommodation for another 500 in case of emergency. Grey and pink volcanic stone was shaped into lintels, arches and gun slits; boulders were carried to reinforce the inside of ramparts, cannon were hauled, and the forest was cut to afford a clear sight of the surrounding sea. By the end of it all, over fifty major structures dotted the twin hills upon the point from which thirty-five mortars and cannon of varying sizes were aimed seaward waiting for the enemy.

In 1854, when the Caribbean had become a valueless backwater of the French and British empires, the last company of regular troops to be stationed there marched through the tall stone gates and down the steep causeway to waiting ships. The garrison from which they sailed, immediately succumbed to the onslaught of the luxuriant vegetation growing over and between the massive walls, tearing at the finely cut volcanic stone and at the clay bricks originally carried out from Britain as ballast for sailing ships. Raiders seeking these useful bricks and fine stone staircases, robbed what they could extricate from the forest. Occasionally a cannon was removed (a couple of them now stand on a lawn in Mobile, Alabama USA), but generally the isolation of the Cabrits made it less accessible to looters than many other historic sites in the Caribbean.

Successive governments of Dominica have from time to time considered the question of how best to utilise the historic remains on the Cabrits and more particularly Fort Shirley. It has been used at various times this century for brief periods as a forestry and agriculture station, a quarantine post and it almost became the island's leper home.

Since 1966, tourism-orientated proposals followed each other in quick succession. Among these were the usual Caribbean politicians' dreams of free ports, casinos, a jet airport and tourist enclaves. One unsuccessful scheme, launched by an American chicken farmer resident in Dominica, proposed to cut the Cabrits headland off from the rest of Dominica by means of a canal and develop a modern freebooters' paradise upon that man-made "Sunday Island." This was followed by an equally hapless venture called Valhalla and another even greater free port fiasco in 1979.

From July 1975, when the Dominica National Parks system was established, the idea of including the Cabrits as one of the island's National Parks took root. Over recent years, the production of studies and project proposals as well as actual work at the Cabrits have intensified. Those involved include the Dominica National Parks Service, the Caribbean Conservation Association's Eastern Caribbean Natural Area Management Programme (ECNAMP), with assistance from the Dominica Conservation Association, the Dominica Institute and Island Resources Foundation in St. Thomas, U.S. Virgin Islands.

Fort Shirley and other historic buildings at the Cabrits are seen as being part of a valuable national resource which can be used for the benefit of modern Dominica. Even in a ruined state, the buildings are tremendous assets.

Slowly the awareness of the economic as well as aesthetic value of our architectural heritage is catching on in the Eastern Caribbean so that governments and aid donors now see the potential and are willing to invest in the promotion of such sites as Brimstone Hill, St. Kitts; Shirley Heights, Antigua; and Fort Charlotte, St. Vincent.

Regular assistance comes, for example, from the British Royal Navy whenever its ships are in port. This began in September 1982 when men from H.M.S. Rhyl responded to a request for a team of sailors to haul a mortar back into place on Fort Shirley, thus setting an example which has been followed by the crews of other visiting ships since then.

The overall plan for the park, entitled "Cabrits 2000," aims at establishing the entire headland as a National Park; improving trails and access; establishing a docking facility on the site of the old wharf area; restoring Fort Shirley with appropriate services as the headquarters for the park; providing a museum and archives as well as a hostel and lecture/activity centre for students and exchange groups from within Dominica and abroad, visiting for work, study and holiday camps.

A section of the beautiful reef and beach along Douglas Bay to the north will be included as a Marine Park within the Cabrits area.

Since the 1960s the Forestry Department helped to keep the major ruins free of bush, but the main thrust towards formal establishment of the park was evident on 12th April 1982 when a small museum was opened at Fort Shirley to commemorate the Battle of the Saints, fought between the French and British fleets just north of the Cabrits exactly 200 years earlier.

Today activity stirs at the forested garrison once more as youth groups and school parties armed with pencils and notebooks make regular visits, following guided tours along trails to outlying batteries, gun emplacements and barracks. Masons blend mortar according to the traditional methods and carpenters chisel out joints and window frames in the fashion of the 18th century, shaping the edifices of war and conflict into a haven of peace and learning for Dominicans of future generations.

TOURIST INFORMATION

AIR TRAVEL
Arriving by air: connecting flights with international airlines (American Airlines, British Airways, Air Canada, Air France, Eastern & Lufthansa), are available at Antigua, Guadeloupe, Martinique, Barbados, St. Lucia and Puerto Rico. Dominica has no jet airport, but the Caribbean airline LIAT, provides several daily scheduled flights for inter-island hopping, both northbound and southbound, enabling connections to be made with the rest of the Caribbean and the world.
The port of entry for cruise ships, Woodbridge Bay, is located at Fond Cole and is approximately three-quarter mile from the centre of Roseau, the capital in the south-west of the island.
Air Guadeloupe has scheduled flights daily, except onSundays, from Guadeloupe to Dominica.
Air Guadeloupe, Air Martinique, Air BVI, Air Carib and Nature Island Airways are available for charters.

CURRENCY
The local currency is the Eastern Caribbean Dollar (EC$)

BANKS
The National, Commercial and Development Bank of Dominica
Banque Francaise Commreciale
Barclays Bank Plc
Credit Union
The Royal Bank of Canada
The Bank of Nova Scotia
Agriculture, Industry and Development Bank (A.I.D.)

BANKING HOURS
Barclays: Monday - Friday 8am - 1pm
Others: Monday - Friday 8am - 12 noon
All reopen on Friday 3pm - 5pm
(Closed Saturdays and Sundays)
Local banks will change the following currencies:
Pound Sterling Deutsche Marks
Trinidad & Tobago Dollars US Dollars
Canadian Dollars Barbados Dollars
French Francs
Cruise ship passengers may change left-over local currency back to other currencies at banks during normal banking hours.

MAIL
Post Office days/hours: Monday: 8am - 5pm Tuesday - Friday: 8am - 4pm
Open during lunch hours

SHOPPING DAYS/HOURS
Monday - Friday: 8am - 4pm
(lunch break included)
Saturday: 8am - 1pm

VISITORS REQUIREMENTS
Proof of citizenship/passport and return ticket

LOCALTRANSPORTATION
Taxis (4 - 6 passengers)
Minibus (15 passengers)
Land Rover & Ford Jeeps (8 passengers)

TAXI FROM AIRPORTS
Melville Hall, 36 miles from Roseau:
1hour 30 mins journey
Canefield Airport, 3 miles from Roseau:
10 mins one way

VISITORS DRIVER PERMITS
may be obtained upon presentation of a valid driver's license to the Police Traffic Dept and at the Immigration Desk of Canefield Airport during office hours. There is a small fee payable
N.B. TRAFFIC DRIVES ON THE LEFT SIDE OF THE ROAD

TELEPHONE, CABLE, FAX, & TELEX
Facilities available at Cable & Wireless Int. and at some hotels.

TAXES
Taxes which concern a visitor: 10% Government tax on alcoholic beverages in hotels. 3% Government Restaurant tax. 10% Government room tax. $20 EC (adult), $10 EC (child) airport embarkation tax.

FOR EMERGENCY CALLS
Police...............82222
Princess Margaret Hospital......82231
Fire & Ambulance.....................82890
Harbour Master........................82610

MEDICAL FACILITIES
CheckMinistry of Health for details

BRIEF OUTLINE
The Princess Margaret Hospital is located at Goodwill, a residential suburb of Roseau. There are small hospitals elsewhere on the island, at Portsmouth, Marigot and Grand Bay, to name a few. Clinics and District Nurses are located throughout the island. The Princess Margaret Hospital (Government), and Harlsboro Medical Centre in Roseau (private), are staffed by a surgeon and several other doctors. There are a few dentists on the island.

PRINCIPAL ATTRACTIONS
View from Morne Bruce
Trafalgar Triple Waterfalls
Emerald Pool Nature Trail
Tour of Roseau and its environs (Historic) including the Botanical Gardens
Carnival parade of costumed bands.
Dancing and music in the streets, (usually the two days before Ash Wednesday)
Plantation/Mountain hotels
The Boiling Lake (second largest in the world)
Valley of Desolation
Sulphur Springs

Local Handcraft shops
Roseau Market
L'Escalier Tete Chien
Fort Shirley - Cabrits National Park
Fresh Water Lake
Boeri Lake
Titou Gorge
Indian River
Scotts Head
Carib Territory

MUSEUMS
One can observe relics of the past, and certain animal species at the Cabrits National Park Museum, and National Parks Office, Botanical Gardens, Roseau. Open Mondays - Fridays.

NEWSPAPERS
The New Chronical on Friday each week

LOCAL CLUBS AND ORGANISATIONS
The Rotary Club of Dominica
True Gospel Businessman's Fellowship
Catholic Youth Movement
Methodist Youth Group
Jaycees Caribbean Pearle Lodge
National Secretaries Association
Free Masons
Lions Club of Dominica
Boy Scouts

ART AND CRAFTS
Prints by local artists
Weaving
Grass mats, bags, dolls, table mats
The Caribs' besides being popular with their basketry, are famous for their dugout canoes.
Leathercraft
Pottery
Candlemaking
Craft work from bamboo, cow horn, coconut shell heads, sea shells, local wood, etc.

PRINCIPAL PLACES OF WORSHIP
The Roman Catholic Church
The Methodist Church
The Anglican Church
Pentecostal Assemblies
International Baptist Mission
Jehovah Witness
Gospel Mission
Christian Union Mission
Seventh Day Adventist
Berean Bible Church

ELECTRICITY
220 - 240 volts AC: 50 cycles

WATER
Visitors can drink water from a tap or faucet

DRESS
IT IS THE CUSTOM NOT TO WEAR SWIMSUITS OR BIKINIS IN THE STREETS

BUSINESS INFORMATION

KEY FACTS
Official title: Commonwealth of Dominica
Head of Government: Prime Minister, Eugenia Charles
Ruling Party: Dominica Freedom Party
Capital: Roseau

COUNTRY PROFILE:
Political system: Executive power rests with the president of the republic, although the holder of the office normally acts on the advice of the cabinet. The president is elected by the unicameral legislature, the House of Assembly for five years, renewable once. A candidate may be elected unopposed if the prime minister and leader of the opposition agree, otherwise a secret ballot is held. The House of Assembly has five members nominated by the prime minister, four nominated by the leader of the opposition, one ex-officio member and 21 members directly elected by the 21 constituencies. parliamentary terms run for five years. The prime minister is the leader of the majority in the House of Assembly and the leader of the opposition is appointed by the president as leader of main grouping outside the government.

MEDIA:
Press: Two weeklies The New Chronicle, (independent) and the Official Gazette.
Broadcasting: Government-operated radio service and one privately-owned religious station.

EXTERNAL TRADE:
Balance of payments deficit is supported by IMF loan and bilateral aid from USA, France and UK.

EXPORTS:
Bananas (44.7% of exports), toilet and laundry soap (22%), coconut products (6.7%), galvanised sheets, citrus products, drinking water, aloe vera, cut flowers, wooden furniture, various light manufactured products (apparel, gloves, footwear).
.Main destinations: UK (has traditionally taken about 75% of banana exports), CARICOM countries.

IMPORTS:
Traditionally machinery, transport equipment, food, manufactured goods.
Main sources: UK, USA, CARICOM countries.

AGRICULTURE:
Sector is mainstay of economy, contributing around 42% to GDP. Bananas are the main crop, with exports destined mainly for the UK. Other export crops include coconuts/copra, oranges, grapefruit and limes. Livestock-raising and fishing are under-developed and geared towards domestic consumption. Over 40% of the total area is covered by forests with a number of commercially viable wood species present. Sector as a whole is still recovering from hurricane damage in 1979 and 1980.

INDUSTRY:
Sector is small-scale and centred on agricultural processing, mainly coconut oil, copra and soap, canned fruit juices, tobacco and rum. Water bottling for export is also important. Tourism is important source of foreign exchange.

ENERGY:
Around 80% of island's electricity needs is met by hydro-power, of which there are plentiful resources.

Membership of international organisations: FAO, GATT, IMF, UN, Commonwealth, Economic Commission for Latin America, Organisation of American States, state associated with the IEC, World Bank. CARICOM

DOMINICA AT A GLANCE

Location and Size: The largest and most northerly of the Windward Islands, between the two French-controlled islands of Martinique and Guadeloupe. Total land area of 289.5 square miles.
History and Government: Discovered in 1493 on a Sunday, thus the name Dominica (pronounced Dom-i-nee-ka). Originally inhabited by the Caribs (who still live on the island). The island changed hands between France and Britain several times before Dominica became a British possession in 1805.

Dominica became an independent republic within the Commonwealth on November 3, 1978. The House of Assembly is elected for up to a five year term. The Prime Minister Mary Eugenia Charles, first won an election in 1980, was re-elected in 1985.

Population: 85,000 (1988 estimate)
Language and Literacy: English is the major language; a French patois is also widely spoken. Literacy is about 90 per cent.
Labour Force: 40,000 (unemployment is about 13%)
Incentives to Investors: Small, stable society. Trainable workforce. Tax holidays for new investors. Good telecommunications, roads and electrical power. Low-cost factory rentals.

COMMUNICATIONS
There are 450 miles (675km) of roads of which 300 miles (450 km) are paved and 150 miles (225 km) are gravel and earth.

SHIPPING
The country's two ports are located at Roseau and Portsmouth. The port at Roseau with a draft of 30 feet can accommodate large vessels and offers modern container facilities. There are plans to upgrade the present facility to accommodate a larger number of ships.
Shipping companies provide a regular service between Dominica and the major international ports in North America, Europe and the Caribbean:
Antilles and Amazon Line, Marine Bulk Services,Bernuth Nedlloyd, Lloyd Lines, Carib Services Inc., Resolve Maritime Corp., Compagnie Generale Maritime, Saguenay Shipping Lines, Concord/Nopal TEC lines, Geest Line, The West India Shipping Co.

AIR TRANSPORT:
Regular scheduled air services are provided daily by the regional airline Leeward Island Air Transport (LIAT) with links to all Eastern Caribbean islands including international airports at Puerto Rico, Antigua, Barbados, Martinique and Guadeloupe. Three additional reliable air freight services to North America via DC-3 and Boeing 707 are provided by Caribbean Airfreight, Seagreen, and Air Carib. There is an airport on the northern part of the island at Melville Hall with a 4,800 foot runway and a handling capacity of 65,000 pounds per square inch. The 2,500 foot airstrip at Canefield, just outside the capital city of Roseau, handles inter-island traffic. The airstrip was completed with grants from the French and British governments.

TELECOMMUNICATIONS:
Telephone , telex ans facsimile services on the island is provided by Cable and Wireless (West Indies) Ltd. The telephone network is automatic. There are VHF and UHF links to St. Lucia, two radio stations and several TV stations.

UTILITIES:
IndustrialWater
U.S. $0.93 per 1000 gallons for the first 50,000 gallons and U.S. $1.19 per 1000 additional gallons.
Electricity
The rate is U.S. $0.11 per KWH for industrial enterprises, and U.S. $0.135 per KWH for commercial users.
75% of electricity is supplied by hydro-electric power. Diesel generators supply to the remainder.

BANKING:
Agricultural, Industrial, and Development Bank (A.I.D.)
Banque Francaise Commerciale
Barclays Bank International, Ltd.
National Commercial and Development Bank
Royal Bank of Canada
Bank of Nova Scotia

FOR FURTHER INFORMATION PLEASE CONTACT THE ADDRESSES OVERLEAF.

The
National Parks
and other Wild Places of
New Zealand

The
National Parks
and other Wild Places of
New Zealand

TEXT BY KATHY OMBLER

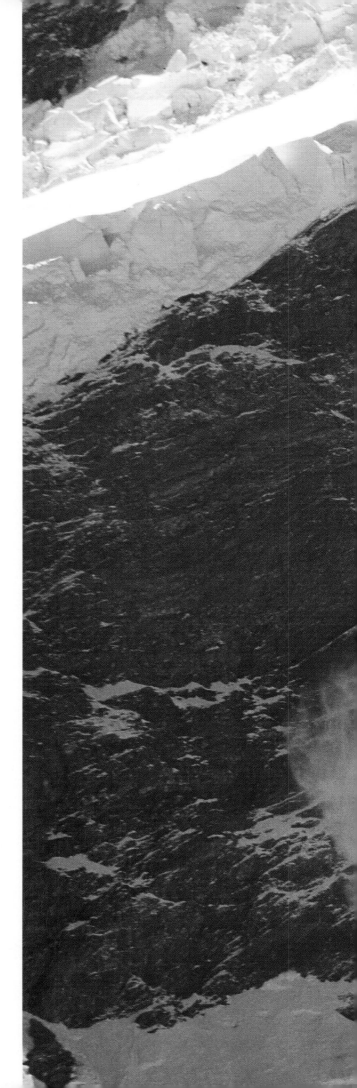

First published in 2001 by New Holland Publishers Ltd
London • Cape Town • Sydney • Auckland
86 Edgware Road, London W2 2EA, United Kingdom
80 McKenzie Street, Cape Town 8001, South Africa
14 Aquatic Drive, Frenchs Forest, NSW 2086, Australia
218 Lake Road, Northcote, Auckland, New Zealand

2 4 6 8 10 9 7 5 3 1

ISBN 1 85974 524 5 (UK)
ISBN 1 87724 627 1 (NZ)

Publisher: Mariëlle Renssen
Commissioning Editor: Claudia dos Santos
Editors: Lauren Copley, Ingrid Schneider
Designer: Claire van Rhyn
Cartographic Concept: John Loubser
DTP Maps: John Hall
Production Manager: Myrna Collins

Reproduction by Unifoto (Pty) Ltd, Cape Town

Printed and bound in Singapore by Tien Wah Press (Pte) Ltd

PUBLISHER'S NOTE
For ease of reference by the general reader, species are for the most part referred to by their
common, as opposed to scientific, names throughout this book. Scientific names can be found in
many of the titles listed in the Further Reading section on page 174. In some instances, however, the
scientific names have been used; in a number of others (where they are likely to prove helpful) both
the common and scientific names are given. The maps published in the book are intended as 'loca-
tors' only; detailed, large-scale maps should be consulted when planning a trip. Although the publishers have made every effort to ensure that the information contained in this book was correct at the
time of going to press, they accept no responsibility for any loss, injury or inconvenience sustained by
any person using this book.

Half title: *The Tuatara, an ancient reptile that evolved at the time of the dinosaurs, is the only reptile
of its kind surviving today.*

Full title: *The seaward Kaikōura Range dominates the Kaikōura coastline.*

Opposite: *An avalanche peels off Mount Sefton in Aoraki/Mount Cook National Park.*

Page 6: *Southern Rātā blooms in January.*

CONTENTS

FOREWORD

New Zealanders pride themselves as a people of the coast, the forest and the mountains. New Zealand, set in the remoteness of the boundary between the South Pacific and the Great Southern Ocean, has known the tread of human feet for less than 1000 years. It was literally the last place on the face of the planet to see human beings, besides Antarctica. Consequently, New Zealand is a place where nature still dominates, and where it can be experienced in so much of its splendour. Thus, it is no wonder that New Zealand's cultural icons are its natural heritage – flightless birds such as the kiwi and kākāpō, the great cathedrals of the northern primeval kauri forests, the splendour of the great carved southern fiords, and the giant peaks of the central Southern Alps. New Zealanders have taken their natural heritage to their hearts and enshrined it in a protected area system unequalled in the world.

It is no accident that Tongariro National Park was the world's fourth national park, and that by the beginning of the last century, New Zealand had also enshrined both Mount Taranaki and the gigantic Fiordland wilderness as additional parks. Over the past 100 years a protected area network has developed to encompass the diverse range of natural ecology. More recently, New Zealand innovation in conservation management has gone beyond the 'park' concept to integrated management across the wider landscape. The country's national reserve system and indigenous species are looked after under the umbrella of a single Department of Conservation (DOC). The benefits of consistency, quality and integration are manifest.

This book, then, is a way for you to enjoy the natural wealth of New Zealand in a vicarious way and hopefully spark a desire to visit. National parks and conservation areas quite properly are looked after by putting nature first. With this proviso, people are encouraged to enjoy, and learn. The ways and byways of the tracks, paths and places in this book all instil a sense of fun, achievement, and above all, appreciation. For through the appreciation of nature and wild places comes the desire to perpetuate and protect.

Hugh Logan

Hugh Logan
Director General, Department of Conservation
New Zealand

INTRODUCTION

Whatungarongaro he tangata Toitū te Whenua

'Man passes on, but the land remains'

MĀORI PROVERB

New Zealand sits in a remote corner of the world, in the southern Pacific Ocean. Small and isolated, the country contains a huge diversity of natural landscapes and habitats, which support a unique ecology.

Only in New Zealand can one find subtropical beaches and rainforests, active volcanoes and geothermal regions, ice-capped mountains and glaciers, all within less than 2000 kilometres (1243 miles) of each other. Add to this vast forests, river systems, lakes, wetlands, a myriad smaller islands and unique endemic wildlife, and it is not surprising that this little country is such a popular tourist destination.

Although young in terms of human settlement, New Zealand was one of the first countries in the world to embrace the concept of conservation. Since its first national park was created over a hundred years ago, New Zealand has developed an impressive network of protected parks, reserves, marine reserves and wildlife sanctuaries, many with well-developed visitor facilities. The World Heritage Status that has been granted to several sites within New Zealand recognizes the immense international significance of the country's natural and cultural heritage.

Isolated Evolution

New Zealand's natural heritage is aptly described by the country's first human settlers, the Māori, as a 'taonga', meaning treasure. And so it is, for the natural environment of this, one of the world's most isolated landmasses, is unique.

For 80 million years, following its breakaway from the ancient super continent Gondwana, New Zealand has developed in isolation and seen the evolution of unparalleled plant and animal life. Safe from predatory mammals, New Zealand's most ancient birds, such as the kiwi, now the nation's national emblem, the kākāpō, the world's largest parrot, and other, now extinct species, evolved into unique flightless browsers. New Zealand's Tuatara, resembling a lizard, is the sole survivor of a line of reptiles that became extinct elsewhere in the world about 60 million years ago.

In New Zealand, invertebrates occupied the niches filled by rodents in other countries: the Giant Weta, which belongs to the same order as grasshoppers and crickets, is one of the world's largest insects; carnivorous land snails are among the world's oldest. The country also has the most diverse lizard population of all temperate zones and three native frog species among the most primitive in the world.

New Zealand's flora has developed in a similarly singular fashion. The country's vast podocarp and beech forests are considered internationally significant by ecologists because they are

Previous pages: Yellow-eyed Penguins (hoiho) make their daily pilgrimage to the sea on Otago Peninsula.

Opposite: Whanganui inlet, which neighbours Kahurangi National Park, is one of the largest and least modified estuaries in New Zealand. Fringed with rainforest, the inlet is regarded as an outstanding marine and wildlife habitat.

Above: New Zealand Fur Seal populations have recovered well after being decimated by seal-skin hunters in the 1800s.

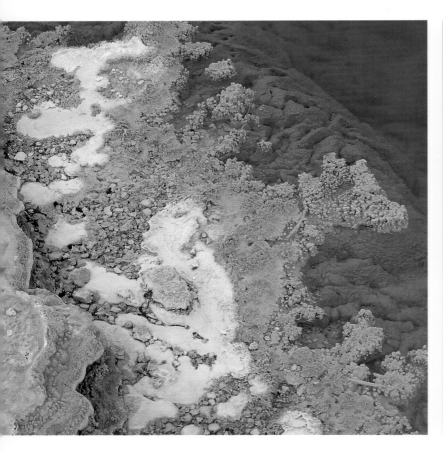

most like the ancient forests of Gondwana. Over 80 per cent of New Zealand's flowering plants are found nowhere else in the world, and 93 per cent of its hardy alpine species are endemic.

Fire and Ice

By far the most visually spectacular aspects of New Zealand's physical development have been the mighty forces of tectonic movement, vulcanism and glaciation.

New Zealand sits above the boundary of two of the earth's great crustal plates, the Pacific and Indo-Australian plates. As these plates jostled and collided throughout geological time, mountains were thrust upwards. The Southern Alps/Kā Tiritiri o te Moana, which form the spectacular mountainous backbone of the South Island, have been elevated by the Alpine Fault which marks the edge of these two plates.

Further north, fiery volcanic mountains and geothermal fields form the volatile southern extent of what is known as the Pacific Rim of Fire, a massive rift of volcanoes – of which several are still active – that extends along the edge of the Pacific crustal plate as far as Tonga and Samoa in the South Pacific. Across the central North Island distinctive landscapes and plant communities are still being created by recurrent eruptions and explosions.

The mighty power of ice has also played a major part in sculpting the landform of New Zealand. Successive ice ages have chiselled and shaped the land, creating valleys, fiords,

lakes, hanging cirques and sharp crested mountain peaks and ridges. In the highest mountains, glaciers still dominate the landscape and continue their powerful sculpting process.

Climatic Diversity

Married to these volatile and varied landscaping forces is New Zealand's huge climatic diversity. New Zealand has the fourth largest maritime area in the world, with thousands of offshore islands scattered throughout territorial waters that extend from subtropical through to subantarctic climes. The New Zealand landmass is exposed to a variety of weather systems: cold winds blowing all the way from Antarctica and, from the north, warm and wet subtropical influences. Coastal habitats are remarkably diverse and over 18,000 kilometres (11,000 miles) of coastline encompass estuaries, inlets, harbours, beaches, rocky cliffs, sounds and fiords.

People of the Land

New Zealand is the last major landmass in the world to have been settled by people. The natural history here has been subject to less than 1000 years of human interference, a meagre period compared with the rest of the world.

Seafaring Polynesians were the first to settle in Aotearoa (New Zealand) and today their Māori descendants are closely bound with the land. Tribal oral histories reflect a deep knowledge of, and spiritual association with, mountains, lakes, rivers,

forests and coastline. In documenting the events which shaped the environment, the Māori also reinforce tribal identity.

European explorers first glimpsed New Zealand in 1642. British expedition leader, James Cook, visited and charted the country in the late 1700s and colonists from European countries, in particular the United Kingdom, settled in New Zealand from the early 1800s. In 1887, New Zealand's first national park was created when paramount chief Te Heuheu Tukino IV (Horonuku), of the tribal group Ngati Tuwharetoa, presented the summits of Tongariro, Ngauruhoe and Ruapehu to the Crown in order to protect their sacred status.

Today the majority of New Zealanders live in the North Island, one of the country's two major islands. One-third of New Zealand's 3.8 million people live in the region of Auckland city, although the capital is Wellington, which sits at the southern tip of the North Island. Tourism, farming, horticulture (including a fast-growing wine industry) and exotic forestry are the mainstays of the economy.

A History of Conservation

The arrival of people, and the associated forest clearance, land development and introduction of animal pests, made an enormous impact on New Zealand's natural ecosystems. On the other hand, the country's isolation spared its environment of the worst effects of atmospheric and marine pollution. From very early times the ethic of conservation has been strong.

Today one-third of New Zealand's land area is legally protected as conservation land and managed by the Department of Conservation (DOC). This encompasses 13 national parks, 20 forest (or conservation) parks and a multitude of reserves, marine reserves and island wildlife sanctuaries.

The Department of Conservation's Māori name is Te Papa Atawhai, which means 'to care for a treasure chest' – a name that reflects the close affinity between conservation and the Māori people and the respect that exists for Māori cultural and spiritual values.

Many places, plants, birds and animals are regarded as 'taonga', or treasures, by the Māori people. Several trees, birds, insects and other species that are common throughout New Zealand have only Māori names, while others have only English names, and many have both. Names of some parks and

Top far left: *Orange-red metal sulphides colour the shallows of Champagne Pool in the Waiotapu thermal area in Rotorua.*

Top centre: *The last rays of sunset catch the flower heads of toetoe, in Tongariro National Park. The seed heads were used by Māori as a dressing for fresh wounds, to stop the bleeding.*

Top right: *The Māori war canoe (waka-taua), on display at Waitangi National Reserve, Bay of Islands, is built to carry 80 paddlers plus 55 passengers.*

landscape features have recently been officially accorded dual Māori and English names, recognizing the significance these places have for the Māori people.

The international significance of New Zealand's natural heritage is recognized by the designation of several World Heritage Sites. These include Tongariro National Park (the first in the world to be granted dual cultural and natural World Heritage status), Te Wahipounamu/South Westland (a massive region that incorporates part of Fiordland, Mount Aspiring, Aoraki/Mount Cook, Westland/Tai Poutini) and the Subantarctic Islands.

New Zealand conservationists have earned an international reputation for restoration of natural habitats, in particular, island sanctuaries which provide safe refuges for some of the country's most distinctive and endangered species of wildlife, such as the giant parrot, the kākāpō, and the beak-headed reptile, the Tuatara. These strategies are now being tested on the mainland, with encouraging early success.

Visiting Parks and Other Wild Places

New Zealand's national parks and other wild places offer visitors an impressive range of outdoor experiences; be it adventurous recreation, solitude, scenic splendour, nature appreciation – or all of these combined – for people of all ages. Ice climbing in the Southern Alps, wandering among tussock and alpine flowers on a mountain pass, skiing the slopes of an active volcano, camping on the shore of a forest-lined lake, cruising the remote southern fiords, watching a Sperm Whale breech, walking beneath ancient podocarp trees, listening to the song of endangered birds on an island wildlife sanctuary – these are but a mere selection of options.

Providing for visitors and recreation is a major part of the Department of Conservation's work. Facilities cater for all ages and fitness levels. DOC provides visitor information centres, huts, walking tracks (trails), campsites, picnic spots, facilities for less mobile people, visitor programmes and advice on park routes, weather and safety. (It should be noted that in New Zealand, hiking or trekking is referred to as tramping, while the term track is used to describe a trail.) The department also oversees commercial operators who run skifields, guided walks, launch trips, wildlife watching, natural heritage tours and other activities.

Parks and most protected areas are open all year round and can be visited free of charge and without a permit. However, payment is required for park brochures, maps and overnight stays in park huts or campsites. In some cases bookings are required for huts and camping areas, and hut passes must be purchased in advance. Where this is not the case, huts are available on a traditional 'first come, first served' basis.

Facilities range from park to park. Many are easily accessible and have comprehensive visitor centres, well developed amenities and established tourist infrastructures. Others are more remote, with few developed tracks or facilities. New

Zealand's premier tramping tracks (and one river journey) are known as 'Great Walks' and include Lake Waikaremoana Track, Tongariro Northern Circuit, Abel Tasman Coast Track, Heaphy Track, Routeburn Track, Milford Track, Kepler Track, Rakiura Track and Whanganui Journey. Guided walks, on these and other wilderness walking tracks, as well as natural heritage and ecotourism tours are available from a host of specialist private operators.

In recent years New Zealand has gained a reputation for 'extreme' outdoor adventure. Many of these pursuits, such as bungy jumping, heli-bungy and river-surfing, take place outside the parks and are not covered in this book.

Hunting (for introduced animals such as deer, pigs and goats which browse and therefore cause serious damage to native forests) and fishing (for introduced Rainbow and Brown Trout) are traditional pasttimes in New Zealand's parks. Guided operations are well established throughout the country, but hunting permits and fishing licences are required. Native freshwater fish are protected and marine recreational fishing rules, including size and catch limits, are monitored by the Ministry of Fisheries.

New Zealand is perhaps one of the few countries in the world where there are no dangerous animals, poisonous snakes or similar such threats lurking in the outdoors. Wasps and a few species of poisonous spiders are the main threats to safety, while pesky mosquitoes and sandflies have earned a fearsome reputation for the unwelcome attention they lavish on park visitors!

When to Visit

The splendid natural features of New Zealand can be appreciated year-round, with seasonal variations in scenery, wildlife watching and recreational experiences. Tramping (hiking), is better suited to summertime (December to March) when tracks and passes are not covered with snow. Avalanche danger for trampers in the South Island mountains is most prevalent in spring. Short walks, scenic cruises and island sanctuary visits are year-round activities.

Visitors should be aware that heavy rain, snow and gales can hit mountain ranges suddenly at any time of the year, even in summer. People exploring high-level mountain tracks need to be well equipped and experienced. Visitors should also be wary of security issues at remote back country car parks, and not leave valuables unattended. New Zealand's parks are beautiful places but, like anywhere in the world, some of its human inhabitants are not.

Opposite far left: *A stream tumbles through Victoria Forest Park.*

Opposite left: *The giant weta, one of the largest insects in the world, has remained virtually unchanged over the last 190 million years.*

Left: *One of New Zealand's flightless birds, the weka is an omnivorous scavenger, whose diet consists of insects, berries, bird's eggs and worms.*

Below: *Ice-encrusted rocks decorate the cold waters of Crucible Lake.*

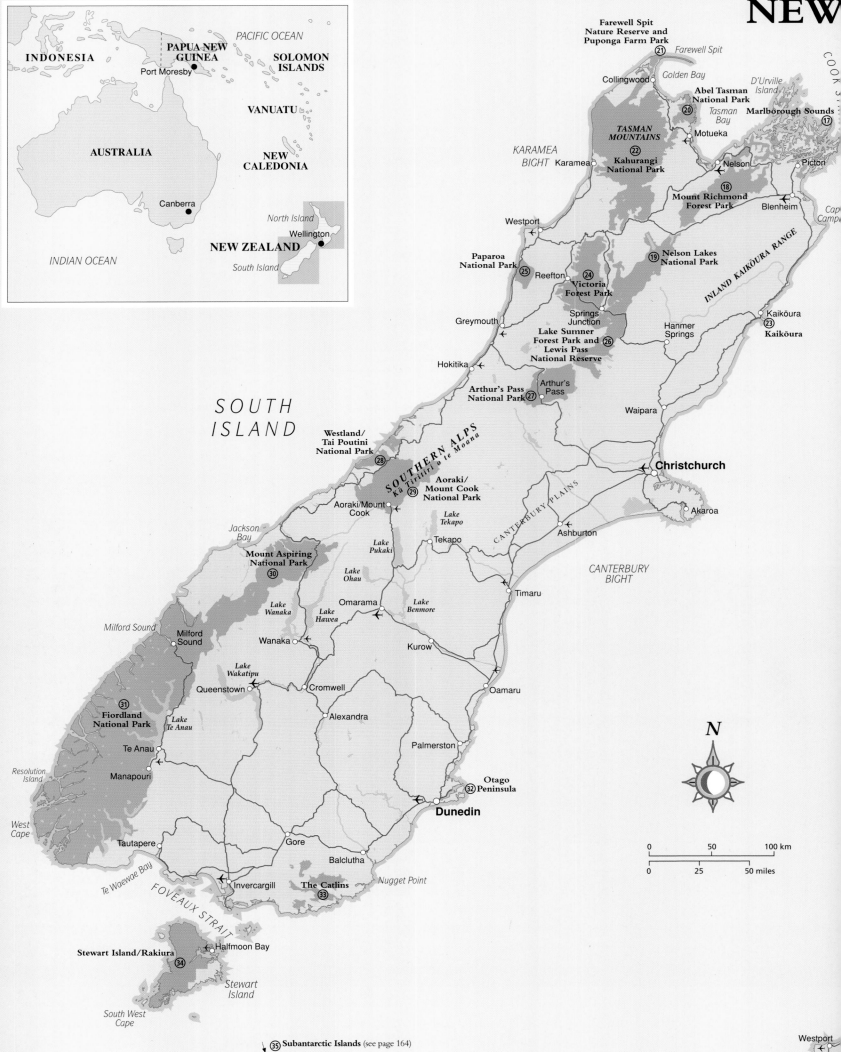

NEW

PACIFIC OCEAN

INDONESIA

PAPUA NEW GUINEA
Port Moresby

SOLOMON ISLANDS

VANUATU

NEW CALEDONIA

AUSTRALIA

Canberra

INDIAN OCEAN

North Island

NEW ZEALAND
Wellington

South Island

Farewell Spit
Nature Reserve and
Puponga Farm Park ㉑ *Farewell Spit*

Collingwood *Golden Bay*

D'Urville Island

Abel Tasman National Park ⑳

Tasman Bay

Marlborough Sounds ⑰

COOK ST

TASMAN MOUNTAINS

Motueka

Nelson

Picton

KARAMEA BIGHT Karamea

⑳ Kahurangi National Park

Mount Richmond Forest Park ⑱

Blenheim

Cap Camp

Westport

Paparoa National Park ㉕ Reefton

⑲ **Nelson Lakes National Park**

INLAND KAIKŌURA RANGE

Greymouth

Springs Junction

Lake Sumner Forest Park and Lewis Pass National Reserve ㉖

Hanmer Springs

Kaikōura ㉓
Kaikōura

㉔ **Victoria Forest Park**

Hokitika

Arthur's Pass National Park ㉗ **Arthur's Pass**

Waipara

SOUTH ISLAND

Westland/ Tai Poutini National Park ㉘

SOUTHERN ALPS
Kā Tiritiri o te Moana

Aoraki/ Mount Cook National Park ㉙

CANTERBURY PLAINS

Christchurch

Akaroa

Aoraki/Mount Cook

Lake Tekapo

Jackson Bay

Lake Pukaki

Tekapo

Ashburton

CANTERBURY BIGHT

Mount Aspiring National Park ㉚

Lake Ohau

Lake Wanaka

Lake Hawea

Omarama

Lake Benmore

Timaru

Milford Sound

Milford Sound

Lake Wakatipu

Wanaka

Kurow

㉛ **Fiordland National Park**

Resolution Island

Queenstown

Cromwell

Oamaru

Alexandra

Palmerston

Te Anau

Lake Te Anau

N

Manapouri

Otago Peninsula ㉜

West Cape

Dunedin

Tautapere

Gore

Te Waewae Bay

Balclutha

Nugget Point

FOVEAUX STRAIT

Invercargill

The Catlins ㉝

0   50   100 km

0   25   50 miles

Stewart Island/Rakiura ✈ Halfmoon Bay

㉞

Stewart Island

South West Cape

↓ ㉟ **Subantarctic Islands** (see page 164)

Westport

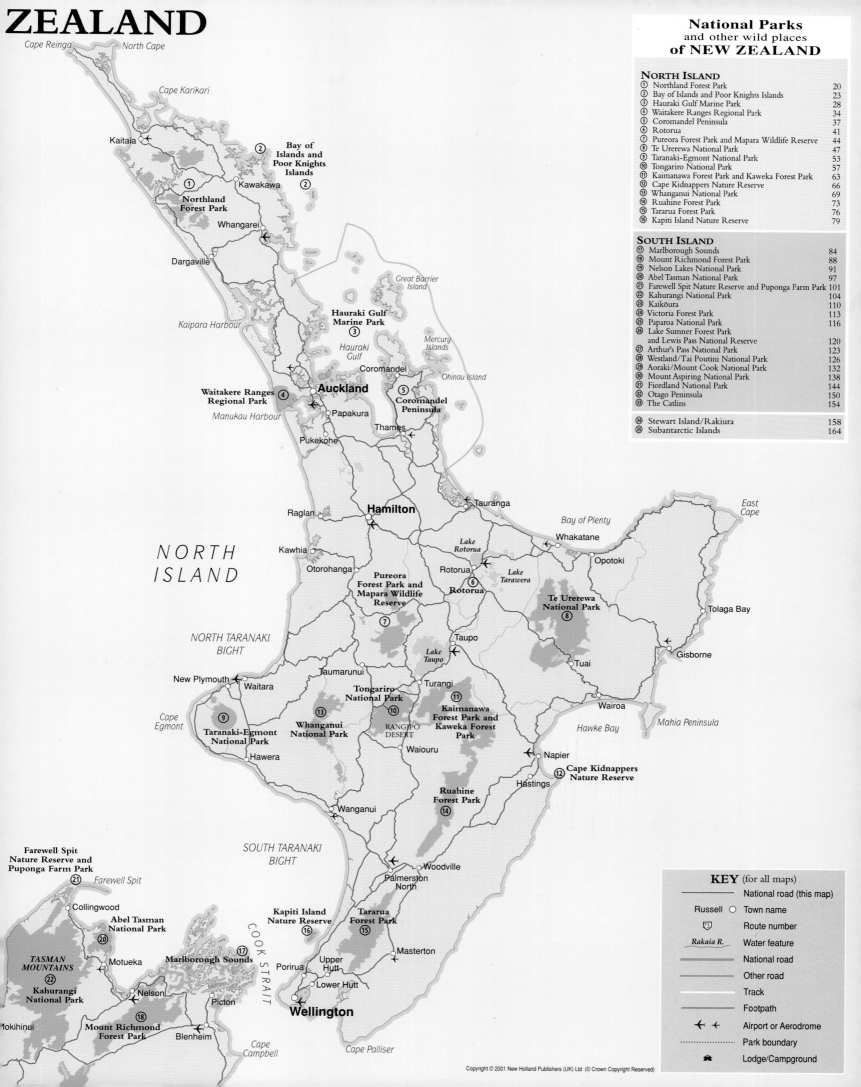

ZEALAND

KEY (for all maps)

————	National road (this map)
Russell ○	Town name
🛡	Route number
Rakaia R.	Water feature
————	National road
————	Other road
————	Track
··········	Footpath
✈ ✈	Airport or Aerodrome
··········	Park boundary
⌂	Lodge/Campground

Copyright © 2001 New Holland Publishers (UK) Ltd (© Crown Copyright Reserved)

NORTH ISLAND
Te Ika a Māui

The North Island is by far the more heavily populated of the two main islands of New Zealand, yet significant areas of natural wilderness remain intact. Over one million people – one-third of New Zealand's population – live in greater Auckland city. Several other cities, including the capital, Wellington, are also in the North Island. Much of the countryside is a mosaic of dairy, sheep and cattle farms, plantation pine forests, horticulture and viticulture crops, and primary industries which are among the country's economic mainstays.

Yet dominating the North Island landscape in many regions are its wide-ranging natural features. These include mountain volcanoes, geothermal fields, subtropical and temperate rainforests, as well as a long mountain axis of rugged, forest-covered ranges and rivers, lakes and beaches. Four national parks, 13 forest or conservation parks, a marine park and many hundreds of reserves and wildlife sanctuaries protect the natural and recreation values of the North Island.

This area has much to offer the nature lover. Standing like sentinels over the central North Island are the volcanic mountains of New Zealand's first national park, Tongariro, a Cultural and Natural World Heritage site. In 1887 the national park became only the fourth to be created in the world.

Recreation opportunities in the North Island parks are similarly diverse and include boating, diving, and nature-watch cruising around the coastline and islands of Coromandel Peninsula, Hauraki Gulf and the Bay of Islands. Networks of tramping tracks (hiking trails) are found throughout the island, while canoeing through forested wilderness on the Whanganui River and skiing at Tongariro and Taranaki–Egmont are other options.

Temperatures are generally higher in the North Island than in the South. This applies especially to the far north where frosts are rare and subtropical rainforests are dominated by one of earth's biggest trees, the kauri.

According to the Māori people, the North Island is a giant fish, hauled from the sea by the legendary fisherman Māui. The fish writhed and thrashed in his grip, then turned solid as the night ended, thus creating this jumbled and rugged land known as Te Ika a Māui, 'the fish of Māui'.

NORTHLAND FOREST PARK

Kauri Kingdom

This park is made up of many separate pockets of rainforest, dominated by New Zealand's largest kauri trees *(Agathis australis)* and filled with an outstanding and diverse collection of plants and wildlife. Northland encompasses a collection of reserves and forest sanctuaries which all feature the majestic and ancient kauri tree.

The largest kauri trees in Northland stand up to 50 metres (165 feet) high and are estimated to be over 1000 years old. Each year, tens of thousands of people, young and old, view the trees as they explore the many scenic short walks in the park. The New Zealand Kauri, reputed to be exceeded in volume only by the Giant Sequoia trees of California, is the largest of 13

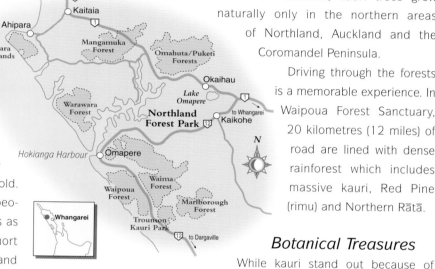

kauri species that grow throughout the Southwest Pacific. Kauri is a member of the genus *Agathis*, which is related to one of the oldest existing conifer families. In New Zealand, kauri trees grow naturally only in the northern areas of Northland, Auckland and the Coromandel Peninsula.

Driving through the forests is a memorable experience. In Waipoua Forest Sanctuary, 20 kilometres (12 miles) of road are lined with dense rainforest which includes massive kauri, Red Pine (rimu) and Northern Rātā.

Botanical Treasures

While kauri stand out because of their size, the lowland forests of Northland are outstanding for their botanical richness and variety. In many ways they are more akin to the tropical rainforests of the Southwest Pacific than to the temperate forests of the rest of New Zealand.

More than 600 different species, including over 100 species of threatened plants and 125 species that grow nowhere else, are found in these northern forests. Beneath the giant kauri trees and peculiar to its forests is a ground cover lily, or astelia plant, with a grass-like appearance – appropriately known as Kauri Grass. The jungle-like forests are characterized by luxuriant profusions of tree ferns, climbing plants, vines, lianes and epiphytes (plants which are hosted by other bigger plants).

The kauri trees themselves support huge communities of epiphytic plants which grow in their lower spreading branches. This botanical richness is matched by the diversity of wildlife. Included among these forests' native bird populations are threatened species such as Red-

Opposite: Tane Mahuta, the world's largest kauri tree, is estimated to be over 1000 years old.

Inserts opposite (top): Kauri bark – nature's artwork.
(bottom): In the early 1900s the collection of kauri sap or gum was a major industry.

Top right: Distinctively shaped Kidney Ferns brighten the forest floor with their transparent green fonds.

Previous pages:
p18: Ngauruhoe (foreground) and Ruapehu volcanoes stand like sentinels over New Zealand's oldest national park, Tongariro.
p19: School of Blue Maomao near Goat Island, Leigh, where New Zealand's first marine reserve was established in 1975.

Location: Northern part of the North Island.

Climate: Mild winters (no frosts), hot summers, rain all year round.

When to go: Anytime.

Access: Trounson and Waipoua forests are on the western side of Northland, 40 minutes' drive north of Dargaville. Puketi/Omahuta forests are near the east coast, 35 minutes' drive north of Kaikohe and 20 minutes' drive from Kerikeri. A tourist bus service travels through Waipoua Forest.

Permits/Reservations: Permits required for hunting.

Facilities: DOC visitor centre at Waipoua Forest, walking tracks, picnic and camping grounds at Waipoua, Trounson and Puketi forests. Some shops, cafes and petrol at Omapere, Opononi and Rawene townships. Range of accommodation throughout the park. Hokianga, harbour cruises, guided night walks in Trounson.

Wildlife: North Island Brown Kiwi, Yellow-crowned Parakeet, New Zealand Pigeon, Kauri Snail.

Landscapes: Big trees, lowland rainforest, forest-lined streams, mangrove-filled estuaries.

Visitor activities: Short walks, overnight tramping, mountain biking, hunting (pigs and goats), surfcasting. A worthwhile visit is the Kauri Museum at Matakohe.

crowned Parakeets (kākāriki) and North Island Brown Kiwi. The forests also support populations of New Zealand's only land mammals – short and long-tailed bats – and a notable variety of native freshwater fish, reptilian fauna, including Hochstetters Frog, and the endemic, ancient and threatened carnivorous Kauri Snail (pūpū rangi).

Devastation

Rich and diverse they may be, today's kauri forests are but a vestige of what existed in Northland and Auckland before human settlers discovered other uses for the great trees. Early Māori who lived throughout this region used some kauri for building canoes and houses and for carving. Kauri gum was also used for starting fires and as a pigment for tattooing.

Kauri milling began in the late 1700s when visiting European explorers and whalers discovered the suitability of kauri for ship spars (masts or poles used for old sailing ships). The arrival of European settlers in the late 1800s increased the demand for construction timber. Logging and fires reduced the Northland kauri forests to a quarter of their original area in just 40 years.

The destruction was exacerbated by the discovery of kauri gum's qualities for making varnish, which sparked a 'gum rush' of up to 10,000 people to the Northland region. Diggers sought gum from fossilized trees under-

ground which had died many hundreds of years before. Climbers collected it in liquid form from mature, living trees. Some cut and bled the trunks until this practice was stopped in 1905 as it endangered the life of the trees.

In the early 1900s the massive onslaught on kauri slowed as gum supplies were depleted and the milling could no longer be sustained. With calls by eminent New Zealand botanists, such as Dr Leonard Cockayne and Professor W McGregor, to halt the further destruction of the trees, the protection of remaining kauri forests and their outstanding wildlife habitats was gradually achieved. Given that the natural values of the great kauri forests meet set national park criteria, these forests may possibly be incorporated into a new national park in the future.

Forest Features

Since 1995, Trounson Kauri Park has been managed as one of the Department of Conservation's (DOC) 'mainland island' forest recovery projects, aimed at restoring the forest ecosystem by intensive control of weeds and animal predators.

In nearby Waipoua Forest, road bridges protect the fragile shallow roots of roadside kauri from vehicle damage. This majestic forest features the biggest kauri tree of all; 'Tāne Mahuta' stands over 50 metres (164 feet) high, has a girth of 13.77 metres (45 feet) and is estimated to be 1500 years old.

The adjoining Puketi and Omahuta forests form one of the largest remaining tracts of kauri forest and feature wonderful short walks. A feature of this kauri kingdom is Hokianga Harbour, a vast drowned river system. Hokianga's treacherous harbour entrance is a spectacular sight, towered over by Kahakakaroa, a massive, golden 200m high sand dune.

BAY OF ISLANDS AND POOR KNIGHTS ISLANDS

Maritime Recreation and Marine Reserve

Outstanding marine life, dramatic seascapes, islands and inlets, national history and a marine reserve with world class diving are the features of these northern maritime conservation areas.

Bay of Islands

As its name suggests, the Bay of Islands is a huge, sheltered bay dotted with a delightful assortment of islands. The bay is framed by rocky headlands, beaches, estuaries and inlets, and many of the islands and surrounding areas are scenic, historic or recreation reserves. Along with conservation, there is also a strong focus on tourism, water-based recreation and historic features in the region.

Marine Life

Thousands of sea birds and an extensive range of underwater life – including up to 57 species of fish and various marine mammals – live in diverse habitats within the Bay of Islands. Marine ecosystems of island lagoons and rocky reefs, mangrove-filled estuaries, volcanic submarine fissures and caves, and the oceanic waters around the outer bay's rocky headlands are enhanced by a sea current that brings warm waters and fish larvae from subtropical climates.

An abundance of colourful reef fish, shrimps, starfish and sea urchins has made 'fish watching' a popular

Top right: A Blue-eyed Triplefin stands its ground. This common but poorly known species prefers areas of broken rock and overhangs free of large algae.

activity. A unique 'Underwater Trail' — designed specifically for snorkelling and the first of its kind in New Zealand — is located in a tranquil, sheltered lagoon on Motuarohia (Roberton Island).

Moving up the bay's marine food chain, school fish such as Kahawai, Kingfish and Trevally attract bigger species, such as Marlin and Mako sharks. Feeding frenzies, where these big fish thresh the water and attack the school fish, are a dramatic sight. This is usually accompanied by hundreds of gulls, terns (tara) and petrels (tītī) wheeling above in search of food scraps. The presence of these game fish has given the Bay of Islands a long-standing, international reputation as a top spot for big-game fishing.

Australasian Gannets (takapu) are often seen 'working the water' (diving for fish) with schools of Common Dolphins, which frequent the outer bay. Over 300 Bottlenose Dolphins, among the largest dolphins in the world, live inside the bay. Several licensed tourist operators offer 'swim with the dolphins' cruises, adhering to strict regulations set by DOC so as not to disturb or harm these fascinating creatures.

Boating visitors in the bay might also catch a glimpse of larger mammals such as Bryde's Whales, Minke Whales, Orca and occasionally Humpbacks and Blue Whales pass the coastline on their annual migrations. Of the whales, the most frequent visitors are the Pacific Ocean-dwelling Bryde's Whales. This particular species breeds throughout the year and does not have a seasonal migration. Although shy and often difficult to spot, Bryde's have been known to come well into the bay.

Map labels

Purerua
Bay of Islands
Moturoa Island
Moturua Island
Urupukapuka Island
Cape Brett
Kerikeri
Waitangi
Motuarohia Island
Rawhiti
Russell
Paihia
to Kawakawa
Auckland
Russell Rd
Whangaruru North
Oakura
Whangaruru Harbour
Helena Bay
Poor Knights Islands Marine Reserve
Tawhiti Rahi Island
Aorangi Island
Kaikanu Rd
High Peak Rocks
Matapouri
Sugarloaf Rock
Tutukaka

Location: Northeast coast of the North Island.

Climate: Hot summers and mild winters. High sunshine hours, sea breezes and gusty winds.

When to go: Anytime. The best time to see young dolphins is spring and autumn, but swimming with dolphins is not allowed if there are calves in the pods. Whales pass by in winter and early summer.

Access: To Bay of Islands by road via SH1. Daily bus services. Daily flights from Auckland to Kerikeri. To Poor Knights, charter boats are available from Tutukākā.

Permits/Reservations: Landing is only permitted on Poor Knights with a DOC permit. Boats may not be tied to any part of the shoreline.

Facilities: DOC camping grounds, one lodge, walking tracks, picnic areas. Paihia, Kerikeri and Russell have a full range of accommodation. Tourist cruises, ecotours, estuary and sea kayaking, air and boat charters, water taxis, game fishing, dive and sailing charters, yacht and kayak hire are available.

Wildlife: Several species of whales, Common and Bottlenose Dolphins, Mako Sharks, marlin, other fish species and marine life, North Island Brown Kiwi. At Poor Knights, many sea bird species, underwater sponge gardens, gorgonion coral fields, stingrays and Manta Rays.

Landscapes: Islands, rocky headlands, estuaries, waterfalls, lagoons, sea cliffs, coastal forests and mangrove forests.

Visitor activities: Boating, cruises, whale and dolphin watching, kayaking, diving, snorkelling, walking, camping, fishing.

Islands of the Bay

The islands here all have their own distinctive character. The largest, Urupukapuka, combines farmland with a large camping area. Some of its features include sandy beaches, sheltered anchorages, good diving and a half-day's walk exploring interesting archaeological sites. Like most of the islands, early Māori settled on Urupukapuka. On neighbouring Moturua one can find more beaches, sheltered anchorages and a walkway.

The regenerating coastal forest on Moturua is now the home of North Island Robins and North Island Brown Kiwi. These threatened species were relocated to the island refuge by conservation staff to ensure their survival and increase their dwindling numbers.

On all the islands rapidly regenerating coastal forest comes alive in summer with the crimson flowers of the prolific pohutukawa, or New Zealand Christmas tree.

Birthplace of the Nation

The Bay of Islands is also referred to as the 'Birthplace of the Nation', for it was here during the 1700s that Māori, New Zealand's first settlers, and European people first made significant contact. Explorers, whalers, sealers and missionaries sailed into the sheltered bay, initiating a volatile period of cross-cultural trading and social interaction.

In 1840 the Treaty of Waitangi — a document that defined the partnership between Māori and the British Crown — was signed by British representatives and 46 local Māori chiefs. The treaty was later taken around the country and signed by many other tribes. Today, the Waitangi National Reserve is an outstanding memorial to this critical period in New Zealand's history. In magnificent grounds overlooking the bay, visitors can explore the restored Treaty House (originally the resident governor's home), and view a traditionally carved Whare Rūnanga (Māori meeting house), the largest taua waka (war canoe) in New Zealand and a visitor centre, with

Right: *New Zealand's geographical isolation has led to a high number of endemic species, like this Giant Centipede. Over 80 per cent of invertebrates and 90 per cent of insects live nowhere else.*

Below: *Islands and headlands of weathered sedimentary rock, lapped by old flooded river valleys, make up the sheltered Bay of Islands.*

audio-visual presentations. Close by, the Waitangi Trust Mangrove Walk penetrates the heart of mature mangrove forest, a feature of the many inlets and estuaries of the Bay of Islands.

Poor Knights Islands

Slightly to the south of the Bay of Islands is a special group of steep, visually dramatic islands and rocky islets (rockstacks) known as the Poor Knights. The islands are a nature reserve and the surrounding sea is a marine reserve, world renowned for its underwater formations, water clarity and marine life.

The islands, eroded remnants of a huge volcano, have been isolated from the mainland for about 18,000 years. Having remained free of almost all introduced animals, they provide a haven for endemic flora and fauna, as well as many species that are now extinct or extremely rare on the mainland. The reptile Tuatara, Giant Weta insects, several lizard species, Flax Snail and a Giant Centipede are the faunal rarities that share the islands with bellbirds (korimako), Bush Parrots (North Island kākā) and Yellow-crowned Parakeets (kākāriki). Millions of sea birds, including nine species of petrel (tītī), breed on the islands. A staggering two to three million Bullers Shearwaters live here; the Poor Knights is the only place in the world where Bullers Shearwaters breed. The migratory birds return from the North Pacific each year to breed, and usually reclaim the same nest.

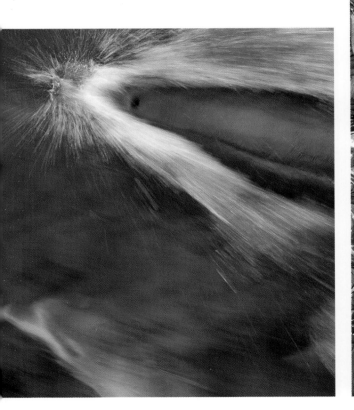

Above: Kayaking through dense estuary mangrove forests is popular in the Bay of Islands.

Left: In the Whare Rūnanga (meeting house) at Waitangi National Reserve, carved panels represent all the main Māori tribes of New Zealand.

Far left: Hundreds of Bottlenose Dolphins, one of the largest dolphin species in the world, live and breed inside the Bay of Islands.

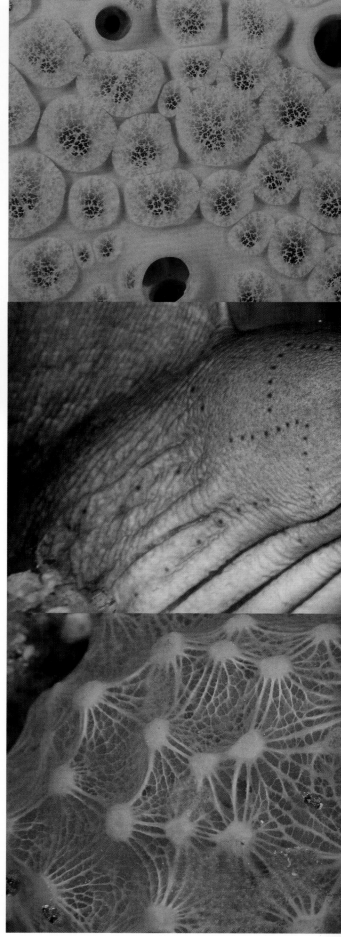

Early Māori, who lived on the two largest islands until the 1800s, cleared the forests for their gardens. However, forests of coastal species such as pohutukawa, karaka and puriri have since regenerated. Distinctive, endemic plants include the coastal shrub, *Hebe bollonsii,* and the gloriously red flowering Poor Knights Lily.

Landing on these islands is not permitted. However, exploring the surrounding water, is encouraged and the Poor Knights Islands Marine Reserve attracts divers from around the world. Beneath the water caves and cliffs that plunge 100 metres (30 feet) below the surface, arches and tunnels provide a great underwater experience. Sponge gardens and gorgonian coral fields are inhabited by myriad fish, shellfish, urchins and anemones, with black coral in deeper water. Many of the subtropical fish living in the reserve, such as the Spotted Black Groper, Mosaic Moray and Lord Howe Coralfish, are found nowhere else in New Zealand. Manta Rays, turtles, different species of dolphins and whales and 'squadrons' of stingrays are regularly sighted.

The reserve extends for 800 metres (2600 feet) around the islands and rock stacks. Underwater visibility of up to 30 metres (100 feet) is usual, especially in winter. Ecotours and diving charters regularly visit the Poor Knights Islands from Tutukākā, 24km (15 miles) away on the mainland.

Hauraki Gulf Marine Park

Wildlife Sanctuaries and Maritime Playground

In the enigmatic Hauraki Gulf, outstanding natural values are found right alongside New Zealand's largest city. Over one-third of New Zealand's 3.8 million people live around the gulf and its islands. It is the traditional 'playground' for thousands of boating Aucklanders, the venue for international yacht races, such as the America's Cup, and is traversed by a busy shipping channel.

Yet the gulf also contains several world renowned wildlife sanctuaries, islands which are among the last refuges for some of New Zealand's most rare and endangered plants and wildlife. Over 50 islands are scattered throughout the gulf. Some are nature reserves with restricted access; others are open sanctuaries, recreation reserves and historic reserves.

Native forests, wildlife habitats, rocky shorelines, beaches, tidal flats and sheltered anchorages are features of these islands, and of the reserves dotted along mainland inlets, bays and headlands throughout the park, which encompasses over 2000 kilometres (1245 miles) of coastline. Numerous archaeological and historic features provide evidence of New Zealand's human history; the gulf was one of the earliest regions in the country where people settled.

Left: Old pohutukawa trees frame the scenic Whangaparapara Inlet on Great Barrier Island, as another day draws to a close.

Top right: Pohutukawa, also known as New Zealand Christmas tree, boasts a blaze of crimson flowers in late December.

There are also three marine reserves within the park, including Cape Rodney–Okakari Point around Goat Island, the first to be established in New Zealand. This area, previously decimated by overfishing, now teems with marine life. Swimmers and snorkellers share the sheltered waters with hundreds of apparently tame fish such as Blue Maomao, snapper, Red Moki, rock lobsters and other species, and the reserve has become an important fish nursery.

The gulf waters range from oceanic waters of the outer gulf to the tidal, reef-strewn, wave-battered inner regions, creating a diversity of nutrient-rich habitats for a huge variety of marine life. Over 100 species of fish are found here, while frequent visitors to the bay are Bottlenose and Common Dolphins, Orca and various species of migratory whales, including Humpbacks, Sei, Minke, and Bryde's whales.

The marine park was established by special legislation in 2000, to integrate management of the islands, coastline and waters of the gulf. The gulf itself hosts an incongruous mix of small pleasure craft, luxury yachts, windsurfers, sea kayakers, racing yachts, fishing boats, merchant ships and passenger ferries. The latter transport people regularly from the bustle of downtown Auckland city to the islands of the gulf, many of which are well known for their distinctive features. Moving from downtown cityscape and traffic bustle to the sounds of bird song and lapping waters of bush-lined bays, the sudden contrast of such a ferry ride is strong.

Location: Auckland, North Island.

Climate: Hot summers, mild winters. Rain year-round with changeable winds.

When to go: Anytime.

Access: Ferries and natural heritage cruises from downtown Auckland and Warkworth to many park islands. Ferry and air service to Great Barrier. Little Barrier visits available only with DOC licensed operator.

Permits: DOC permits required for landing on Little Barrier Island and Mokohinau Group (except Burgess Island). No fishing or disturbance of marine life is permitted in marine reserves.

Facilities: Full range of accommodation and services throughout Shops and accommodation on Great Barrier and Waiheke Islands. Park information centres in Auckland, Warkworth and Kawau. Walking tracks, camping and picnic areas throughout the park.

Wildlife: Numerous rare and endangered birds on island sanctuaries, plus tui, fantail, New Zealand pigeon and sea birds. Dolphins and whales occasionally visit. Abundant marine life in marine reserves.

Landscapes: Islands, inlets, beaches, coastal cliffs, estuaries, rocky shorelines, coastal and pohutukawa forests, volcanoes.

Visitor activities: Walks, bird watching, camping, sailing, boating, sea kayaking, windsurfing, tramping, mountain biking, snorkelling, diving, visiting historic sites.

Precautions: Take care to prevent accidental introduction of mice, rats, cats or other pests onto islands.

Map labels

Mokohinau Island
Great Barrier Island
Little Barrier Island
Rakitu Island
Goat Island
Leigh
Warkworth
Hauraki Gulf Marine Park
Kawau Island
Cuvier Island
Motuora Island
Great Mercury Island
Whangaparaoa
Tiritiri–Matangi Island
Red Mercury Island
Rangitoto Is.
Motutapu Is.
Waiheke Island
Coromandel
Whitianga
Auckland
Aldermen Islands
Firth of Thames
Coromandel Peninsula
N
Thames

Little Barrier Island (Hauturu)

Little Barrier is one of the country's oldest and most important nature reserves, a refuge for rare and endangered plants, birds and animals. The steep-sided, circular volcanic island is covered with large leftover pristine rainforest and has one of the highest diversities of plant-life in the country.

With nearly 50 bird species breeding on the island, the forest rings with birdsong. Endangered saddlebacks (tïeke), stitchbirds, Brown Kiwi, Great Spotted Kiwi (roa) and Blue Wattled Crow (kōkako) have been relocated from threatened mainland habitats to help ensure the survival of these species. Fourteen species of Tuatara reptiles, skinks (lizards) and geckos, as well as Short- and Long-tailed Bats and a Giant Weta insect species also live here on the island.

Extreme care is taken to keep Little Barrier free of animal pests and weeds. Landing is strictly forbidden without a permit and day visitors are carefully monitored by conservation staff.

Great Barrier Island (Aotea)

New Zealand's fourth largest island, 'The Barrier' is so named because it shields the Hauraki Gulf from the vast Pacific Ocean. With its rugged landscape, the volcanic island is dominated by forest-covered hills, steep rocky pillars and bluffs. The coastline is a smorgasbord of unspoilt beaches, estuaries, harbours, scenic offshore islands and steep cliffs.

Two-thirds of the island is reserved, thus protecting what is New Zealand's largest possum-free forest. Although the island's kauri forests have been logged in the past, these are fast regenerating and more than 50 species of threatened plants now thrive on the island. Great Barrier is a stronghold for many threatened birds, including Bush Parrot (North Island kākā), Black Petrel, New Zealand Dotterel and one of the world's rarest ducks, Brown Teal (pateke). The 30-centimetre-long (12-inch) Chevron Skink, New Zealand's largest and rarest skink, lives only on Little and Great Barrier Islands.

Motels, camping grounds, tramping huts and safe anchorages accommodate visitors to Great Barrier. Visitor activities include tramping, mountain biking, fishing, surfing, bathing in hot springs, diving and visiting historic sites, such as the restored Kaiarara kauri dam.

Kawau Island

About one-tenth of Kawau Island is reserved. In the 1860s the island became famous as the home of New Zealand's Governor Grey, who left a legacy of exotic, animals and birds, including peacocks and wallabies.

His grand home, now known as Mansion House, is partially restored and forms the main visitor attraction. A former copper mine is also restored, and sheltered anchorages are popular for recreational boating in the summertime. A DOC cottage can be hired, but beware of the noisy Little Blue Penguins (kororā) nesting under the floorboards! Native Woodhen (weka) and North Island Brown Kiwi also live here.

Tiritiri–Matangi Island

This tiny island, where the dawn chorus seems to continue all day long, has a special conservation story. Over a decade, thousands of tree-planting volunteers transformed the formerly cleared, 220-hectare (543 acres) island into a forest-covered sanctuary. The island has since been cleared of animal pests and now provides refuge for many rare and endangered birds.

The island is bestowed with rare 'open sanctuary' status and has become a world renowned bird-watching venue. The public is free to visit and observe birds unlikely to be seen on the mainland, for example, takahē, saddleback (tīeke), Blue Wattled Crow (kōkako), stitchbirds and Little Spotted Kiwi. Including sea birds, 77 species of birds have been recorded on the island. DOC asks visitors to take special care to prevent the accidental reintroduction of mice, rats, cats or other pests.

Left: *New Zealand has one of the most diverse lizard populations in the world. Duvaucel's Gecko, pictured here, is one of 13 species found on Great Barrier Island.*

Left: *Little Barrier Island, one of New Zealand's most important wildlife sanctuaries, is a stronghold for a number of threatened animal species.*

Right: *Volunteers from community conservation groups have undertaken massive revegetation programmes on some of the Gulf islands.*

Rangitoto Island

This well-known Auckland landmark dominates the inner gulf and is considered botanically unique for the plants which cover its lava base. Rangitoto is the largest and youngest of the 50 volcanoes in the Auckland volcanic field and its eruption, about 600 years ago, was witnessed by Māori people living on neighbouring islands. Since then a remarkable variety of over 200 plants, dominated by summer-flowering pohutukawa, has colonized the harsh, lava scoria rock that covers the island. In recent years, ridding the island of possums and wallabies has made a significant difference to the growth of pohutukawa in this area.

Rangitoto, in particular its summit walk, has long been a popular day trip venue for Aucklanders. Great views, lava caves and pohutukawa forest are features of the summit walk. An old World War II gun emplacement dominates the summit clearing. The island's tracks and roads were hewn out of sharp volcanic rock by prisoners during the 1920s. Islington Bay, beside neighbouring Motutapu Island, is one of the most popular sheltered anchorages in the gulf.

Below: *The flightless Takahē is just one of the rare endangered species which enjoys sanctuary on predator-free Tiritiri-Matangi Island.*

Motutapu Island

Joined by a causeway but very different from its volcanic neighbour, is the sedimentary, largely forest-free Motutapu Island. Numerous archaeological sites reflect the island's intensive former settlement, first by Māori people — whose villages were covered with thick ash layers during the eruption of Rangitoto — then later by European farmers.

During World War II, the island was a major military base. Today the island is a recreation reserve and is popular for picnics, short walks and education camps.

Other Special Places

Other, smaller islands and reserves also contain significant features. Browns Island (Motukorea) is a well preserved 'volcano in miniature', with remains of several stone walls from early Māori gardens and some remnants of defensive ditches.

Motuora Island, currently undergoing a major revegetation programme, provides a predator-free habitat for the highly endangered wading bird, the Shore Plover.

To the north of the Great Barrier, most of the remote islands in the Mokohinau group are wildlife sanctuaries surrounded by some of the most spectacular dive spots.

Above: Mosses cling to volcanic scoria rock. Many of the gulf islands are volcanic in origin.

Left: The mass arrival or departure of thousands of migratory birds to or from the Miranda tidal flats is an awe-inspiring sight.

WAITAKERE RANGES REGIONAL PARK

Wilderness beside a City

Location: On the west coast, beside Auckland city.

Climate: Mild winters, hot summers, rain year-round.

When to go: Anytime.

Access: Several roads provide access from Auckland city, via Henderson and Titiriangi. Muriwai is reached via SH16.

Permits/Reservations: Required for camping, bookings for barbecues and picnic sites advisable.

Facilities: In the park – Arataki Cultural and Heritage Centre (displays, audiovisual presentations, information and Environmental Education Centre), walking tracks, camping and picnic grounds, outdoor education camps. Natural heritage tours and guided walks available. Surf lifesaving clubs at Piha, Karekare and Muriwai. Small shops at Huia, Piha, and Muriwai. Small museums at Huia and Rose Hellaby House. Full services throughout Auckland city.

Wildlife: Australasian Gannets, Fur Seals, sea birds, common forest birds. Present but unlikely to be seen are Kauri Snail, Long-tailed Bats and Hotchstetter Frogs.

Landscapes: Kauri forest, streams, waterfalls, seascapes (huge cliffs, surf beaches, caves, blowholes, rock stacks and rocky headlands, dunes), lagoons, sheltered bays, great view points.

Visitor activities: Short walks, tramping, bird watching, swimming, surfing, surfcasting, scenic drives.

Precautions: The west coast seas can be dangerous and very unpredictable. Take care when swimming and surfcasting.

This forest-covered Auckland regional park dominates the western skyline of Auckland city. The sprawling suburbs, motorways and buildings of concrete and steel contrast sharply with the wild west coast on the other side, beyond the great green 'buffer' of the ranges. Here, towering sea cliffs are the dominant structures and beaches, wetlands, rocky islets and dunelands are the 'suburbs' – the natural domain of numerous native sea birds and wetland birds.

The park provides a welcome, wilderness retreat from New Zealand's largest city. Within less than an hour's drive from the bustle of downtown Auckland, visitors can walk among mature kauri trees on a forest track, swim in a clear pool beneath a waterfall, or watch the surf thundering onto a desolate, windswept beach.

Waitakere is the largest of 18 regional parks managed by the Auckland Regional Council. In a foresighted move in the 1890s, sections of the park were first reserved to protect mature native kauri forest from further logging operations. For over 60 years, one-third of the area that is now parkland was closed to the public for water catchment protection, leaving the forests to regenerate without human disturbance. Local landowners also donated areas for parkland and, in 1940, Waitakere Ranges regional park was formally established to commemorate Auckland city's centenary.

Top left: *The Pied Stilt is one of the many birds found in the wetlands between the Karekare and Whatipu dunes.*

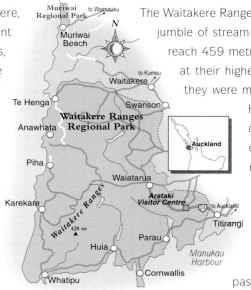

Te Kawerau a Maki, the Māori people who first lived along the Waitakere coast, call the park Te Wao Nui o Tiriwa, the 'great forest of Tiriwa'.

Waitakere Volcano

The Waitakere Ranges today consist of a convoluted jumble of stream-dissected, low-lying hills which reach 459 metres (1500 feet) above sea level at their highest point. Millions of years ago they were much higher. The ranges are the heavily eroded eastern flank of the Waitakere Volcano, which once stood a massive 3000 metres high (9800 feet).

This volcano, centred on the seabed 20 kilometres (12 miles) offshore from the present coastline, is reputed to have been much larger, in the past, than the combined mass of New Zealand's three big modern volcanoes, Ruapehu, Tongariro and Ngauruhoe.

About 16 million years ago, the Waitakere Volcano was thrust above the sea by tectonic movement, and volcanic vents erupted across its eastern flank, shaping the basis of the park landscape we see today. Explosion craters, bounded by towering lava cliffs, line the west coast and form spectacular beach settings such as Karekare and White's Beach. Lava cliffs that border Mercer Bay reach a dizzying height of 300 metres (980 feet). Solidified lava flows, constantly lashed by pounding seas, have formed caves, chimneys and prominent landmarks such as Lion Rock, at Piha. Inland, waterfalls tumble over erosion-resistant layers of volcanic conglomerates at popular picnic spots such as Kitekite, Karekare and Fairy Falls. The high volcanic cliffs and rocks once formed ideal defence sites for the Māori people. Today, many of these spots are features of the park tracks.

Coastal Forest and Kauri Trees

Kauri, the biggest of all New Zealand's trees, once covered the Waitakere Ranges. However, logging from the 1840s to the early 1900s all but decimated these forests. The good news is that some mature kauri have remain untouched, in particular in the park's Cascades/Kauri region, where the one-hour Auckland City Walk leads to some of the park's finest kauri. Elsewhere groves of young kauri, known as rickers, are regenerating with vigour and beginning to penetrate the forest canopy.

Relics of the logging era remain, a legacy of the determined efforts made to extract the huge trees from this formidable environment. The remains of Black Rock Dam in Piha Stream, plus the sight of huge kauri logs jammed in a nearby gorge, tell of the partly successful attempts to flush kauri logs down dammed waterways to the coast. Old railway spikes and a tunnel through a rocky headland (now a convenient walking track) remind visitors of a tramway built along 14 kilometres (nearly 9 miles) of the treacherous, cliff-lined coast to transport kauri to Whatipu wharf.

Throughout the ranges, a healthy mix of regenerating trees and coastal rainforest now show little sign of logging history. Along with kauri, Northern Rātā and the podocarps; Red Pine (rimu), tōtara and White Pine (kahikatea) emerge above a tropical-like canopy of tree ferns, Cabbage Trees, Nikau Palms and the broadleaf trees: Celery Pine (tānekaha), mahoe, New Zealand Honeysuckle (rewarewa) and puriri, a relative of Teak. In spring, splashes of flowering white clematis and Tree Daisy, then yellow kowhai, can light up entire hillsides. Summer-flowering pohutukawa (New Zealand Christmas tree) flourish in sheltered areas. Understoreys are rich with ferns, vines, orchids, grasses and lilies, and on the coastal cliff tops flaxes, karaka and kānuka trees and native grasses such as toetoe, grow in defiance of the onslaught of salt-laden winds that sweep the area.

Plants which grow only in the Waitakere Ranges include *Celmisia major*, a relative of New Zealand's alpine daisies, West Coast kowhai and the shrub, *Hebe bishopiana* (koromiko).

Diverse Habitats

In the southwestern ranges, between Whatipu and Karekare, dunes that extend far out to sea from the coastal cliffs support a special community of native plants and wildlife. These sands are a distinctive black colour, made of magnetic iron oxides eroded from the Taranaki volcanic zone and swept north by sea currents. Native sedges (a grass-like plant growing in wetland areas), herbs and sand-binding plants such as spinifex and the golden-coloured pingao grow across the Whatipu dunes. Associated wetlands provide a habitat for birds such as Whitefaced Heron, Little Shags, Caspian Terns, Pied Stilts, Bittern, Banded Dotterel and the much rarer New Zealand Dotterel.

Above: Kowhai, a native forest flower, is a favourite of the honey-eating birds.

Below left: The dramatic cliffs off White's Beach are legacy of the area's violent volcanic past.

Below: Wetlands are a fertile habitat that support many wading birds.

Tui, New Zealand Pigeon (kererū), Fantail (pīwakawaka) and Grey Warbler (riroriro) are prolific native birds, while endangered Bush Parrots (North Island kākā) from Great Barrier Island and the Hunua Ranges southeast of Auckland city, have been known to visit from time to time. Offshore, Australasian Gannets (takapu) diving for fish are a common spectacle.

Muriwai

Australasian Gannets likely come from Muriwai, just north of the park, where New Zealand's northernmost mainland gannet colony has become established on offshore rock stacks and, recently, overflowed to mainland cliff tops. Excellent walkways, viewing platforms and information panels show the colony and its spectacular setting to its best advantage. White Fronted Terns (tara) nest on cliffs near the gannets, and Fur Seals occasionally haul out on the small offshore islands.

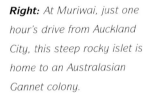

Above: *Moonlit Manuka trees bend in the predominant westerly winds. These trees often form extensive areas of shrub that protect regenerating forest seedlings.*

The Waitakere forests also support an interesting diversity of birds and invertebrates. An amazing 120 species of native land snails, including the carnivorous Kauri Snail, are found in the park. The small, seldom seen and endangered native Hochstetters Frog lives on stream margins, Long-tailed Bats can be seen at dusk on forest edges, the large insect Cave Weta lives in caves and hollows, and forest geckos live throughout this zone.

Muriwai is also a regional park, attracting thousands of people each year to see the gannet colony, surf or swim on Muriwai Beach, a long, windswept expanse of sand which extends 50 kilometres (30 miles) to the north. They simply 'blow out the cobwebs' in this spectacular coastal setting.

Right: *At Muriwai, just one hour's drive from Auckland City, this steep rocky islet is home to an Australasian Gannet colony.*

Coromandel Peninsula

Islands, Rainforests and Heritage

A forest park, several island nature reserves, a marine reserve, farm parks, recreation reserves and a network of walkways are all part of the conservation estate of Coromandel Peninsula. They protect significant ecological values as well as cater for the tens of thousands of holidaymakers who visit the area.

The peninsula has long been one of New Zealand's most popular holiday regions. Its extensive coastline, with beaches, bush-lined bays and rocky headlands, forest-covered ranges, tramping tracks (hiking trails), and subtropical climate attract thousands of visitors each year, particularly from the large population of the neighbouring Auckland region.

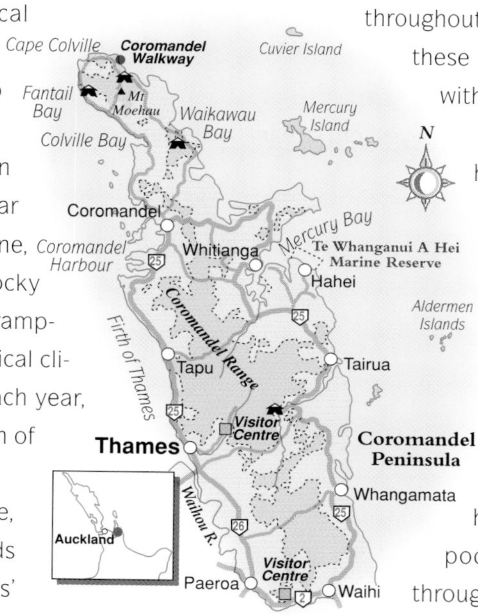

Cape Colville
Coromandel Walkway
Cuvier Island
Fantail Bay
Mt Moehau
Waikawau Bay
Mercury Island
Colville Bay
N
Coromandel
Mercury Bay
Whitianga
Coromandel Harbour
Te Whanganui A Hei Marine Reserve
Hahei
Aldermen Islands
Coromandel Range
Firth of Thames
Tapu
Tairua
Visitor Centre
Thames
Coromandel Peninsula
Whangamata
Auckland
Waihou R.
Visitor Centre
Paeroa
Waihi

From an ecological perspective, the peninsula and its offshore islands provide refuge for some of the islands' rarest and most endangered wildlife. The forest park protects remnants of the great kauri forests which once covered the Auckland and Northland regions. Mount Moehau, the peninsula's highest point, rates as an internationally significant ecological area.

Peninsula History

The local Māori people also consider Mount Moehau as *tapu*, or sacred, because they believe a revered ancestor lies buried near the summit. The peninsula was heavily populated by early Māori. Over 3000 pre-European archaeological sites have been recorded here, including some of the earliest known settlements in New Zealand. Food sources from the forests and surrounding sea were plentiful, and Māori names for landscape features throughout the peninsula are testimony to these earliest settlers' long association with the region.

The arrival of European settlers heralded dramatic changes to the landscape. The big kauri trees, many of them over a thousand years old, were felled, first for use as ships spars for whaling and trading vessels, then increasingly for construction timber. Today, healthy stands of regenerating kauri, some more than one hundred years old, grow alongside podocarp and broadleaf trees throughout Coromandel Forest Park.

In Manaia Sanctuary, a vestige forest of mature kauri includes New Zealand's sixth largest kauri tree, 'Tanenui', which has a girth of over 10 metres (32 feet) and a height of 47 metres (154 feet).

In the Kauaeranga Valley, where extensive logging took place, popular tramping tracks (hiking trails) lead to old tramways and remains of 'kauri dams', which were built to flush felled kauri logs down dammed waterways to the coast. The tracks also focus on the many natural features of the valley, which include regenerating forests, waterfalls, swimming holes and spectacularly jagged volcanic peaks such as The Pinnacles.

Gold in the Hills

The southern Coromandel ranges are a series of old, weathered volcanoes. The discovery of metals such as

Top right: *The Dancing Creek dam was one of many built during logging days to flush kauri trees down dammed waterways to the coast. Kauri is now protected on the peninsula.*

Location: East of Auckland.

Climate: Hot, humid summers and mild winters. Rainfall year-round.

When to go: Anytime.

Access: From Auckland follow SH1, SH2, then SH25. Regular bus services from Auckland and Hamilton. Several roads on the peninsula are narrow and gravelled.

Permits/Reservations: Advance booking required for Waikawau Bay Farm Park camping area during Christmas holidays. At other times, and for other camping grounds, campsites are allocated on a first-come first-served basis.

Facilities: Three towns on the peninsula, Thames, Coromandel and Whitianga, have a range of shops, restaurants and accommodation (motels, camping grounds, tourist lodges). There are several DOC-managed camping grounds at reserves, farm parks and in Coromandel Forest Park, as well as picnic facilities, walking tracks, toilets, interpretative information and one tramping hut. A DOC visitor centre at Kauaeranga Valley. Other DOC offices are in Thames, Coromandel and Tairua.

Wildlife: The most endangered wildlife, such as Archey's and Hochstetters Frogs, Red-crowned Parakeet and North Island Brown Kiwi are unlikely to be seen. Visitors are more likely to spot Bush Parrots, Tui, Bellbird and Fantail. Sea birds are prolific.

Landscapes: Forest-covered ranges, regenerating kauri forests, volcanic formations (sea arches, pinnacles), sandy beaches, bays, rocky headlands, islands.

Visitor activities: Tramping, snorkelling, diving, fishing, sea kayaking and horse riding.

gold, silver, copper and other minerals in the 1800s instigated a Coromandel gold rush. Although quartz mines were scattered throughout the region, the most productive mines were located further to the south, outside the borders of the forest park.

A former mining settlement within the park at Broken Hills has since been developed as a recreation area. In this forested, riverside setting visitors can now enjoy a popular camping and picnic ground and several short walks, which incorporate interesting mining relics. Recent proposals to reopen mines within the park met with intense opposition from the DOC and local residents, who now prefer to focus on protecting the region's outstanding ecological values. Ecology encompasses more than just wildlife; it describes the overall interaction of natural organisms with one another and their surroundings. Tourism, rather than mining and logging, has become the economic mainstay of the Coromandel.

Natural Values

Despite its logging and mining past, the Coromandel has retained its important wildlife values. Bush Parrot (North Island kākā), Red-crowned Parakeet (kākāriki), New Zealand Falcon (kārearea), North Island Brown Kiwi and small populations of Blue Wattled Crow (kōkako) live in the ranges. Wading birds include the variable Oystercatcher and endangered New Zealand Dotterel.

Two of New Zealand's native frog species, Hochstetters and the very rare and smallest of New Zealand's four species of native frog, Archey's Frog, find refuge in the northern Coromandel forests of Mount Moehau, together with another faunal rarity, the Coromandel Stag Beetle. Mount Moehau is one of the few places in New Zealand where browsing by introduced possums does not impact on the forests. Montane vegetation and a small subalpine herb field near the summit of Mount Moehau include several plants which normally grow much further south, and at higher altitudes.

Two walking tracks on Mount Moehau reward climbers with great coastal views as they pass through a variety of forests, from subtropical nikau palms, kohekohe trees and tree ferns to subalpine vegetation. These tracks climb from opposite side of the peninsula, bypassing the sacred Moehau summit.

Te Whanganui A Hei Marine Reserve

On the eastern Coromandel coast, Te Whanganui A Hei Marine Reserve protects several kilometres of reefs and underwater caves as well as complex communities of marine plants, sponges, crustacea, molluscs, fish and deep water corals. Onshore, the rock archways of Cathedral Cove are a feature of the walking tracks which provide access to the beaches lining the marine reserve.

Island Sanctuaries

The coastline walking tracks of the eastern Coromandel are good vantage points from which to view three groups of island nature reserves.

Off the tip of the peninsula is Cuvier Island. All of the introduced animal pests, such as goats and cats, have been removed and the island is now a stronghold for birds such as the endangered Red-crowned Parakeet (kākāriki) and the North Island Saddleback (tīeke), which were liberated there some 30 years ago.

Further south is the Mercury Group, of which five islands are nature reserves. These rat-free islands support a diverse population of invertebrates and lizards. On tiny Middle Island, for example, just 13 hectares (32 acres) in size, are 10 lizard species, a rare carnivorous centipede, one of the rarest and only omnivore of all New Zealand weta species, the Giant Tusked Weta and, star resident, the Tuatara. A remnant of ancient times,

Right: Tramping and mountain biking are popular recreational pursuits in the Coromandel Ranges.

Below: Coromandel's offshore island nature reserves provide refuge for New Zealand's living fossil, the Tuatara. This is the sole survivor of a reptile order that became extinct elsewhere in the world about 60 million years ago.

this 'beak-headed' reptile resembles a lizard, but is actually a member of its very own early order of reptiles. The Aldermen Island group, which lies even further south, is another refuge for Tuatara, as well as for New Zealand's largest colony of White-faced Storm Petrels.

Although members of the public are not permitted to land on these island reserves, it is comforting to view them from the mainland and to be aware that these are special places. They provide an insight into what the New Zealand mainland might have been like before the modification of natural habitats and the introduction of animals and pests displaced so much of the native fauna. They also provide hope for the survival of some of the native species whose mainland habitats have been destroyed.

Back on the mainland, Waikawau Bay and Cape Colville farm parks provide a unique opportunity for members of the public to visit working farms, in remote coastal settings on farmland that is interspersed with coastal and lowland forest.

ROTORUA

Steaming Geothermal Geyserland

Geothermal fields and a strong association with Māori culture have been the cornerstones of a long tourism tradition based in and around Rotorua city. Rotorua's 17 lakes, some of which are located within reserves and wildlife refuges, have also long been popular draw-cards for holidaymakers.

From an ecological perspective, the special habitats in this region – geothermal ecosystems, lakes, freshwater wetlands and rem-nant podocarp/hardwood forests – support an outstanding range of native flora and fauna, including unique geothermal-associated plantlife.

Deceptive Tranquillity

At first glance, Rotorua seems a tranquil place, at peace with nature, with its picturesque lakes surrounded by forest-clad hills that ring with the sound of native bird-song. But look closer, and detect the traces of steam wafting skyward. Sniff the air, and note the slightly pun-gent odour. These subtle hints suggest something far less tranquil has transpired – and is still continuing – in this region. Rotorua sits directly on the Taupo Volcanic Zone. This narrow but fiery belt of volcanic and geother-mal energy, aligned with the meeting of two crustal plates, extends from the central North Island volcanic mountains to the very active volcano of White Island.

Top right: *Māori cultural performances are one of the high-lights for visitors to Rotorua.*

Throughout the Rotorua region, the earth's crust is a fragile 10 kilometres (6 miles) thick, compared with the average 20- to 25-kilometre (12- to 15-mile) thickness of nonvolcanic regions.

Most of the tranquil lakes are, in fact, filled depressions and craters, blasted by volcanic eruption. Many of the surround-ing hills are volcanic domes and the wafting steam and pungent odour emanates from several geothermal fields. This makes Rotorua a volatile region of boiling mud pools, silica terraces, steam-ing vents (fumaroles), geysers, and hot mineral springs.

Much of the landscape has been shaped by the devastating eruption in 1886 of Tarawera, a volcano located 25 kilo-metres (15 miles) southeast of Rotorua city. The blast tore a massive 17-kilometre (10-mile) rift in the earth's surface, covering the land for kilometres around with boiling mud and ash, burying villages, killing 108 people and devastating surrounding forests. With explo-sions that were heard as far away as Auckland and Christchurch, the eruption also destroyed the then famous pink and white terraces – stunning silica forma-tions, in contrasting colours of pink and white that had attracted tourists from around the world – and created a new and volatile hydrothermal field at Waimangu.

The pink and white terraces may have disappeared, but tourists kept coming to Rotorua, as Waimangu and other geothermal fields at Whakarewarewa, Wai-o-tapu and Hell's Gate continued to enthral with erupting geysers, bubbling lakes, steaming cliffs and variously coloured silica formations. The geyser flat at

*Bottom: A section of the vast
Mount Tarawera crater that
blasted open when the volcano
erupted in 1886. Māori owners provide tours of the area.*

Whakarewarewa at the city boundary ranks alongside the geysers of Yellowstone National Park as one of the few geyser fields left in the world.

Mineral springs have also been a major attraction; for over a hundred years tourists have come to Rotorua for the therapeutic benefits of hot sulphur springs – or simply to relax in a naturally heated pool. A striking Tudor-style building, now the city's museum, was originally a much-visited spa known as The Bath House. Within the city today, alkaline springs form warm public paddling lakes at Kuirau Park and Government Gardens.

For many years tourists have been guided through the geothermal fields by local Māori people, Te Arawa. These people relate the origins of Rotorua's *ahi tipua*, 'sacred volcanic fire', to the actions of their ancestral explorer, Ngatoroirangi. He called to the gods of his homeland for warmth when climbing through snow and ice on Mount Tongariro and the gods responded by sending fire. This travelled beneath the Pacific Ocean, then burst to the surface along the 'Rim of Fire.'

That the geothermal features hold great spiritual significance to local Māori is confirmed by the names and stories they have for hundreds of individual pools, geysers and lakes. Their own uses for bathing, cooking, medicines, dyes and rituals in these pools are recognized as an integral part of Māori tradition.

The hosting and guiding traditions of local Māori have since developed to the extent that showcasing Māori culture is now a major facet of tourism in Rotorua. At the hotels and local villages there are many opportunities to watch stirring performances of *kapa haka* – Māori song and dance which relates local stories and traditions – and to partake in traditionally cooked *hangi* meals. In the New Zealand Māori Arts and Crafts Institute, at Whakarewarewa, tourists can watch students practising traditional carving and weaving skills. Customs, lifestyles and tribal history are shared with tourists in local villages and extended family homes. Māori-owned tourist organizations guide visitors in helicopters, boats and four-wheel-drive vehicles to the volcanic and geothermal features that have had such strong influence in shaping their people's past. It is a blend of the past and present; a story of nature's powerful impacts and human response.

The Lakes

There are 11 major lakes and six smaller lakes within the Rotorua region – many surrounded by forested reserves. Many are also well stocked with introduced Brown and Rainbow Trout and this area is an internationally renowned fishery. Boating pursuits such as kayaking, water-skiing, sailing, rowing and jetskiing are popular, and there are several lakeside camping areas and walkways.

The lakes and adjoining wetlands support notable populations of freshwater fish and native waterfowl, including the threatened mātā (fernbird). Although much of the mature forest in the region has been cleared for farmland and exotic plantation forest, forested reserves surrounding the lakes support endangered species: the Blue Wattled Crow (North Island kōkako), Saddleback (tīeke), North Island Brown Kiwi, Wood Pigeon (kererū), Bush Parrot (North Island kākā) and woodhen (weka).

In one such reserve, Kaharoa Forest, local residents keen to help the small kōkako population have formed a trust and are working with DOC to raise funds for control of animal predators. Many forests of the region have regenerated since being devastated by the

Tarawera eruption. Because of their specialized habitats, geothermal sites often support bird species that are not commonly found together, such as the Banded Dotterel, and the Black-billed and Red-billed Gulls that breed at the Sulphur Point Wildlife Sanctuary on Lake Rotorua.

Also present here are threatened New Zealand Dabchick, Pied Stilts and Caspian Terns. On the lake, Mokoia Island has populations of threatened bird species such as woodhen, saddleback, North Island Robin and stitchbird.

The warm and acidic soils of the geothermal fields support a unique plantlife, characterized by a prostrate form of kanuka tree and rare frost-tender ferns with tropical affinities. The dark orange coloration commonly found on geothermal vegetation is actually a fungus. In Waimangu Valley, where hot springs and crater lakes were created when Tarawera erupted, the plant life is of particular interest to scientists because it is the only geothermal field in the world whose origin can be pinned down to the exact day.

Throughout the region, DOC walking and tramping tracks explore the forests, lakes, wetlands, rivers, waterfalls and historic sites. The major geothermal fields are commercially operated but there are parks and reserves where people can wander among hot pools and steaming vents. While the Polynesian Baths are the city's main mineral springs complex, many hotels and motels have their own private thermal spas.

Above: Geothermal features include geysers, mud pools, and vividly coloured terraces and springs, such as the Champagne Pool at Wai-O-Tapu.

PUREORA FOREST PARK AND MAPARA WILDLIFE RESERVE

Saving the Podocarps

Location: Central North Island.

Climate: Mild to hot summers, frost and occasional snow in winter.

When to go: Anytime.

Access: Pureora Forest Park visitor centre is at Pureora Village, 4km (2.5 miles) off SH30, 56km (35 miles) from Te Kuiti and 85km (53 miles) from Taupo (just under an hour's drive from each place). Tramping access off the Western Bays Highway (SH32), one hour's drive from Turangi. Mapara Wildlife Reserve is on Mapara South Road, south of Te Kuiti. (Pureora and Mapara are close to main roads, but there is no public transport.)

Permits: Required for hunting.

Facilities: Pureora Village has a visitor centre, DOC camping ground, cabin accommodation, and a large lodge nearby. There are two other roadside picnic and camping areas, plus several trampers' huts. There are no shops within the park.

Watching wildlife: Blue Wattled Crow, Bush Parrot, Yellow-crowned Parakeet, North Island Robin.

Landscapes: Podocarp forest, bush-covered hills and two eroded volcanoes with low-growing subalpine shrublands. Forest-lined rivers.

Visitor activities: Tramping, short walks, picnicking, camping, bird watching (there is a bird watching tower near Pureora Village), hunting, botanizing, mountain biking and off-road driving on old logging roads.

Pureora contains some of New Zealand's finest podocarp forest. Majestic tōtara, Red Pine (rimu), Black Pine (mataī), miro and White Pine (kahikatea) trees, up to 40 metres (130 feet) high and many hundreds of years old, dominate the park. The park is also one of the last remaining habitats of the endangered Blue Wattled Crow (kōkako), its recent history including one of the most significant (and successful) conservation battles in New Zealand.

Botanizing, bird watching, tramping and hunting are the main reasons why people visit the park, which extends over 60 kilometres (some 40 miles) along the ridges and valleys of the Hauhungaroa Range, the vast western watershed of Lake Taupo. There is also ample opportunity for scenic drives and short walks through the majestic podocarp conifer forests, for camping and picnicking next to clear-running, forest-lined rivers and for walking in forest that resounds with birdsong. Chances of spotting two of New Zealand's colourful native parrots, the Yellow-crowned Parakeet (kākāriki) and Bush Parrot (kākā) are high, particularly from the 12-metre-high (40 feet) bird-watching tower near the park visitor centre.

Day walks lead to the summits of the park's two eroded volcanoes. Titiraupenga (1042 metres, or 3420

Map: to Te Awamutu; Turangi; Mangatutu Ecological Area; to Te Kuiti; to Aramatai; Mapara Wildlife Reserve; Pureora Headquarters; Waimiha; to Taumarunui; Waipapa Ecological Area; to Mangakino; Pureora Forest Park; YMCA; Ongarue R.; Mt Pureora; Boginn; Rata-Nunui Ecological Area; to Mangakino; Maramataha Ecological Area; Hauhungaroa Range; Waihaha; N; Whenuakura Ecological Area; Kuratau; to Taumarunui; to Turangi, Lake Taupo

feet, above sea level) and the park's namesake, Pureora (1165 metres or 3824 feet above sea level). Both climbs lead through a varied altitudinal range of vegetation that includes dense podocarp forests, goblin-like lichen, kāmahi forests and low-growing, spring-flowering subalpine shrublands. The all-round summit views of the central North Island, taking in the bigger volcanoes of Tongariro National Park, are stunning. Looking down from these heights the rich and varied greens of Pureora's native forests contrast sharply with the more uniform greens of adjoining farmland and plantation forest.

A feature of Pureora is its buried forests: well-preserved trees that lie beneath volcanic ash blasted 50 kilometres (30 miles) from the cataclysmic Taupo eruption, some 1800 years ago. The preserved state of these buried trees gives evidence of the ancient podocarp forests of Celery Pine (tānekaha) and Mountain Cedar (kaikawaka) and even details of the insect life, that survived here 2000 years ago. One particular example, was accidentally uncovered in 1983 by a bulldozer. In Pureora's post-Taupo eruption forests, there is no Mountain Cedar and only a little Celery Pine. This massive eruption had cleared the stage for the majestic podocarps to dominate as regrowth.

Premier Podocarps

International botanists have rated New Zealand's podocarp forests among the finest in the world. Eminent New Zealand naturalist, Sir Charles Fleming, used the term 'podocarp gothic' to compare them to the great

Top left: In the shaded recesses of the park's 'goblin forests' variously coloured fungi, such as the Blue Capped Fungus, grow on host trees or decomposing forest litter.

cathedrals of Europe, while British botanist Professor David Bellamy has called them 'dinosaur forests'.

It is perhaps ironic that Taupo's massive eruption, which destroyed entire forests in the region, simultaneously provided the fertile ash foundation which produced the mighty podocarps of Pureora and nearby Whirinaki Forest Park. These are acknowledged as New Zealand's two most impressive podocarp forests.

These forests are vestiges of far more extensive podocarp forests which covered the central North Island until large-scale land clearance for farming began in the 1800s. Later, during the mid-1900s, the big trees of Pureora were progressively clear-felled and the land planted in exotic pines — until 1978, when protesting 'tree-sitting' conservationists moved in. These 'tree-sitters', who perched themselves high in the tree tops as loggers threatened to fell the trees, ignited public opinion, which led to a government-imposed moratorium on clear-felling. Following this, a three-year study on the impact of selective logging of native forest led to the end of native forest logging in the park. The roar of saws and bulldozers was thus silenced, both here and in Whirinaki, where similar protest action by conservationists also achieved its goal.

The conservation story continues at Pureora today. Saving the podocarps also helped safeguard the habitats of several native bird species, including Blue Wattled Crow (kōkako), Bush Parrot (kākā), Yellow-crowned Parakeet (kākāriki), North Island Brown Kiwi, New Zealand Falcon (kārearea), North Island Robin, New Zealand Pigeon (kererū), Blue Duck (whio) and a host of more common native birds such as tui and bellbird (korimako). The park is now the focus of intensive animal pest control and revegetation programmes, in particular in the northern Waipapa area, where DOC scientists are refining new techniques of restoring the ecosystems of large mainland areas, through a concept described as 'mainland islands'.

Mapara Wildlife Reserve

Introduced animal pests, such as possums, rats, ferrets and stoats, have had a detrimental impact on natural habitats and native species throughout New Zealand. These and other pests destroy native vegetation and prey on eggs, chicks and adult native birds, thus severely affecting their long-term survival.

Unlike predator-free offshore islands, mainland habitats are subject to continual reinvasion by animal pests. The concept of mainland islands therefore involves intensive, ongoing management of herbivorous and carnivorous pests in areas with physical 'boundaries' such as lakes, rivers and farmland separated by fencing.

Above left: *Huge matai and tōtara trees, several hundred years old, are part of the magnificent podocarp forest of Pureora.*

Above: *Descending the boardwalk that leads almost to the summit of Mt Pureora.*

Below: *The rare Blue Wattled Crow (kōkako), one of New Zealand's most ancient bird species, is renowned for its beautiful song.*

Right: Sunrise over a
podocarp forest. Rich
volcanic soils and a cool
climate enable these ancient
conifer trees to attain great
size and height.

New Zealand's first successful mainland island project,
and the place where visitors are now more likely to hear
or see kōkako than in neighbouring Pureora, is Mapara
Wildlife Reserve, just 30 minutes drive west of the park.

The Blue Wattled Crow, one of New Zealand's most
ancient birds, belongs to the endemic wattlebird family.
Other wattlebirds are the now extinct huia and the saddleback (tīeke), which now survives only on predator-free
offshore islands. The Blue Wattled Crow is a poor flier —
it hops and runs through branches — but is renowned for
its hauntingly beautiful song. Loss of large areas of forest
habitat and the introduction of predatory animals have
brought this once common bird to the brink of extinction.

However, the conservation management programme
initiated at Mapara has turned the tide. Since 1989,
intensive animal pest control operations and boundary
fencing have substantially increased the reserve's
formerly declining Blue Wattled Crow population. To help
the species' chances of survival, several birds have now
been moved from Mapara to offshore islands and other
mainland areas. The DOC is also refining its animal
control techniques at Mapara with the aim of maintain-
ing a healthy forest ecosystem. A short one-hour loop
track that climbs gradually through a section of the
reserve enables the public to hear and occasionally see the
Blue Wattled Crow.

Right: This forest observa-
tion tower in the park gives
visitors a chance to view
the giant podocarps from
a lofty height.

TE UREWERA NATIONAL PARK

Land of the Mists

Te Urewera, a remote expanse of forest-covered ranges, rivers and lakes, is New Zealand's fourth largest national park and part of the single largest tract of native forest remaining in the North Island. Despite the isolation – just one long and winding road penetrates the heart of the park – Te Urewera's magnificent track on Lake Waikaremoana is one of the country's great walks.

The Tuhoe People

Te Urewera is filled with the presence of Tuhoe, the 'people of the land' *(tangata whenua)*, many of whom still live in isolated enclaves throughout the park. The use of Tuhoe names for landscape features, settlement sites and sacred places in the park reflects an association with the land which extends back many centuries.

Tuhoe people also have a notable tradition of resistance to European influences. In 1906 Rua Kenana, their charismatic religious leader, established a settlement, independent of the European world, at Maungapohatu, deep in the heart of Te Urewera country. Today Maungapohatu, at the foot of the sacred Mount Maungapohatu, still remains a Tuhoe-owned enclave within the national park.

Tuhoe's refusal to allow prospectors and surveyors into Te Urewera, at a time when logging and farm devel-

opment were decimating other New Zealand forests, meant the region's natural integrity was retained. Conservationists' moves to protect this large tract of forest led to negotiations with the Tuhoe people and, in 1954, the national park was created. Since then, significant additions have been made to the park, although the Tuhoe presence remains strong throughout the region.

Forest-covered Ranges

Te Urewera's jumbled mass of forest-covered ranges reach a maximum height of just 1392 metres (4361 feet). The dominant Huiarau and Ikawhenua Ranges are made up of ancient and uplifted greywacke, a hardened sedimentary rock. To the south, younger sandstones overlaid by softer mudstones have created a series of distinctive landscape features.

Several layers of ash, thrown from eruptions from the central North Island volcanoes, cover the entire park and form the fertile base for Te Urewera's unbroken mantle of forest. There are very few clear areas, even on summit ridges. These misty, cloudy places are covered with tangled, gnarled Silver Beech forests, mixed with some Mountain Beech in drier places. Below about 900 metres (3000 feet), Red Beech and Red Pine (rimu) dominate, while lower still, Northern Rātā, rimu, tawa and kāmahi are the main big trees.

The huge forests contain more than 650 native plants, including many rare or vulnerable species. This is one of the few places where the red-flowering *Clianthus puniceus* (kakabeak shrub) still grows in the wild.

Top right: *The koru – the young curved tree fern frond that represents new life – is a well-known symbol of New Zealand.*

Prolific Birdlife

Because of its size and range of natural habitats, Te Urewera supports a collection of wildlife as comprehensive and intact as any left on the New Zealand mainland. Nearly all the native birds present in North Island forests live in Te Urewera, including several threatened species – North Island Brown Kiwi, Blue Duck (whio), Yellow-crowned Parakeet (kākāriki), Bush Parrot (North Island kākā), New Zealand Falcon (kārearea) and Blue Wattled Crow (North Island kōkako). Te Urewera's remote northern forests contain about half of the national population of this highly endangered wattle

bird. The Northern Te Urewera Ecosystem Restoration Project, an intensive programme to control possums and other animal pests, is being undertaken by DOC to enhance the kōkako population, as well as those of other threatened species.

Other interesting fauna in the park includes New Zealand's only land mammals – Short and Long-tailed Bats – giant land snails and a tusked weta, a species that is yet unnamed. At least nine species of native freshwater fish, including threatened kōaro and short-jawed kōkopu, live in the park's rivers and lakes. The juvenile forms of these fish are known as whitebait.

Left: *Australian possums, introduced to New Zealand in 1848 for a fur trade, have become a major pest as their browsing has devastated native forests. Possum control is now a major focus for conservation staff.*

Left: *Te Tangi a Hinerauu falls at Aniwaniwa, one of the area's scenic waterfalls.*

Waikaremoana

Lake Waikaremoana is a gem in the heart of Te Urewera; it is a major focus for recreation and, like everywhere in the park, steeped in tradition.

Waikaremoana means 'sea of dashing waters'. According to Tuhoe this name refers to the actions of Haumapuhia, the daughter of an ancestral chief, who gouged the furrows and channels that form the lake during a struggle with her father. Haumapuhia is said to have turned to stone in a narrow gorge nearby, blocking a stream which filled the channels she had gouged, and thus creating the lake.

Scientists would explain that Lake Waikaremoana was formed about 2400 years ago, when a massive landslide occurred, blocking and damming a gorge of the Waikaretaheke River.

The vast 5,439-hectare (13,439 acres) lake is popular for boating, kayaking and fishing (for introduced trout). Red and Silver Beech forests, waterfalls, secluded bays and the view from the top of Panekiri Bluff are features of the Lake Waikaremoana Track, which circles two-thirds of the lake and takes three to four days to complete. The park's main visitor centre is located beside Waikaremoana at Aniwaniwa. There are also numerous short walks in the vicinity.

Nestling in a smaller basin above Waikaremoana is a smaller but no less beautiful 'gem', Lake Waikareiti. There are six islands dotted across this lake, which is one of the few lakes in the North Island that is free of

Above: *Several species of native freshwater fish, such as the Short-jawed kōkopu, are protected by law.*

Opposite: *The forested hinterland of Te Urewera; known as 'the land of the mists'.*

Left: *A quiet spot of fishing in the calm of a Lake Waikaremoana inlet.*

Below: *A DOC official checks hut passes of trampers staying in the park. Many of these officials are volunteers.*

introduced aquatic life. And on the largest island there is yet another lake! A walking track which climbs gradually to Waikareiti passes through forests of Red Pine, Northern Rātā, tawa, then Red and Silver Beech. While beech forest covers the basin surrounding Waikareiti, nearby clearings and wetlands are a vegetation curiosity of Te Urewera. Plants normally associated with subalpine areas and South Island west coast wetland swamps (which are known as *pakihi*), grow in this area. In the Urewera this vegetation curiosity is referred to as 'the tundra'.

In northern Te Urewera, the park's main river valleys, Whakatane and Tauranga, offer tramping routes, kayaking and fishing. There are also walks suitable for wheelchairs in two areas of the park. More remote rugged tracks follow old Tuhoe trails, such as Rua's Track to Maungapohatu, which should be tackled only by those with considerable tramping experience.

Above: A highlight of the Lake Waikaremoana track is the spectacular view from the bluffs of Panekiri Range.

Right: Beautiful, forest-lined Lake Waikareiti is one of the country's few lakes with no introduced aquatic life. There are six forest-covered islands on this lake, one with its own small lake.

TARANAKI-EGMONT NATIONAL PARK

Volcanic Symmetry

The mountain Taranaki, also known as Mount Egmont, dominates the landscape, the weather, the history and the economy of Taranaki province. The perfectly cone-shaped volcano, an imposing sentinel that stands in splendid isolation on the westernmost tip of the North Island, is also the dominating feature – the raison d'être in fact – of Egmont National Park.

From a distance the park looks simple; a symmetrical, cone-shaped mountain blanketed white with snow in winter and flanked by a near-perfect circle of green forest. But look closer, or try walking up, down or around the mountain tracks, and a very different picture emerges. The composition of this perfect-looking mountain is the result of thousands of years of two powerful and complex natural forces at work – volcanic buildup and weathering erosion.

There are streams, rivers, lakes and swamps; immense lava bluffs, deep gorges, waterfalls and unstable slips. The steep summit is a world of rock, ice, moss and lichens. The upper slopes are covered with tussocks, subalpine shrubs and flowers. Descending further, there are dramatic-looking, wind-blown Mountain Cedar (kaikawaka) forests, while in the lower regions, dense forests of kāmahi, rātā and Red Pine (rimu) are festooned with epiphytic plants, filled with ferns, vines and

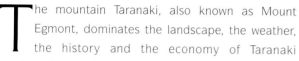

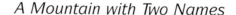

Top right: Most of New Zealand's moths, like this Zebra Moth, live in the mountains. They are masters of camouflage and play an important role in plant pollination.

smaller trees, and echo with native birdsong. And even that is very much a simplification of the varied and complex ecosystems that occur throughout the park.

As New Zealand's second oldest national park, Egmont was created in 1900 to safeguard both the mountain's natural integrity and the great outdoor playground that was, even then, popular among local people. Today, nearly 400,000 visitors from all over the world arrive each year to experience the great range of scenic and natural delights found on the many walking tracks, climbing routes, skifields and scenic drives on what is the second highest mountain in the North Island.

A Mountain with Two Names

Taranaki is the Māori name for this mountain. Unknown to the British explorer Captain Cook when he sailed along the coastline in 1770, he named the mountain Egmont, after the then first lord of the British Admiralty. Today, both names are officially acceptable.

The mountain is the most recent of a chain of andesitic volcanoes in the region which have variously erupted over the past two million years. To the north, the older, eroded volcanoes of Pouakai and Kaitiaki also lie within the park, adding significantly to the landscape variation and disrupting the otherwise perfectly circular boundary.

As the Taranaki volcano built up in a series of violent eruptions of lava over several thousand years, volcanic debris mantled the surrounding land and laid a fertile foundation for what is now an intensive regional farming

Location: West coast of the North Island.

Climate: Generally hot in summer and cold and frosty in winter. Stormy cold weather can occur at any time of the year. Rainfall increases and temperatures decrease with altitude.

When to go: Summer for walks, tramping, alpine flowers. Winter for skiing and snow climbing.

Access: Daily air and coach services to New Plymouth City, which is located on SH3. There are three main road entrances to the park: North Egmont near New Plymouth, Pembroke Road and Dawson Falls (Hawera). Public shuttle transport is from New Plymouth. Other roads lead to more remote walking tracks.

Permits: Required for goat hunting. Licences required for fishing.

Facilities: Park visitor centres, restaurants. at the three main entrances Accommodation within the park includes tourist hotels, lodges and tramping huts. Local towns provide a full range of services. Guided walks and climbs available. Ski field and climbing equipment available.

Wildlife: Alpine flowers, native birdlife.

Landscapes: Volcanic landforms, very steep mountain (snow-covered in winter), lava bluffs, deep gorges, subalpine shrublands, rainforest, wetlands, streams and waterfalls.

Visitor activities: Tramping, short walks, scenic drives, climbing, rock climbing, skiing, hunting.

Precautions: Be wary of sudden changes in weather, particularly on the exposed slopes above bushline. Steep terrain, ice and snow require climbing expertise.

industry. The mountain has erupted eight times in the last 500 years; the last blast of ash occurred in 1775.

Although often described as dormant, few geologists believe that Taranaki's volcanic life has ended. Scientific experts and Māori elders both hold the view that, one day, the mountain may again erupt in violent upheaval.

Taranaki is a symbol of great majesty and spiritual power to the many Māori tribes who have lived around the mountain since around the 14th century. These people have their own way of describing the volcano's arrival. They believe that Taranaki once lived among the other mountains gods of the central North Island. He fled to his present location following a battle with the mighty Tongariro over the love of the 'beautiful mountain maiden' Pihanga. As he fled, Taranaki gouged the bed of the Whanganui River, but was trapped from further flight by the old volcanoes Kaitiaki and Pouakai.

According to the tribal personification of their revered mountain, Taranaki's summit, or head, is a sacred place. Māori describe the summit rocks and ice as Taranaki's skull; the low-growing subalpine shrubs are his hair, the hardened lava ridges his bones, the rivers and streams his life-giving veins, and the mantle of forest his cloak.

It is an apt analogy, for the streams and rivers surely are the mountain's lifeblood. They feed the forests and are a critical element that contribute to the ongoing land-sculpting process. While volcanism has built the mountain, water continually erodes it away.

A feature of the park is its extremely high rainfall. Taranaki acts as a giant magnet to passing weather systems, and as moisture-laden winds meet the mountain they are forced to rise. They cool, then deposit rain. At higher, cooler altitudes, this often turns quickly and dramatically to snow and ice. Winds, too, become strong with increasing altitude and diminishing shelter, while katabatic flows of cold air blast down the lower valleys.

Such temperamental and tempestuous weather can cause problems for careless trampers and climbers in the park. The incredible steepness of Taranaki and the easy accessibility from road ends to dangerous, exposed terrain are added factors which visitors must consider if they are to safely enjoy their park experience. Cold rain or snow, bad visibility, steep slippery ice and huge bluffs are dangerous combinations! Technical expertise and equipment are essential for mountain climbers.

But the park also enjoys a high percentage of sunshine, while the 140-kilometre (87 miles) network of short walks and tramping tracks provides ample opportunities to explore its varied landscapes and forest types.

Right: *Winter snows cover Taranaki's upper slopes. From season to season, even day to day, the mountain's weather can change dramatically.*

Distinctive Vegetation Types

The vegetation here is significantly different from other parks in New Zealand. The changeable weather patterns, extreme altitude range and Taranaki's isolation from other mountains and forests have resulted in the growth of distinctive vegetation types. No beech forest grows here; instead the lower slopes are clothed with dense rainforest, dominated by lofty rātā and Red Pine (rimu) that are festooned with a range of epiphytic plants unequalled throughout the rest of the country.

'Goblin Forest' or cloud forest are oft-used descriptions for the tangled, lichen-covered (kāmahi) montane forest that grows at higher levels. Then, from about 1000 metres (3300 feet), the striking deep greens of Mountain Cedar (kaikawaka) dominate. Above the bushline there is a paucity of subalpine species compared with other North Island mountains, yet some plants growing here are found nowhere else in New Zealand. Two endemic alpine flowers, Mountain Foxglove (*Ourisia*

Above: 'Goblin Forest' is dominated by lichen-covered kāmahi, one of several distinctive vegetation types found in the park.

Left: The symmetrical cone of the Taranaki–Egmont volcano is the central focus of the park. The mountain is viewed here from the Pouakai Range.

Right: Nearing the summit during a winter climb on the extremely steep Mount Taranaki. The skis carried by this climber will ensure a fast descent.

Bottom right: The delicate Mountain Foxglove (Ourisia macrophylla) is one of two alpine flowers that grow only on Taranaki.

Below: Despite the snow cover, this hut at Fanthams Peak will be a welcome sight for weary hikers who have braved the elements to climb here.

macrophylla) and the Mountain Buttercup *(Ranunculus nivicola)*, make a delightful show in early summer.

Park wetlands are of particular botanical interest with regard to the variety of plants that have adapted to these special conditions. Over 260 plant species, including some endemic varieties, grow in the Ahukawakawa Swamp between Mount Taranaki and the Pouakai Range.

In terms of wildlife, the range of natural habitats within the park support some of New Zealand's rarer species, such as the North Island Brown Kiwi, fernbird (mātā) and New Zealand Falcon (kārearea), plus a host of more commonly seen New Zealand Pigeon (kereru), tui, bellbird (korimako) and rifleman (tītitipounamu).

The park has a long history of recreation. Climbing, tramping, skiing (on the small club field) and short forest walks that lead to scenic features such as waterfalls, have been popular activities for generations. Road ends lead to park tracks, of which the main three are North Egmont (which features a comprehensive information display and audiovisual presentation) as well as Stratford and Dawson Falls.

TONGARIRO NATIONAL PARK

A Gift to the Nation

Active volcanoes, snow-covered mountain peaks, a diversity of volcanic, alpine and desert landscapes, beech and podocarp forests, wetlands and waterfalls distinguish Tongariro, New Zealand's oldest national park and also a World Heritage Site; in 1993 it became the first site in the world to be granted dual status for both its natural and cultural values.

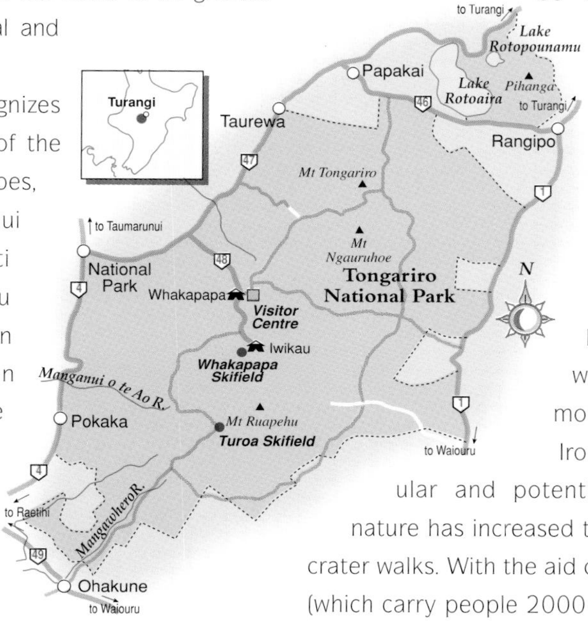

The cultural status recognizes the very special significance of the park to the local Māori tribes, Ngati Tuwharetoa and Atihaunui a paparangi. It was Ngati Tuwharetoa chief Te Heuheu Tukino IV (Horonuku) who, in 1887, gifted the mountain peaks of Tongariro, Ngauruhoe and Ruapehu to the Crown, in an attempt to prevent the sacred mountains from falling into private ownership and to preserve them in perpetuity.

Today the park's landscapes, skifields, climbing opportunities and network of tramping tracks and short walks attract more visitors to Tongariro than to any other national park in New Zealand.

Volatile Volcanoes

Ruapehu, Tongariro and Ngauruhoe, form the nucleus of the park. These three volcanoes stand at the southern end of the Pacific Rim of Fire, along a vast zone of volcanic and earthquake activity, which results from tectonic movement of the great Pacific crustal plate.

Top right: Rare Blue Ducks, one of only four species of torrent duck in the world, live in some of the park's fast-running mountain streams.

The highest volcano, Mount Ruapehu (2797 metres, or 9177 feet), dominates the surrounding countryside and is the only North Island mountain with glaciers (albeit small). Ruapehu's volatile, steaming crater lake is one of the few hot crater lakes in the world to be surrounded by snowfields. Ruapehu is an extremely active volcano, sometimes erupting every few years.

As recently as 1996, massive showers of ash, rock and steam were blasted hundreds of metres from the Crater Lake and lahars (rivers of mud and water) streamed down the mountain slopes.

Ironically, perhaps, this spectacular and potentially life-threatening act of nature has increased the popularity of summertime crater walks. With the aid of guides and skifield chairlifts (which carry people 2000 metres, or 6500 feet, up the mountain), even walkers of moderate experience and fitness can climb to view the crater lake. Reassuringly, park staff have installed a sophisticated monitoring system to provide early warning of eruptions and lahar flows. If there is any sign of volcanic activity, it is best to stay well clear!

Mount Tongariro (1968 metres, or 6459 feet) may be lower than Ruapehu but its huge massif extends over 18 kilometres (11 miles) in length and encompasses numerous craters, steaming fumaroles, geothermal springs and volcanic vents, one of which is in fact the higher, classical cone-shaped Ngauruhoe (2291 metres, or 7519 feet).

The Tongariro Crossing, a popular though longish (seven to eight hours) day walk which climbs between Ngauruhoe and Tongariro, ranks as one of the country's

Map labels: to Turangi, Lake Rotopounamu, Papakai, Lake Rotoaira, Pihanga, to Turangi, Turangi, Taurewa, Rangipo, Mt Tongariro, to Taumarunui, Mt Ngauruhoe, Tongariro National Park, National Park, Whakapapa, Visitor Centre, N, Manganui o te Ao R., Iwikau, Whakapapa Skifield, Pokaka, Mt Ruapehu, Turoa Skifield, to Waiouru, to Raetihi, Mangawhero R., Ohakune, to Waiouru

Location: Central North Island.

Climate: Huge seasonal variations. Summer (January to March) can be very hot but conditions can quickly change, especially at high altitudes. Winters are cold; expect snow and frost. Year-round rainfall.

When to go: Summer for tramping and seeing alpine flowers, winter for skiing and climbing.

Access: Whakapapa Village is one hour's drive from Turangi via SH47. Main southern entrance is via Ohakune township. Ohakune Mountain Road and Bruce Road are sometimes closed in winter.

Permits: Required for hunting.

Facilities: Tracks, huts, skifields. Guided walks and ski instruction available. Park information centres at Whakapapa, Ohakune and Turangi. Various accommodation and restaurants at Whakapapa. Specialist climbing, skiing or tramping gear is available for hire.

Wildlife: Blue Duck, Long-tailed Cuckoo and common native birds, bats, alpine flowers.

Landscapes: Active volcanoes and snow-covered mountains, volcanic features, lakes, mountain streams and waterfalls, subalpine shrub and tussocklands, desert, beech and mixed podocarp/rainforests.

Visitor activities: Tracks, huts, walks, skiing, snowboarding, alpine climbing, rock climbing.

Precautions: Be wary of sudden weather changes. In the case of volcanic eruption, move quickly to high ridges. Follow the advice of DOC staff.

most interesting day walks and is popular with most visitors. The spectacular track traverses stark, lunar-like volcanic terrain, climbs old lava flows and moraine walls and passes beside steaming craters and the stunning Blue Lake and Emerald Lakes. It is part of the Tongariro Northern Circuit, and is regarded as one of New Zealand's 'Great Walks'.

While these three major volcanoes dominate the park other, smaller, volcanoes such as Hauhangatahi, Pihanga and Kakaramea are dotted around the park's extremities. However, by far the biggest volcanic effect on the region's landscape resulted from a huge eruption outside the park in AD186. The immense crater which has since been filled by the benign-looking Lake Taupo, was the source for what is reputedly the biggest volcanic eruption to have occurred on the planet in the past 5000 years. The cataclysmic blast devastated every one of the surrounding forests, blanketed much of the North Island with pumice and ash and caused darkened skies that may have been recorded as far away as China and Rome.

Flora and Fauna

The forests have since recovered and now blanket the park's lower slopes. However, in the southern part of the park there is a remnant stand of podocarp forest that was sheltered from the Taupo eruption by Mount Ruapehu. Here a wheelchair-standard walk meanders among ancient rimu, miro and mataī trees, beneath which grows a tangled profusion of understorey trees, shrubs and vines typical of healthy podocarp forest.

Other, younger, podocarp and broadleaf forests now grow around the extremities of the park while, at higher altitudes, beech forest dominates. This in turn gives way to tussocklands, subalpine shrubs and wetlands. In a vast area east of Ruapehu, known as the Rangipo Desert, strong winds have prevented forest recovery following denudation by frequent human fires and volcanic disturbance. Growing throughout these diverse landscapes are over 550 species of native plants, most of which are endemic to New Zealand.

The park's forests, open areas, rivers and lakes provide habitat for many native birds, including threatened

species such as the North Island Brown Kiwi, Blue Duck (kōwhiowhio), New Zealand Falcon (kārearea), Bush Parrot (kākā), North Island Robin, Fernbird (mātā) and Long-tailed Cuckoo (koekoeā). Also present are populations of New Zealand's only native land mammals, Short- and Long-tailed Bats.

That the Tongariro mountains are of deep spiritual significance to the local Māori people, who have lived in the region for nearly a thousand years, is evidenced by traditions woven around the origins of volcanism in the park. Such traditions give clear evidence of the depth of Māori knowledge and innate understanding of the natural processes and geological formations of the Tongariro region.

There is the story of the high priest Ngatoroirangi, who first explored this area to claim it for his people. When Ngatoroirangi spied a challenger for the land he called for help from his gods, who sent dark clouds and snow. Later, when Ngatoroirangi neared the summit of Tongariro he was frozen in a snowstorm and called to Hawaiki, his traditional Polynesian homeland, for warmth. Fire duly arrived via the underground passage – known today as the Pacific Rim of Fire – and erupted from a crater at the summit. This tenuous juxtaposition of fire and ice is one of the unique features that makes Tongariro such a special place today.

The park is also the birthplace of rivers with strong Māori spiritual associations, such as the Whanganui, lifeblood of the Te Atihaunui a Pāpārangi people. Tradition relates how the Whanganui's course was gouged by the personified mountain Taranaki as he fled from the central North Island, after losing a 'mighty battle with the venerable old Tongariro over the love of the fair mountain maiden Pihanga'. After this battle, Tongariro is said to have been considerably lowered in height – a reference to the immense size of Tongariro before major eruptions.

While the Ngati Tuwharetoa triple-summit gift to the Crown protected the mountain's sacredness, the creation of Tongariro National Park also cleared the way for protection of lower altitude forests from milling, as European settlers arrived to farm in the region surrounding the mountains. Tourism soon became a major activity in the park; huts were built for trampers, the first skiing pioneers explored the Whakapapa slopes in 1913, and in 1929, the imposing-looking hotel now known as The Grand Chateau was built at the foot of Mount Ruapehu.

Today the park hosts nearly one million visitors each year. Major drawcards are the two commercial skifields – Whakapapa and Turoa – and their associated network of ski lodges and cafes.

Opposite: *Now still and silent in their snow-covered grandeur, the Tongariro volcanoes have been prone to violent and spectacular eruptions.*

Above: *In 1998, local Māori tribes dedicated this plaque to commemorate Tongariro National Park's dual cultural and natural World Heritage status.*

Left: *Climbers watch the sunset from Paretetaitonga, one of the peaks bounding the crater of Mount Ruapehu.*

A comprehensive network of tramping tracks links with park huts around the three mountains. Major circuits are the Tongariro Northern Circuit, a New Zealand 'Great Walk' (mentioned in previous pages) and the Round the Mountain Track which circumnavigates the forests, lakes, waterfalls, and subalpine shrublands of Mount Ruapehu. These tracks can be negotiated throughout the year, though snow and ice climbing expertise is needed for winter journeys. Other, shorter walks provide easy opportunity for people of all ages and levels of fitness to explore the park's diverse landscapes. Park information centres provide an excellent selection of brochures and maps detailing tramping and walking options.

Above: *Rotopounamu (meaning greenstone lake) nestles on the eastern extremity of the park.*

Above right: *Karamu (Coprosma lucida) provides year-round fruit for many native birds.*

Right: *Ngauruhoe's summit cone. According to legend, when Māori ancestor Ngatoroirangi climbed the mountain he called to his Hawaiki homeland for fire to warm him. Hawaiki responded with hot molten lava and rock.*

KAWEKA AND KAIMANAWA FOREST PARKS

Beech Forests and Tussock Valleys

These adjoining parks encompass the Kaimanawa and Kaweka mountain ranges and form a vast area of wilderness in the central North Island. Their mantle of beech forests, tussock grasslands and subalpine tops are rather more typical of South Island mountains, with the notable difference that layers of volcanic pumice and ignimbrite have poured over these ranges from the neighbouring Taupo volcanic zone and significantly affected landforms and vegetation patterns. These ranges are part of the North Island main divide; the highest peaks 1500 to 1700 metres (4900–5580 feet) above sea level.

Major North Island rivers, the Mohaka, Ngaruroro and Rangitikei, which have their beginnings in the heart of these mountains, are popular for wilderness rafting expeditions. Hunting, for introduced Red and Sika Deer, tramping, and short walks are other recreational pursuits in these parks. Many roads lead to park entry points, where there are picnic and camping areas, and walking tracks, while aerial access is also a commonly used option.

Sedimentary greywacke rock forms the basis of these mountains, which have been pushed upwards and contorted by fault lines, and are constantly eroded by rain, frost and wind. To the south of the Kaweka

Range, on a series of small plateaus which are remnants of eroded earth surface known as a peneplain, younger limestones and sandstones overlie the greywackes. A belt of older, metamorphic schist that extends through the heart of the Kaimanawa Ranges is the only occurrence of schist in the North Island.

Volcanic Legacy

Throughout both parks the presence of charcoal and charred, buried tree stumps is telling evidence of the devastation brought about by a series of huge volcanic eruptions. Outcrops of ignimbrite rock in several of the parks' headwaters have come from massive showers of hot, molten rock that exploded from Te Whaiti, near Taupo, about 300,000 years ago and covered a radius of hundreds of square kilometres. Just under 2000 years ago masses of hot pumice from eruptions of Taupo were blasted over the mountain ranges and into river valleys. Large pumice terraces, up to 20 metres (65 feet) thick, are still preserved in the headwaters of the Ngaruroro and Mohaka rivers.

The spectacular gorges and waterfalls along the Tongariro River were formed from volcanic ignimbrite and andesite rocks, thrown from eruptions on Mount Tongariro. In the eastern Kaweka ranges, over 70 kilometres (43 miles) from the volcanoes, several layers of volcanic deposits have been carried by easterly winds. And as recently as 1996, yet another mantle of ash covered the Kaimanawa and Kaweka mountains from a violently erupting Mount Ruapehu.

Top right: *A Tobacco Pouch Fungus brightens the forest floor in Kaimanawa Forest Park.*

Location: Central North Island, east of Lake Taupo and west of Napier.

Climate: Can be extreme – hot and dry in summer, snow and heavy frosts during winter – but snow can fall at any time of the year.

When to go: Anytime, though climbing experience is advisable on snow-covered tops in winter.

Access: Roads lead to Kaimanawa Forest Park from Taupo and Turangi, and to Kaweka Forest Park from Napier. There are daily air and bus services to Taupo and Napier. Aerial access is available to an airstrip on the boundary between the two parks.

Permits/Reservations: Permits required for hunting and licences for fishing.

Facilities: In the parks – huts, tracks, camping areas and information signs. In the nearby towns of Taupo, Turangi and Napier there is a full range of accommodation, restaurants, shops and services; also DOC visitor centres. Fishing, hunting and rafting guides and charters available.

Wildlife: Bush Parrot, Yellow-crowned Parakeet, Blue Duck, New Zealand Falcon and North Island Robin might be seen. Tui, Bellbird, Fantail and kererū are more common.

Landscapes: Mountain ranges (snow-covered in winter), beech forests, wide tussock-filled valleys and uplands, subalpine tops, regenerating manuka and kanuka forests, big clear rivers, gorges and waterfalls.

Visitor activities: Tramping, short walks, rafting, hunting, fishing, camping, hot swims.

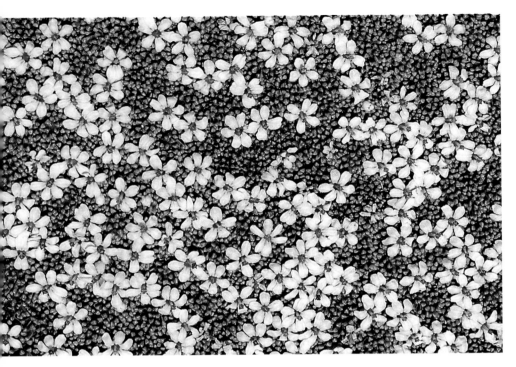

Above: *Montane Rock Cushion Flowers; over 90 per cent of New Zealand's alpine plants grow nowhere else in the world.*

Below: *Conservation staff are working to maintain viable populations of the North Island Brown Kiwi in Kaweka Forest Park.*

(matai), Brown Pine (miro) and Red Pine (rimu) – grow around the lower altitude margins.

In the upland valleys, such as the headwaters of the Ngaruroro and Waipakihi rivers, trapped cold air and heavy frosts have discouraged the regrowth of forests. Instead, these wide, open valleys are now filled with Red Tussocks, Snow Tussocks and alpine podocarp trees such as bog pine and mountain toatoa. Other valleys similarly filled with tussocks and alpine grasses are a legacy of fires, started not by natural causes, but by early Māori and later European settlers – either accidentally or in deliberate but misguided attempts to develop these remote valleys for farming.

These valleys are now delightful places to wander. Or perhaps to pass the time of day on the verandah of a park hut, many of which are strategically set to overlook the wide tussock flats, framed by mountain peaks. In winter the mountain tops will be snow-covered, yet in summer they come alive with delicate-looking yet hardy alpine flowers, such as edelweiss, celmisias and gentians.

Fragile Nature

The eastern 'front country' of the Kaweka Ranges, already subject to natural erosion with its soft sedimentary base overlain with unstable volcanic soils, has also been affected by attempts to farm the land. During the late 1800s, the southern plateaus and eastern Kaweka Ranges were extensively burnt, and sheep were driven high into upland basins to graze. Stripped of much of its vegetation cover, the mountains eroded even faster, so efforts to stabilize the steep slopes were made by planting a quick-growing, introduced pine species. As these pines quickly started to overtake the native plants, the folly of this misguided plan was realized. Conservation staff have worked hard to rid park land of these invasive trees, and lowland areas that were burnt are now well covered with regenerating manuka and kanuka forests.

The two parks contain the only herd of Sika Deer in the Southern Hemisphere. These strange-sounding whistling deer have joined Red Deer and possums on the list of introduced animal pests who browse and damage the park's native vegetation. Recreational hunting, encouraged by DOC as a means to reduce deer numbers, has become one of the most popular activities in these parks.

The cycle of land abuse witnessed in these parks, followed by protection and restoration, has been oft repeated throughout the past 200 years of New Zealand's history, as new settlers rushed to 'tame' the

Entire forests, smothered and scorched by the earlier volcanic blasts, gradually became re-established. In other, similarly devastated areas in the volcanic region, such as Whirinaki and Pureora, impressive podocarp forests emerged from the fertile pumice soils. But in the cooler, higher altitudes of the Kaimanawa and Kaweka mountains, beech forests took hold, spreading from sheltered stands that had survived the eruptions. Red and Mountain Beech is predominant throughout both parks, and Silver Beech is present on the northern slopes. Scattered pockets of podocarps – Black Pine

land for farming no matter how remote, steep, or poor the soils. At the same time, game animals were introduced for the traditional 'sport' of hunting, without thought of likely consequences to the natural ecosystems. Fortunately attitudes have changed in recent years and the natural qualities of these special areas are now recognized, valued and legally protected.

There are significant natural qualities in the huge expanse of mountains, forests and river valleys that make up the Kaweka and Kaimanawa wilderness. Kaweka Forest Park is significant as the southernmost habitat for North Island Brown Kiwi. Threatened Bush Parrots and Yellow-crowned Parakeets are still relatively common, rare Blue Duck (kōwhiowhio) frequent the remote headwaters, and New Zealand Falcons (kārearea), North Island Robins and fernbirds (mātā) have been recorded in both parks. Common forest birds, such as tui, Bellbirds (korimako), Fantails (pīwakawaka) and New Zealand Pigeons (kererū) live throughout the region.

An area of fragile wetlands and tussocklands in the southwestern corner of Kaimanawa Forest Park contains many unique and threatened plants, including 16 species which have been lost elsewhere and 11 which are endemic to this region. A difficulty faced by conservationists in this area is the presence of a wild horse herd, which causes significant damage to the threatened plants. DOC measures to remove these horses, and protect the fragile wetlands, are monitored carefully by horse enthusiasts, who believe the isolated herd to be genetically significant.

While a network of tracks and huts link most of the mountains, valleys and forests of the two parks, two 'Remote Experience Zones' have been set aside to be retained in their natural, undeveloped states – these are in the Makino catchment, a tributary of the Mohaka, and in the upper Rangitikei catchment of Kaimanawa Forest Park. The presence of sulphur hot springs beside the Mohaka River is a natural feature that strikes a popular chord with trampers and rafters.

Below: *The Kaweka Ranges tower over the western boundary of Hawkes Bay, causing a rainshadow effect which helps a thriving wine-growing industry on the eastern plains.*

CAPE KIDNAPPERS NATURE RESERVE

Gannet City

The world's largest mainland concentration of gannet colonies is established amidst a spectacular coastal setting of sea cliffs and reefs at Cape Kidnappers Nature Reserve, in the North Island region of Hawke's Bay.

Nearly 7000 pairs of Australasian Gannets nest at the Cape, in three main colonies and increasingly, as their population grows, on adjacent outlying areas. The mainland location and ease of public access make the Cape one of the better places in the world to view these ocean-going birds – well known as majestic fliers and for the dramatic spectacle they present as they dive into the sea from great heights and at high speeds for fish.

Highlights for the tens of thousands of people who visit the Cape each year include close-up views of nesting gannets (and chicks), a look at interesting geological formations, and the approach walk or ride along a scenic piece of coastline. Views across the seascape of Hawke Bay, swimming, fossicking in tidal pools and seeing other sea birds are added attractions. Birds that also frequent this area are White Fronted Terns (tara), Variable Oystercatchers, Reef Herons and Spotted Shags.

Opposite: Cape Kidnappers is one of the best places in the world to see Australasian Gannets. Nearly 7000 pairs nest in colonies amidst a spectacular coastal setting of cliffs and reefs.

Top right: A gannet pair guards its nesting site. Adult birds usually return to the same site each year to breed.

The Cape's Gannets

Apart from South Africa and the North Atlantic, Australasian Gannets are one of very few species of gannets found throughout the world. While there are about 20 colonies in New Zealand, most are established on islands or rock stacks. Some of these are joined to the mainland at low tide, while others are located as far as 60 kilometres (37 miles) offshore. Aside from the tidal shellbanks of Farewell Spit, and a recent mainland extension to the island gannetry just off Muriwai Beach, Cape Kidnappers is the only true mainland location where Australasian Gannets nest.

Gannets were first recorded at the Cape in 1856. At that time, just 50 birds were living on what is now known as the Saddle Colony, on the sea cliffs near the very tip of the Cape. Since then, their numbers have increased considerably. Today, several thousand pairs live in three main colonies, in spectacular locations on top of the Cape's high cliffs and on the nearby rock stacks of Black Reef.

The gannets base themselves at Cape Kidnappers from July, through summer, until April–May. During winter most disperse around coastal waters. Nest preparation, courting and egg-laying occurs from July to November. Chicks are hatched from early November, then mature through stages of white fluffy down to grey, speckled juvenile birds.

Gannets usually fish close by, though birds from Cape Kidnappers have been known to forage up to 200 kilometres (125 miles) away. Anchovy, pilchard, Yellow Eyed Mullet, garfish and other small fish and squid make up a gannet's diet, which is regurgitated to feed the chick when the parent returns to its nest.

Location: Hawke's Bay.

Climate: Usually dry throughout the year, very hot in summer. Sometimes windy.

When to go: Best gannet viewing time (for seeing chicks) is late November to February. The colonies are closed to the public from July to late October.

Access: Daily air, road and rail services operate daily to Napier. Public transport can be arranged from Napier and Hastings cities to Clifton, where beach access to the Cape starts. Public access is via the beach and only feasible at low to mid-tide. Commercial tours are available along the beach and overland through private farmland.

Permits: Not required.

Facilities: At the Cape – public shelter, water, toilets, walking track and interpretative signs. At Clifton – camping ground, shop and a sign advising tide times. All services – a full range of accommodation, restaurants, shops and wineries are located in and around Hastings and Napier cities.

Landscapes: Dramatic coastal formations – cliffs, reefs, rock stacks and beaches, seascapes, farmland.

Watching wildlife: Australasian Gannets, Red Billed Gulls, Black Backed Gulls, Variable Oystercatchers, White Fronted Terns Spotted and Black Shags.

Precautions: Avoid disturbing the gannets, keep a minimum of about five paces from nesting sites. The coastal cliffs are unstable, so beware of slipping.

Visitor activities: Watching gannets, nature photography, scenic walks, swimming, shellfish gathering.

Right: Majestic fliers.

Below left: For over 50 years a family-operated company has been offering tractor tours to the colonies.

Below right: Geological history in the form of coloured horizontal layers of various deposits is 'written' on the Cape's sea cliffs.

When the chicks have matured, at about 15 weeks, most leave for the eastern seaboard of Australia. Those who survive the challenging flight, return to the Cape after two to three years. Up to 75 per cent perish!

Each year, adult birds return to the colony to breed, generally to the same nesting site. The gannets' lengthy life span (an average of 20 years) and healthy breeding record compensates for the high mortality rate of young birds. Activity at the Cape colonies is constantly

North Island. Shell layers tell of periods of higher sea levels. This entire horizontal system has subsequently been thrust upwards and tilted by tectonic movement, then has been cut vertically with fault lines that can be clearly seen cutting through the entire height of the cliff face.

The geological journey continues at Black Reef, where gannets nest on top of dark-coloured rock stacks

Below: A Spotted Shag in breeding plumage.

busy. Birds fly in and out, pairs carry out courting, bowing and mutual preening ('kissing') rituals, parents incubate eggs, then feed fluffy white chicks and grey speckled juveniles, while the occasional disagreement flares between neighbouring adults. Although the birds usually seem unperturbed by the close proximity of visitors, they can become hostile if approached too closely.

A Geological Journey

Access to the Cape follows the coast, a narrow, eight-kilometre (5-mile) length of ever-changing sandy beach, mudstone platforms and rocky shore that is only passable from low to mid tide.

This coastal route is hemmed by towering sea cliffs, on which distinctive patterns 'write' the story of geological history. Coloured horizontal layers show the sedimentary deposits which have been laid down here over hundreds of thousands of years. Dark river gravels and even darker fossilized plants contrast with pale layers of volcanic ash, thrown here by massive eruptions from the Taupo volcanic zone, far away in the central

of older, erosion-resistant sandstone. At the Cape itself, the towering cliffs are made of fine, grey siltstone, or papa. As these fragile cliffs are constantly eroding – sometimes by massive slumps which collapse into the sea – visitors should keep to the formed tracks (trails)!

People at the Cape

Deposits found in banks around the coastline near the Cape are of more recent origin, left by humans. These are the shells and bones of middens, or rubbish dumps, from times when early Māori lived here. The Māori name for the Cape, Te Kauae o Māui, refers to the hook used by the ancestor Māui when, according to legend, he fished Te Ika a Māui (the North Island) out of the sea.

The name Cape Kidnappers dates from 1769, when British explorer Captain Cook sailed close to shore and local Māori attempted to make off with a Tahitian boy travelling as an interpreter on board Cook's ship. No people live at the Cape today, but visitors can walk here or choose from various four-wheel-drive, motorbike or tractor tours of the gannet colonies.

WHANGANUI NATIONAL PARK

The Flow of History

The focus of this park centres on a long and historic waterway, the Whanganui River, and the huge tract of forest through which the river flows for much of its 300-kilometre (186-mile) journey from the central North Island mountains to the sea. The forest in the park is the North Island's largest remaining area of native lowland forest. A park tramping track traverses the heart of this wilderness, along the Matemateaonga Range. Another leads through the Mangapurua Valley, where grassy flats of abandoned farms merge with regenerating native forest. Here, the visitor can embark on several short walks to explore scenic and historic features around the margins of the park. However, it is the Whanganui River itself that is the feature 'track' of this park.

The Whanganui is the longest continually navigable river in New Zealand. Each year, many thousands of people canoe some or all of the 170 kilometres (106 miles) of river that flows through the park. Nearly half of this journey passes through remote, forested wilderness. The river flows through several striking, deep-cut gorges, yet its gradient is gentle. While there are 239 named rapids between Taumarunui and Wanganui, most have little more than a metre fall and the river is known for its suitability for beginners. This river trip is known as the Whanganui Journey and is part of the New Zealand Great Walk network.

Great journeys have been a feature of the Whanganui's history, starting right from the time of the

Top right: The tiny, friendly North Island Robin often accompanies walkers in the forest.

land's creation. The Māori people believe the riverbed was gouged by the mountain god Taranaki, as he fled his original place alongside the central North Island mountains after a lost battle over his mountain maiden. After Taranaki halted his flight, on the coast north of the Whanganui, streams of water sprang from the side of Tongariro to fill and heal the wound Taranaki had made in the earth, thus forming the Whanganui River.

Te Atihaunui a Pāpārangi are the Māori people who have lived along the Whanganui for centuries. In early days the river formed a natural transport route between the coast and interior. Food was plentiful, from both the forests and the river, and Māori lived in *kainga* (villages) along its length. They travelled in *waka* (canoes) and built large and sophisticated *utu piharau* (weirs) to trap lamprey, a blind, eel-like fish that moves upstream to spawn. Today, fewer Māori people live along the river. The remote middle reaches are deserted with no road access. However, spiritual links with the river remain strong. Rapids, gorges and landforms throughout the park all have names associated with Māori history. The name, Whanganui, refers to the 'big (*nui*) wait (*whanga*)' of the ancestral chief, Haunui a papa rangi. Wanganui, the city, is a misspelt but entrenched version of the river name.

The river's use as a transport route continued with the arrival of European settlers and missionaries in the mid-1800s. Mission stations established at riverside villages are still in evidence today and continue to carry Māori versions of biblical names, such as Koriniti (Corinth) and Atene (Athens).

Location: Mid-west North Island.

Climate: Mild with few extremes, subject to moist, westerly airflows but also long periods of fine weather. Snow is rare.

When to go: Anytime; the river trip is most popular in summer.

Access: Daily air and bus services to Wanganui City. Daily road and rail services to Taumarunui. Road access (winding and partly unsealed) from Wanganui and Raetihi to the village of Pipiriki.

Facilities: In the park – huts, campsites, tracks, information panels, small museum and visitor centre at Pipiriki (open in summer). A range of accommodation, shops, restaurants and services available in Wanganui and Taumarunui. Riverboat museum and restored riverboat trips in Wanganui. Guided canoeing trips, scenic jet boat tours and River Road tours on offer. Canoes available for hire.

Wildlife: Common forest birds; also North Island Brown Kiwi, North Island Robin, Yellow-crowned Parakeet, North Island kākā, whitehead. Long-tailed Bats, eels, lamprey.

Landscapes: River, river gorges and bluffs, waterfalls, huge expanse of unbroken forested covered ridges and valleys.

Permits/Reservations: Permits are required for hunting (introduced fallow deer, goats and feral pigs) and fishing (introduced trout are present, mainly in the upper Whanganui reaches and Manganui o te Ao River).

Visitor activities: Canoeing, jet boating, camping, tramping, short walks, scenic and historic drives.

Precautions: The Whanganui can rise quickly. Even if is not raining on the river, rain elsewhere in the catchment quickly affects the flow.

Above: *The park's land-scape is distinctive for its deep-cut gorges, steep bluffs and waterfalls.*

Right: *Tree ferns, such as this Mamaku Fern, are a special feature of the park, which protects one of the largest tracts of unmodified lowland forest in the North Island.*

Then came a lively era of riverboats and tourism. Tourists travelled on a three-day cruise with overnight stays in Pipiriki House, a grand hotel which has long since burnt down, and a salubrious riverboat hotel, moored further upstream. Up to 12 vessels plied the river, the largest was over 100 metres (30 feet) long and carried up to 400 passengers. The riverboats also provided transport for Māori people and for farmers attempting to settle in the remote areas of the middle reaches.

When the main trunk railway line was completed in 1908, the Whanganui's importance as a transport route diminished. Tourists were enticed to other areas, remote farms were abandoned and urban drift saw the Māori population dwindle. Today there are many historical features both within and close to the park. In Wanganui City, two restored riverboats and an impressive museum focusing on the subject are the work of an enthusiastic riverboat restoration trust. In the park, a restored flour mill and the Mangapurua 'Bridge to Nowhere' are now tourist attractions.

River reserves were first established during the riverboat era, with the aim of safeguarding scenic qualities for tourism. Gradually, more of the forest throughout the huge Whanganui basin became protected and, in 1986, the collection of reserves and state forest was gathered together to become Whanganui National Park.

The river is legally not part of the park, but nevertheless integrally linked to it. Its special characteristics – its often muddy-like appearance, fearsome floods, and deeply gouged gorges, bluffs and waterfalls that have so impressed generations of tourists – are all natural phenomena related to the geological make-up of its vast catchment.

The river starts high on the volcanic mountains of the central North Island, but for over half its journey, flows though the jumble of heavily dissected hills, ridges and valleys that make up the park. The hills are formed of sedimentary sandstones and mudstones, known locally as papa, which is soft and easily eroded by water. As erosion continues its relentless work, the created landscape is distinctive for its sharp crested ridges, deep-cut gorges, sheer papa bluffs and numerous striking waterfalls.

The tangled maze of rivers and streams that feed into the Whanganui carry huge loads of papa sediment, which accounts for the river's often muddy appearance.

In times of heavy rain, the Whanganui valley has witnessed some tremendous floods, which have damaged roads and park huts and campsites.

Unbroken Forests

A mantle of fertile volcanic ash that overlays the Whanganui basin, combined with the park's moist, mild climate, have produced the extensive lowland forest that covers the park. Tall New Zealand Honeysuckle (rewarewa), Northern Rātā and podocarps trees emerge above a uniform canopy of kāmahi, tawa, hinau and pigeonwood trees. There is a great diversity of understorey plants, trees, shrubs and vines, while a multitude of ferns, mosses, creepers and orchids grow on the forest floor and as epiphytes in the trees. Tree ferns are a feature of the park.

The steep banks of the Whanganui, and many of its tributaries, are matted with shrubs, creeping plants, kiekie (a climbing shrub valued for weaving by Māori), lichens and mosses. On drier banks Mountain Flax, cutty grass (toe toe) and yellow-flowering kōwhai are prominent, while on shaded, damp slopes the distinctive herb, parataniwha, with its varying lime-green through to bronze-red colouring, is a feature. A continual natural cycle of growth, erosion and regrowth occurs on these papa banks; only those walls which have recently slipped are ever completely devoid of vegetation.

Below: *Jetboats are a popular means of transport, for local families and tourists, on the long wilderness reaches of the Whanganui.*

Below: *Large numbers of native freshwater crayfish live in the river's smaller side-streams.*

Native Wildlife

The Whanganui, its tributaries and the huge forest of the park support a range of native wildlife. Most common North Island native forest birds thrive. There are also significant populations of North Island Brown Kiwi and North Island Robin, while threatened species present are Yellow-crowned Parakeet, Bush Parrot, New Zealand Falcon and whitehead. Long-tailed Bats are sometimes seen at dusk, flitting over the river.

The rare Blue Duck lives in some tributaries. Native aquatic life is plentiful. Large numbers of eels live in the park's waterways until they leave for their epic, once-in-a-lifetime journey to the Pacific Ocean to spawn. In contrast, blind lamprey live in the sea, then migrate up the Whanganui to spawn. Several species of galaxiid, or whitebait, are present and freshwater crayfish live in the smaller sidestreams.

RUAHINE FOREST PARK

Rugged Mountain Ranges

A series of steep mountain ranges, deeply gorged rivers, and a diversity of lowland rainforests, montane beech forests, subalpine shrublands, wetlands and tussock tops make up Ruahine Forest Park. A vast network of walking tracks, tramping routes and back country huts has been developed throughout the park, which has a strong tradition of recreational tramping and deer hunting.

The forest park encompasses the main Ruahine mountain range and four subsidiary ranges which are part of the North Island's main divide. Long and narrow, the park is bordered by the Kaweka Ranges in the north and, 90 kilometres (56 miles) south, the Tararua Ranges continue the north-south mountain axis of the island. The Ruahine Range rises sharply from surrounding plains. Steep and craggy peaks, snow-covered in winter, are a stark contrast with the adjacent lowland farms and townships.

The shaping of these mountains is an ongoing process, witnessed at times by landslides that collapse entire forest-covered hillsides. The geologically young, unstable greywacke mountains are subject to constant uplift and simultaneous erosion by streams and rivers, a natural process aided by high rainfall, strong winds, snow and frosts. The narrow summit ridges are all that remain of an old peneplain, thrust upwards thousands of years ago by earth movement and scoured away ever since by the constant action of water.

Introduced animals have also had an impact. In the early 1900s, Red Deer populations exploded and their browsing seriously damaged the forests, which in turn increased erosion. Government animal control operations reduced deer numbers and today recreational hunting and commercial helicopter hunting are methods used by park management to keep deer under control. Conservation staff now face the problem of possums. These Australian marsupials were liberated into New Zealand's forests for the well-meaning but misguided plan of creating a fur industry, and have now overtaken deer as the prime culprits in vegetation damage.

Despite the impacts of these introduced animals, the park is filled with a range of plants and native wildlife. Several tracks which climb to the open tops pass through a full altitudinal range of forest types. Within a few hours' walking, hikers can view key elements of New Zealand's mountain flora.

The best example is Sunrise Track, on the eastern, Hawke's Bay side of the park, where the track climbs from farmland on the park boundary into dense rainforest. Lofty podocarps – Red Pine (rimu), tōtara and White Pine (kahikatea) – and Red Beech trees tower above a profusion of understorey shrubs, ferns, vines and epiphytic plants. Higher up, Mountain Beech becomes the dominant tree and there are few understorey plants. At about 1000 metres (3200 feet) the beech trees become stunted, then give way to scattered Mountain Cedar (kaikawaka) and subalpine shrubs. On the high, open tops there are sprawling tussock fields, rocky crags, scree slopes, herb fields and, in summer, alpine flowers – ample reward for the effort of the climb!

However, the tops in the southern part of the park, where the ranges are of lower altitude, are covered with

Top right: Kamahi (Weinmannia racemosa) one of New Zealand's most common native flowers, blooms in early summer.

Map labels:
Conservation Land
Rangitikei R.
Mokai Rd.
Mangatera R.
Ruahine Forest Park
Mangaweka
Ruahine Range
N
Rangiwahia
Apiti
Tunupo
Pohangina Field Centre
Pohangina R.
Norsewood
Ruahine Range
Maharahara
Dannevirke
to Palmerston North
Hastings

Location: Lower North Island.

Climate: Cool, cloudy, frequent strong winds, especially around the tops. North westerly winds dominate, mixed with cold southerly winds. Rainfall heavier on the tops and in the west than on the rain-shadowed, eastern foothills. Snow usually lies above 1400m (4600ft) during winter.

When to go: Anytime – summer for alpine flowers and tramping on tops.

Access: The nearest cities are Napier (one to two hours' drive from park entrances via SH50 and SH2) and Palmerston North (30 minutes drive from southern end of the park). Several roads lead to park picnic areas and track entrances. Helicopter charters to huts are available.

Facilities: Huts, tracks, camping and picnic areas, interpretative panels. DOC field bases and information at Ongaonga and Pohangina (staffed at variable hours). A range of accommodation, shops and services in surrounding towns and cities – Dannevirke, Napier, Taihape, Feilding and Palmerston North.

Visitor activities: Tramping, short walks, hunting, cross-country skiing (winter), camping, mountain biking (on Takapari Road and Yeomans Track), four-wheel driving (Takapari Road), fishing for introduced trout.

Wildlife: Blue Duck, North Island Kākā, New Zealand Falcon plus tui, Bellbird and Fantail.

Landscapes: Steep, mountain ranges with forests covering lower levels and rocky peaks above the tree line, broad tussock tops, subalpine herbfields, deep river gorges.

Permits/Reservations: Hunting permits and fishing licences required.

the largest, unbroken mass of Leatherwood in New Zealand – an area of some 50 square kilometres (19 square miles). This low-growing, gnarled, and leathery-leafed tree daisy thrives in areas with high rainfall and cloud cover – and the southern Ruahine is one of the cloudiest (and windiest!) places in New Zealand. On the lower southern slopes the dominant trees are Red Pine (rimu), miro, kāmahi and Northern Rātā. In contrast with the steep, craggy peaks of the central Ruahine Range,

Right: The hunting of deer, which have caused large scale damage to forests since their introduction in the early 1900s, is a long-time tradition in the park.

the tops of the northern Hikurangi and Mokai Patea ranges are broad, covered with alpine bogs and various tussock species such as Red Tussock and Mid-ribbed Snow Tussock.

Forest Splendour

Extensive stands of Mountain Cedar in northern lime-stone areas are considered some of the finest forests of their kind in New Zealand. Mixed with Pink Pine and Hall's Tōtara, these are remnants of upland podocarp forest that once covered the central North Island plateau country. The sight of the distinctive, dark and cone-shaped Mountain Cedar (kaikawaka), which also grows near the forest line throughout the park, is often welcomed by trampers as a signal that they have reached the end of a long haul up a steep forest track.

A feature of the park is Lake Colenso. Sheer, 150-metre high (492 feet) high limestone bluffs enclose a basin filled with dense lowland podocarp forest and the green, pristine waters of the lake. The forest in the basin supports one of the largest varieties of native birds in the park. Over 20 species, including threatened birds such as Bush Parrot (North Island kākā), Yellow-crowned Parakeet (Kākāriki), North Island Robin, Long-tailed Cuckoo (koekoeā) and Blue Duck (whio), have been recorded here. The park is noted for the healthy breeding populations of the rare Blue Duck which finds refuge in the tumbling rapids of several headwater streams and rivers. Lake Colenso was originally called Kōkopunui by early Māori people, who fished here for native fish (kōkopu) and tuna (eels). Early Māori lived around the Ruahine foothills in seasonal hunting camps, gathering birds and berries from the forest and native fish from the waterways. Their close association with the ranges is reflected in the names they have given to peaks, rivers and other park landforms. Early Māori also established various routes across the ranges, although these were used infrequently.

The first European to explore the Ruahine ranges was William Colenso, a zealous missionary, explorer and botanist. During his Ruahine journeys in the mid-1800s, Colenso collected and sent hundreds of native plant specimens to botanists at London's Kew Gardens. The lake and several plants are named after Colenso.

The missionary's epic Ruahine crossings are emulated today by trampers, who sometimes follow marked tracks but often rely on navigation skills and experience to negotiate popular routes along ridge tops and riverbeds. The weather plays a critical part in such journeys as clouded tops and flooded rivers are not conducive to safe travel. There is also scope in the park for

easier walking – many high standard walking tracks leave from a number of road access points.

Cross-country skiing is an occasional park pastime. A ski tow, installed by local enthusiasts in the 1930s on the slopes near Rangiwahia Hut, has long gone. The legacy of those hardy pioneers, along with several other local tramping club enthusiasts who physically carried heavy hut construction materials to sites high on the mountain slopes, lives on in the park's history.

Above: A tent provides supplementary shelter for trampers alongside one of the tiny huts located above the bush line.

Left: Small alpine lakes (tarns) on the open mountain tops can be welcome spots for trampers.

TARARUA FOREST PARK

Natural Wilderness on the City's Edge

From the heart of downtown Wellington, New Zealand's capital city, one can look north and see the craggy peaks of the Tararua Ranges. These sometimes snow-covered mountains, with their tussock tops, dense forests and deep-cut river gorges, make up New Zealand's first proclaimed forest park. The close proximity of this natural wilderness to such a large population has been a major reason why 'the Tararuas' hold a special place in the history of New Zealand's traditional tramping lore.

Tararua Tramping Club, formed in 1919, attracted a number of urban-dwellers seeking to explore the natural world during weekends and holidays, and was the first of many tramping clubs that have since been formed throughout New Zealand. The club eventuated after local, forward-thinking 'tourist committees' developed tracks and encouraged people to appreciate the mountain ranges for their natural and aesthetic qualities, rather than for their value in terms of millable timber.

Soon more Tararua tramping clubs became established, and throughout the early 1900s enthusiastic members cleared tracks and built huts, manually carrying heavy building materials to remote valley or mountaintop sites. Their efforts set the foundation for the very popular track and hut network that extends throughout the park today. Their concerted calls for official conservation measures for the Tararua Ranges led to the formation of the forest park in 1954, thus protecting the water catchments, natural values and recreation values of the ranges.

Despite its popularity, tramping on the Tararua Ranges is fraught with notoriously severe and suddenly changing weather. As the southern limit of the North Island's main divide, the ranges are affected by weather systems from all directions, as many trampers have found to their misfortune. Prevailing northwesterly winds that sweep through Cook Strait bring gales and heavy rainfall, while cold southerly winds dump snow on the southern ranges. Cloud and mist cover the Tararua summits for around 200 days each year, making travel over the tops suitable only for experienced trampers.

Nevertheless, the weather is an essential part of the natural environment, and Tararua's heavy rainfall in protected catchments provides water supplies for surrounding towns. In good weather, the Tararua tops are stunning places in which to wander, and the idyllic river gorges great for wading or swimming. Even if the weather is inclement, the lowland river flats, sheltered valleys and forest walks around the park's margins are suitable for people of all ages and experience who wish to escape the city confines.

Like many of New Zealand's mountains, the Tararua mountain range consists of sedimentary greywacke rocks that have been thrust upwards by fault movement. Four major, parallel fault lines run through the ranges.

Opposite: Silver Beech trees dominate the drier eastern and southern slopes of Tararua Forest Park.

Top right: Speargrass, an alpine plant with a beautiful flower, but needle-pointed spines, can be the bane of walkers on Tararua's upper mountain slopes.

Location: Near the southern end of the North Island.

Climate: Very changeable with high winds throughout. Prevailing moist northwesterlies bring heavy rainfall on the western side; drier on the east. Mild summers, cold winters. Some snow during mid-winter. Cloud and mist on the tops year-round.

When to go: Anytime, though snow sometimes covers high-level tracks in winter.

Access: Several roads lead into the ranges from SH1 on the western side (main access is Otaki Forks) and SH2 on the eastern side (main access is Mt Holdsworth). The main southern access is Marchant Road, 40 minutes' drive north of Wellington City.

Permits/Reservations: Permits are required for hunting, licences for fishing

Facilities: In the park – huts, tracks, bridges, road end picnic and camping areas. Towns and cities surrounding the park provide full services, including a range of accommodation.

Wildlife: Common forest birds plus Paradise Shelduck and New Zealand Falcon. Native land snails.

Landscapes: Mountain ranges, steep ridge lines, tussock tops, beech and podocarp forests, open river flats, river gorges.

Visitor activities: Tramping, short walks, school education camps, camping and picnicking, hunting (for introduced Red Deer), rafting and kayaking, some mountain biking, fishing (introduced trout).

Precautions: Be wary of changeable and stormy weather.

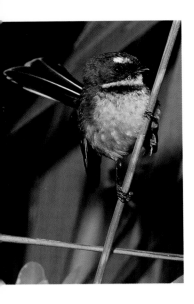

Above: *The fantail is probably the most friendly of all the native birds; it hovers close to forest walkers looking for the insects disturbed by their footsteps.*

Right: *Blue Range Hut, one of an extensive network of huts in the park.*

Below: *Walking the open ridge tops of the Jumbo–Holdsworth route is particularly popular.*

The highest Tararua peaks reach just over 1500 metres (5000 feet). Between the peaks and ridge lines, the easily eroded sediments of the ranges have been washed into streams and rivers by rain and carried away to pile up on river terraces flanking the ranges.

Apart from the Tongariro volcanoes, the Tararua Ranges are the only North Island mountains affected by glaciation. The headwaters of rivers around the highest peaks show the distinctive U-shaped profile typical of past glaciation, and some tarns occupy hollows formed by glacial ice.

In the lower reaches, where rivers break out of the ranges and onto surrounding plains, deep-cut gorges are a feature. While these gorges make great natural swimming holes, they can impede river route tramping for all but the hardiest adventurers – and they can be fearsome when in flood.

Vegetation Contrasts

The Tararua Ranges rise abruptly from the plains, and with their mantle of dense forest, form a marked contrast to surrounding lowland farms. While the foothill forests suffered from milling during the early 1900s, from about 350 metres (1150 feet) upwards the steep slopes are covered with mature forest. On the western side, with its particularly heavy rainfall, dense temperate rainforests of White Pine (kahikatea), Red Pine (rimu) and rātā, mixed with kāmahi, tawa and Silver Beech, give way to a cloud-covered band of thick subalpine shrubs dominated by the gnarled, impenetrable leather-

wood, *Olearia colensoi*. On the drier, eastern ranges Red, Silver and Hard Beech (tawai) dominate then gives way abruptly to open tops of tussocks, herb fields, speargrasses, and flowering alpines such as North Island Edelweiss, which appropriately forms the emblem of the Tararua Tramping Club. Special plants find refuge in the dense forests of the ranges, such as several species of nationally threatened mistletoes.

Some of the most interesting native animals in the park are giant land snails, similar to those found in the Nelson region. Other native curiosities are giant weevils and slugs that live in the subalpine shrubs and snow tussocks, and mostly venture out at night.

It is perhaps an ironical claim to fame that the Tararua Ranges were the last known refuge of the now extinct wattlebird (huia). The last official recording of this species was in 1907 on the track to Mount Holdsworth. The conservation ethic in New Zealand has since turned around. Instead of destroying the habitats of native birds, intensive efforts are now being made to rebuild populations of threatened species by reducing threats to their natural habitats and relocating them to sanctuaries such as offshore islands.

The Tararua Ranges support a diversity of native bird life, such as the tiny forest dwellers Riflemen (tītitipounamu), whiteheads (pōpokatea), Grey Warblers (riroriro), fantails (pīwakawaka) and Yellow-crowned Parakeet kākāriki, while Paradise Shelduck, Pipit (pīhoihoi) and the self-introduced immigrants Spur-winged Plovers and Welcome Swallows are well established on the open river flats. New Zealand Falcon (Kārearea) and North Island kākā are sometimes seen and heard above the forests and flats.

KAPITI ISLAND NATURE RESERVE

A Conservation Success

Kapiti is one of New Zealand's most significant nature reserves and arguably one of the world's most successful conservation stories. The island is a large, predator-free refuge for some of New Zealand's most endangered native birds, and its recent history of forest recovery and predator control has been at the forefront of international conservation achievement.

Kapiti is the only large island sanctuary between Auckland's Hauraki Gulf and Stewart Island. It is also one of the country's more accessible island nature reserves. Each year, several thousand visitors welcome the opportunity to observe prolific birdlife, including many species that are either rare or absent from the mainland.

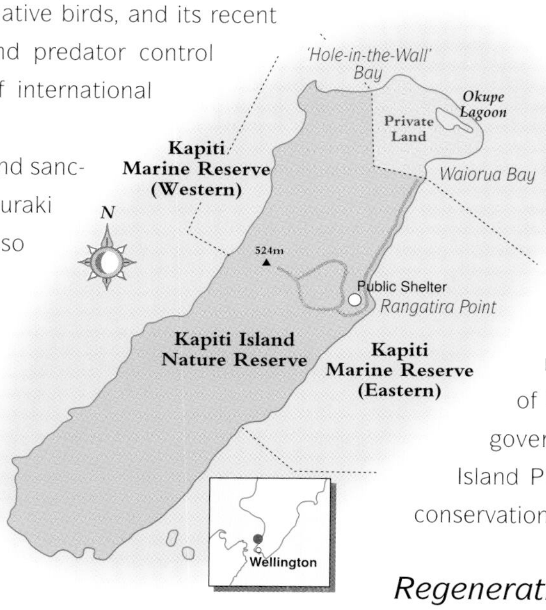

Over the past hundred years, since Kapiti was declared a public reserve, some of New Zealand's most eminent conservationists have been involved in the island's restoration. There has also been strong community support throughout – in recent years, local volunteers and financial sponsors have helped conservation staff tackle the mammoth task of animal predator control. Critical to the Kapiti conservation story has been the support and commitment of three Māori tribal groups (*iwi*) who have a long, traditional association with Kapiti Island. With its long history of Māori occupation, Kapiti is a place of very special significance,

Top right: The honey-eating bellbird may be tiny, but it has a surprisingly loud and resonant birdsong.

both spiritual and strategic, to these *iwi*. Whalers and sealers based themselves on the island during the 1800s, however, it was farming that dramatically changed the island's landscape. While some of the island's virgin forest had been cleared for Māori gardens, farmers in the 1800s drained swamps and destroyed much of the island's forest.

But farming on this isolated, rugged island was never a viable option. In 1897 several far-sighted naturalists, realizing even then the importance of island sanctuaries, persuaded the government to establish the Kapiti Island Public Reserve. Since then, several conservation milestones have been achieved.

Regeneration of an Ecosystem

Kapiti's forests have made a remarkable recovery since the early 1900s and the island is now covered with fast regenerating temperate rainforest. Some huge, ancient Northern Rātā and mataī that survived in deep gullies and steep spurs are surrounded by a forest of kokekohe, tawa and White Teatree (kānuka) and a dense understorey of ferns and shrubs. Forest recovery was helped by the early removal of cattle, sheep, deer, goats, and pigs from the island.

In the early 1900s Little Spotted Kiwi were fortuitously released on Kapiti. Except for the recent release of nine Little Spotted Kiwi into Karori wildlife sanctuary in Wellington, the bird is now extinct on the mainland. A population of about 1000 pairs flourishes on the island. Relocation of endangered birds continued in the 1980s, when North Island Saddleback (tīeke), stitch-

Location: North Island west coast, north of Wellington City.

Climate: Warm summers, cool winters; rain throughout the year.

When to go: Anytime. Birds are most vocal in spring (October–November) but most species are easily seen throughout the year.

Access: Two DOC licensed operators run launch trips from Paraparaumu. Private boats are not permitted to land on Kapiti Nature Reserve.

Permits/Reservations: Visitors require DOC permits. During weekends and summer demand is heavy so apply well in advance (not more than three months in advance). Visitors can be more sure of a booking in winter.

Facilities: Public shelter, toilets, information, walking tracks. Guided walks available. No overnight accommodation.

Visitor activities: Bird watching, photography, walks, picnics.

Wildlife: Prolific birdlife – tui, bellbird, New Zealand Pigeon, North Island Robin, North Island kāka, North Island Saddleback, stitchbird, weka, Red-crowned Parakeet, fantail, whitehead, Long-tailed Cuckoo (summer only), Little Spotted Kiwi (nocturnal)

Landscapes: Hillsides covered with regenerating rainforest (eastern side). Steep, impenetrable bluffs, windshorn shrubs (western side).

Precautions: Inspect your luggage to ensure rats, mice or other animals are not accidentally transported to the island. Launch trips may be cancelled because of rough weather.

Map labels: 'Hole-in-the-Wall' Bay · Okupe Lagoon · Private Land · Kapiti Marine Reserve (Western) · Waiorua Bay · N · 524m · Public Shelter · Rangatira Point · Kapiti Island Nature Reserve · Kapiti Marine Reserve (Eastern) · Wellington

Right: *Bold and raucous kākā parrots, with their vividly coloured underwings, make a lasting impression on visitors to the island.*

Opposite top: *The tenacity of conservation staff who have trekked over the island monitoring the wildlife and controlling animal pests can be appreciated by this aerial view of the island's rugged northwest corner.*

Right: *A colony of ascidians, or sea squirts, live around Kapiti's marine reserve. attaching themselves to surfaces such as rocks.*

Opposite bottom: *As dusk descends over the Tasman Sea, the island reserve resounds with birdsong.*

birds, Blue Wattled Crow (kōkako) and takahē were transferred from threatened mainland habitats and other islands to Kapiti.

In the 1980s, Kapiti's forest recovery was remarkably enhanced by the first ever successful island eradication of possums. In a six-year period an incredible 22,500 possums were removed from the 1,960–hectare (4,843 acres) island.

And the story gets better. In 1996 rats were totally eradicated from Kapiti, in a carefully researched and tightly controlled poison operation that was the largest island rat eradication of its kind in the world. Rats are a major predator of native birds and their raids on nests have been blamed for the critical state of many bird populations. They also cause serious impacts on native forests by eating a range of flowers, fruit and seedlings.

Within months of the Kapiti rat eradication, the forest ecosystem was rejuvenated. Native invertebrates and lizards became more conspicuous and bird numbers rocketed. Saddleback numbers increased from nine pairs to 20, when previously they were declining; while survival of young stitchbirds increased from an average of 33 per cent to 78 per cent. Breeding records for the island's Bush Parrot (kākā) population have also shown healthy improvement, considering 50 per cent of their nests were previously preyed on by rats.

The removal of rats has paved the way for other, highly endangered birds, reptiles and invertebrate fauna to be released on Kapiti, and this internationally acclaimed scientific management of an island ecosystem is now being applied to other large island reserves.

Exploring Kapiti

Kapiti Island is only a 20-minute launch trip from Paraparaumu, on the mainland, and all visitors disembark at Rangatira Point, where there is a DOC residence and public shelter.

The island's prolific and special bird life generally makes its presence known very quickly. Within a five-minute walk from landing, visitors are likely to have come across impressive numbers of New Zealand Pigeon (kererū), woodhen (weka), tui, bellbirds (korimako), North Island Robins, saddleback (tīeke) and kākā. With their size, loud screeching and brightly coloured underwings, the kākā usually make a memorable impression. (Feeding birds is not permitted and kākā are no longer as persistent at begging for food as they once were.) In summer, huge numbers of melodious songsters, tui and bellbirds, feed in frenzies on flowering rātā.

There are three public tracks on Kapiti. Two head uphill and join before reaching the 520-metre high (1707 feet) island summit, Tuteremoana. The return trip takes about three hours, but a quiet, slow walk, with plenty of stops, is recommended to maximize bird-watching opportunities. The third track follows the coast

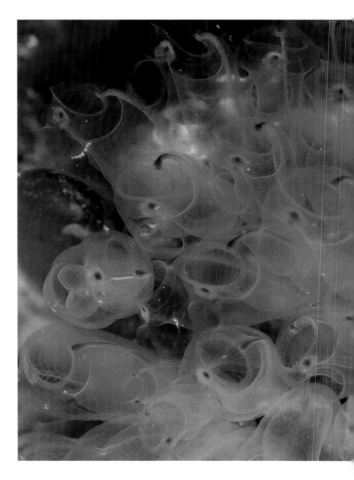

to Okupe Lagoon, at the north end of the island, where resident waterfowl include the Spotless Crake, now uncommon on the mainland. An enclave of privately owned land here belongs to descendants of the island's Māori people.

Kapiti Marine Reserve

This marine reserve protects some of the finest underwater scenery in the Wellington region. Three distinctive marine habitats all exist in close proximity in the reserve. These are the bouldery, sandy and sheltered reef habitats, homes to a variety of sponges, seaweed beds, starfish, corals, shellfish and fish.

Since the establishment of the marine reserve in 1992, marine scientists have recorded significant increases in the size and numbers of fish, abalone (pāua) and rock lobsters. Fish have become relatively tame and rock lobsters will move out of their underwater caves to observe divers that come to view the marine life. Scuba diving is most rewarding on the outer northwestern end of the island, where spectacular underwater features include an interesting rock archway known as the Hole in the Wall. Those with snorkels can explore the rocks close to the shore of Kapiti Island.

SOUTH ISLAND

Te Waka o Aoraki

Mountains, snowfields, glaciers, rugged foothills, vast forests and great glacial-fed rivers and lakes dominate the natural landscape of the South Island. The Southern Alps/Kā Tiritiri o te Moana form the island's great mountainous divide. They are crowned by Aoraki/Mt Cook, New Zealand's highest mountain, which rises to 3754 metres or 12,315 feet.

Ngāi Tahu, the main Māori tribe of the South Island, revere Aoraki as a god. They say the capsized canoe (*waka*) of Aoraki is the South Island, and that Aoraki and his brothers climbed to the high side of their wrecked canoe and became the great mountains of the Southern Alps/Kā Tiritiri o te Moana. The South Island is also known as Te Wai Pounamu ('the land of greenstone') and Te Waka o Māui ('the canoe of legendary fisherman, Māui').

Compared with the North Island, the South Island is sparsely populated. However, cities and towns that line the east coast serve major farming, horticulture and viticulture industries. Tourism is also a major industry in the South Island, with the national parks and other wild places being key attractions for visitors.

Four national parks here make up the Te Wahipounamu/South-west New Zealand World Heritage Site, which encompasses a vast and spectacular natural wilderness of mountains, ice and snowfields, glaciers, luxuriant rainforests, upland beech forests and lakes, fiords and wetlands. There are a total of eight national parks in the South Island, including New Zealand's three largest parks, plus six forest or conservation parks and many other reserves and conservation areas.

On the east coast, seals, penguins, albatross, dolphins and whales are the stars in coastal habitats such as Otago Peninsula, the Catlins and Kaikōura, while on the northern tip of the South Island, bird watchers relish the chance to visit Farewell Spit, one of New Zealand's largest, internationally significant wetlands.

The South Island's well developed tourism infrastructure offers a wide range of accommodation and natural heritage tours that include guided glacier walks and tramping tracks such as the world-renowned Milford Track, in Fiordland National Park. Climbing, skiing, rafting and eco-cruises are also popular visitor activities.

MARLBOROUGH SOUNDS

Forest-fringed Waterways and Islands

A vast labyrinth of waterways, bays, inlets and forest-covered islands and promontories makes up the Marlborough Sounds, at the very northern end of the South Island.

Within this extensive and tangled 1400 kilometres (870 miles) of coastline is a network of island wildlife sanctuaries, one marine reserve and some 50 scientific, scenic and historic reserves. They safeguard over 50,000 hectares (124,000 acres) of native forest, wildlife habitats, marine environments and historic sites. Conservation and ecotourism are happy partners in the Sounds, where sea kayaking, sailing, tramping, short walks and natural heritage cruises are popular visitor activities.

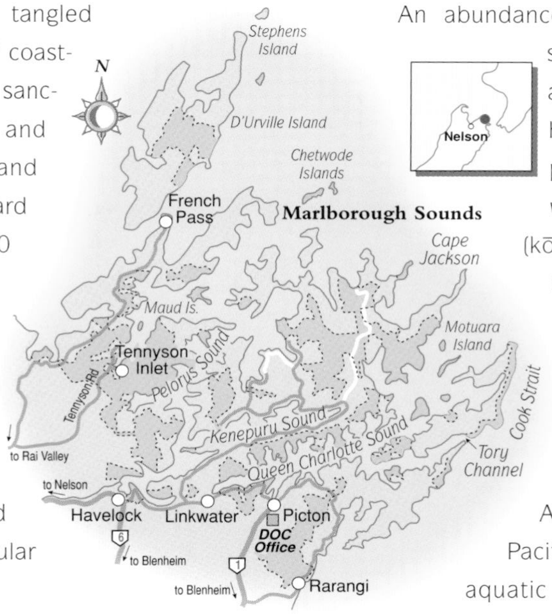

The Sounds are essentially a marine environment: a maze of waterways inhabited by a huge variety of sea birds and marine mammals. New Zealand Fur Seals (kekeno) are common in many areas and Leopard Seals occasionally call from Antarctica. Orca

Opposite: Sunset across the outer Marlborough Sounds, The area is a complex network of waterways, inlets and islands formed when river valleys were drowned by rising sea levels.

Top right: A juvenile saddleback. This species has been saved from extinction by relocation to predator-free areas in the Sounds.

Previous pages:
p82: Dawn breaks over the 'backbone' of the South Island, the mighty Southern Alps/Kā Tiritiri o te Moana.
p83: A Sperm Whale dives off the coast of Kaikōura.

visit annually, migrating Pilot and Humpback Whales (paikea) pass by the outer islands and several dolphin species, including a pod of the world's smallest and rarest Hector's Dolphin live in the Sounds.

An abundance of seafood and numerous sheltered spots for breeding and roosting provide an ideal habitat for sea birds – including petrels (tītī), terns (tara), shearwaters, gulls, gannets, shags (kōau) and Little Blue Penguins (kororā). Many species that live in the Marlborough Sounds are endemic to New Zealand, but there are also a fair number of ocean-going migratory visitors from Siberia, Antarctica, Australia and the Pacific Ocean. The world's rarest aquatic bird, the endangered New Zealand King Shag, lives on a select few isolated reefs and some outer islands.

Island Refuges

The islands of the Sounds are particularly significant from a conservation point of view. Many are the last refuges for some of the world's rarest animals that no longer survive on the mainland because of habitat destruction and the presence of introduced predator pests, such as rodents, cats and possums.

These islands are carefully managed as wildlife sanctuaries, where DOC is working to maintain small populations of rare and unique species. Under the department's care are the Tuatara, New Zealand's 'living dinosaur' that is the sole survivor of a line of reptiles that became extinct elsewhere in the world some 60 million years ago, Maud Island and Hamilton's Frogs, considered two of the world's most primitive and

Map labels: Stephens Island, D'Urville Island, Chetwode Islands, French Pass, Marlborough Sounds, Cape Jackson, Maud Is., Motuara Island, Tennyson Inlet, Tennyson R., Pelorus Sound, Cook Strait, to Rai Valley, Kenepuru Sound, Queen Charlotte Sound, Tory Channel, to Nelson, Havelock, Linkwater, Picton, DOC Office, to Blenheim, to Blenheim, Rarangi, Nelson

Location: The northeastern tip of the South Island

Climate: Mild, sea-warmed temperatures with few frosts. Rain likely throughout the year.

When to go: Anytime. Spring and summer for bird watching.

Access: By road via SH1 from Christchurch and SH6 from Nelson. By sea via Cook Strait ferries from Wellington. By train daily from Christchurch and by air daily flights link Wellington with Blenheim and Koromiko (near Picton). The main entrances to the Sounds are Picton and Havelock.

Permits: Permits are required for landing on the Chetwodes and Maud Island groups. These are issued only through ecotourism operators.

Facilities: Informaton centres, range of accommodation, restaurants and shops are based in the towns of Picton and Havelock. Roads, water taxi and float plane. services provide transport within the Sounds. Sea kayaks, yachts and motorboats available for hire.

Watching wildlife: Sea birds and forest birds. Hector's, Bottlenosed and Dusky Dolphins, New Zealand Fur Seals, plus Orca, Pilot and Humpback Whales .

Landscapes: A tangled maze of waterways, bays, inlets and channels; Beaches, rocky coastline.

Visitor activities: Tramping, scenic drives, sea kayaking, boating, fishing, swimming, mountain biking, hunting, camping, picnicking.

rarest amphibians: Giant Weta, the world's heaviest weta: and several other endemic species of geckos, lizards and insect fauna.

Some of New Zealand's most endangered birds – the large Flightless Parrot (kākāpō), Yellow-crowned Parakeet (kākāriki), takahē, Okarito Brown Kiwi, saddleback (tīeke), Little Spotted Kiwi and South Island Robin – have been deliberately released onto some of these predator-free islands as part of DOC's management programme to protect them from extinction.

Sea birds live on the islands in prolific numbers, and thousands of years of guano deposits have developed fertile soils which now support many plant species that were once widespread before browsing animals were introduced on the mainland.

Several of the island sanctuaries are open to the public without restriction and have good picnic and short walk facilities. Others can be visited only with

licensed ecotourism operators. To protect their fragile environments, landing is not permitted on some of the more remote, outer island groups.

The rocky shores, reefs, sandy floors and open waters of the Sounds make up a complex marine ecosystem and range of habitats for marine life. Protecting a small portion of this is a marine reserve which surrounds Long and Kokomohua islands. To allow the ecosystem here to function naturally, fishing and shellfish gathering are not permitted in this reserve.

On the mainland, more common native birds live throughout the forests, which comprise a varied mix of beech on the higher and drier ridge lines, and lush coastal forest and regenerating Tea Tree (manuka) and White Tea Tree (kanuka) which grow to the water's edge of much of the Sounds coastline.

Mount Stokes (1203 metres, or 3948 feet), the Sounds' highest point, is the region's only subalpine environment and supports species of snow tussock and mountain daisy found nowhere else. A small population of yellowhead, also known as the Bush Canary (mohua), which was once widespread throughout the South Island, also survives on Mount Stokes.

Geological Oddity

Unlike the glacier-gouged fiords of Fiordland at the opposite end of the South Island, the maze of waterways that comprise the Marlborough Sounds are actually drowned river valleys. While the rest of the New Zealand land mass is slowly being pushed upwards, the Sounds represent a geological oddity by sinking, in a process now hastened by rising sea levels.

The Māori people, who have lived in the Sounds for many hundreds of years, have their own way of relating these geological land forming processes. They describe the South Island land mass as the capsized canoe of ancestral explorers, the Marlborough Sounds being the intricately carved prow which shattered and partially sunk when the canoe capsized.

Another story relates to the forest-covered ridge lines as yet uncovered by the drowned river valleys. These are described as the tentacles of Wheke, the octopus who was killed in a mighty battle with the ancestor Kupe. Several Māori tribes settled throughout the Sounds. They made good use of the plentiful food sources (seafood, berries and forest birds) and traded argillite rock – valued material for making tools – from quarries on D'Urville Island. Today tourist lodges, campsites and private holiday homes are scattered throughout the Sounds on the very same places where archaeological remains indicate former Māori occupation. Nothing's changed – those settlers of olden times sought the same north-facing and sheltered waterside locations, close to good fishing spots, as have their holidaying counterparts, hundreds of years later.

During the 1800s the Sounds briefly became one of the Pacific's main whaling ports. Today, little remains of shore-based whaling stations and people come to watch the whales, not kill them. Farming settlers tried but largely failed, to develop the remote, forest-covered outreaches of the Sounds into farmland. Much of the forest they cleared has since regenerated and their laboriously carved bridle paths now form popular tramping and mountain biking tracks.Most popular of these is the Queen Charlotte Walking Track, a 69-kilometre (43 miles) forest walk along the narrow isthmus of land flanked by Queen Charlotte.

Except for holiday homes and a few remote farms, the Sounds themselves are sparsely populated. However, in recent years a comprehensive tourism infrastructure has developed from the local towns. A major industry revolves around aquaculture or the marine farming of Green-lipped Mussels and salmon, which finds its way to many local restaurants.

Left: *A natural heritage cruise visits Motuara, an island reserve that provides sanctuary to rare species such as saddleback birds, green geckos and Maud Island Frogs.*

MOUNT RICHMOND FOREST PARK

The Forgotten Park

Mount Richmond, New Zealand's second largest forest park, is made up of a wilderness of mountain ranges, forests and rivers. In the park is a well developed network of tramping tracks and huts, as well as several short walks, picnic areas, natural swimming holes and historical features that are within easy reach of the nearby cities of Nelson and Blenheim.

Mount Richmond is sometimes referred to as the 'forgotten park'. Despite the wealth of natural features and outdoor recreation it offers, it is a comparatively little visited park. This anomaly is most likely the result of its location in a region well endowed with three national parks and the popular Marlborough Sounds maritime area.

In many ways the park's landscape resembles North Island mountain ranges more than other parts of the South Island. This is largely due to the less extensive glaciation which occurred here, because of the region's drier and more northerly location. Most valleys in the park exhibit the 'V' shape of river erosion, rather than the 'U' shape typical of glacier-carved landscapes. One

exception is the glaciated upper Motueka River, in the southwest of the park. Glaciation has also left its mark on some of the forest park's higher peaks, most notably on the summits of Mounts Fishtail, Rintoul and Richmond.

The park's mountains have an interesting and diverse geological make-up. One of its geological features is the red-tinged Dun Mountain and Red Hills, known as the park's 'mineral belt'. These distinctive regions of iron and magnesium-rich rocks are generally described as 'ultramafic'. Distinctive shrubby, stunted plant communities grow in the harsh, toxic soils of these areas, including many endemic species which have adapted to the peculiar conditions.

Exactly the same rock types are found 500 kilometres (160 miles) to the south, in western Otago. This geological phenomenon is attributed to lateral displacement along the South Island Alpine Fault during the past 25 million years; before then, these two now distant areas were contiguous. The Alpine Fault runs along the Wairau Valley, on the park's southern boundary. Subsequent tilting of the earth's crustal block north of the fault has resulted in the raising of the mountains of the park's Richmond Range, and in the drowning of river valleys to form the Marlborough Sounds, which are situated further to the north.

The presence of mineral-rich rocks throughout the park has resulted in a significant history of mining. Argillite, a hard, metamorphosed mudstone found in the park's mineral belt, was prized by early Māori for its use as sharp-edged tools and weapons. Several argillite 'quarries' were established in the region.

Opposite: Day dawns over the Richmond Range, which lies in New Zealand's second largest forest park, Mount Richmond.

Above right: Mountain daisies are the largest of New Zealand's native plant family. Although they include shrubs and small trees, most native daisies are alpine plants.

Location: In the northeast of the South Island.

Climate: Hot summers, cold winters (frosts, occasional snow on mountain tops), generally drier than most. Frequent summer droughts.

When to go: Anytime (snow sometimes covers the mountain tops in winter).

Access: From Nelson, Havelock and Blenheim, roads turning off SH6 lead into the park. Southern access roads, via North Bank Road, are unsealed and climb through private forests which may be closed during high fire risk periods.

Permits/Reservations: Permits required for hunting (for introduced deer and pigs), licences for fishing (for introduced trout).

Facilities: In the park – huts, tracks, picnic areas, camping areas. Full range of accommodation, shops and services in Blenheim and Nelson.

Wildlife: Most common forest birds, plus South Island Bush Parrot, Mountain Parrot, Yellow-crowned Parakeet, New Zealand Falcon, weka and Blue Duck.

Landscapes: Mountain ranges, broad tussock tops of Red Hills, beech and podocarp forests, glaciated landscape (Motueka River), deeply gorged, blue-green coloured rivers.

Visitor activities: Tramping (for experienced people), day walks, short walks, picnics, mountain biking.

Precautions: Be wary of high wasp populations in summer.

In the mid-1800s Europeans focused on the mining of chromite on Dun Mountain. Chromite was used for dye in the cotton industry. Interestingly, when the American Civil War halted the cotton trade, the English cotton industry collapsed, which in turn led to the demise of chromite mining at Dun Mountain.

Gold mining took its place. Throughout the late 1880s there were three main gold mining regions in what now comprises forest park, the Waikakaho/Cullen Creek area, the north bank of the Wairau River and the Wakamarina Valley which, for its size, was one of the richest gold fields in New Zealand.

Mining activity has left a mixed legacy in the park: regenerating forests, old mine shafts, stonework remains of former mining villages, relics of mining machinery and well-graded miners' trails that now afford easy walking in the park's foothills. Many of these have been maintained by park management, and follow clear-running rivers that are dotted with delightful, emerald-coloured swimming holes.

There are also good mountain biking opportunities on some of these old mining trails. The Wakamarina Track, as well as being popular for weekend tramping, attracts increasing numbers of bikers. For fit and experienced trampers, the park's more remote ridge lines and mountain tops offer scope for multi-day trips, traversing a variety of landscapes with a good network of tracks, poled routes and huts. Two popular walks are the Pelorus Track, encompassing river gorges and changing forests, and what is known as the Alpine Route, which traverses a circuit of peaks and scree slopes above the bush line. Good navigation skills are needed to safely negotiate this latter route, especially in stormy weather and when visibility is poor.

The park's highest peaks stand between 1500 and 1790 metres (4900 and 5870 feet) high, and are sometimes covered with snow in winter. In summer, these peaks represent small 'islands' of tussock and alpine grasslands, with species of flowering hebe shrubs and mountain daisies endemic to the Richmond Ranges.

These 'islands' of tussock tower above beech and, at lower altitudes, mixed podocarp forests. Covering about 85 per cent of the entire park, they provide an extensive habitat for a variety of native birds. The large forest tracts harbour birds such as the New Zealand Falcon and South Island Mountain Parrot.

On short riverside walks near the park fringes, it is sometimes possible to encounter the endangered Blue Duck. Three of the Nelson and Marlborough region's biggest rivers, the Motueka, Pelorus and Waimea, have their origins high in the park and their steep, mountainous characteristics provide ideal habitat for this endangered species.

Another distinctive wildlife habitat is Lake Chalice, which contains a large population of just one species of native fish, kōaro. Lake Chalice, formed by a massive slide which blocked the Goulter River, about 2200 years ago, is completely landlocked, therefore preventing the passage of other, migratory native fish.

NELSON LAKES NATIONAL PARK

Blue Lakes, Beech Forest and Birdsong

Mountains, beech forest, lakes and wide open river valleys: this classical landscape combination so inherent in South Island national parks is particularly well represented at Nelson Lakes National Park.

Situated at the very northern end of the Southern Alps/Kā Tiritiri o te Moana, this park attracts many thousands of people each year with its large number of outdoor recreation opportunities. Tramping, climbing and skiing throughout the park's 75-kilometre long (47 miles) expanse of mountain ranges, boating on the lakes, fishing, camping and wandering along a delightful selection of easily accessible short forest walks are but a few of the most popular activities in the park.

Glaciated Landscapes

Nelson Lakes is named for its two lakes, Rotoiti and Rotoroa (meaning 'small lake' and 'long lake' respectively), which nestle in picturesque grandeur between steep, forest-covered mountains that long ago were thrust upwards by tectonic forces along the South Island's Alpine Fault. The lakes rank as two of the largest in New Zealand with largely unmodified catchments.

Above right: *The sturdy black buttress of a Red Beech tree. Beech forests dominate the lower altitudes of the Nelson Lakes National Park.*

Rotoiti and Rotoroa are also the most obvious legacies which show how the park's landscape has been moulded by the mighty force of ice. Some time between 10,000 and 20,000 years ago, the lakebeds were gouged by glaciers, then filled with water as the ice retreated. The park's major valleys – the Travers, Sabine, D'Urville and Matakitaki – are classical U-shaped, glacier-scoured formations, lined along their entirety by mountain ranges with ice-shaped peaks, cirque basins and alpine meadows where tarns and wetlands have formed in depressions left as the great glaciers retreated.

These ice-sculpted landscapes are enhanced today by vast beech forests that clothe the mountainsides and valley floors. All four of New Zealand's beech species grow in the park's forests, which are filled with the rich and varied greens of subcanopy trees. Also growing here are shrubs and ferns, mosses and lichens that can seem almost fairy-like in the ever-changing light that is so characteristic of beech forests.

Natural Ecosystems

Nelson Lakes' forests support a great diversity of wildlife, including some of New Zealand's more significant and threatened species, such as Long-tailed Bats, Giant Weta and land snails. Visitors are more likely to see the big, playful and colourful Bush Parrots, (kākā), the smaller Yellow-crowned Parakeet (kākāriki), New Zealand's only endemic raptor, the New Zealand Falcon (kārearea), and friendly ground-hopping South Island Robins (kakaruai). The prolific presence of honey-eating tui and bellbirds (korimako) tune in daily for their 'dawn

Location: Near the northern end of the South Island.

Climate: Relatively mild temperatures but with year-round rainfall. Snow in winter. Above the bush line, snow and storms can occur suddenly at any time of the year.

When to go: Summer for tramping, winter for skiing and climbing. Year-round for short walks.

Access: Park headquarters and the main park entrance is at St Arnaud, beside Rotoiti, on SH63. The second main entrance is at Rotoroa, west of St Arnaud.

Permits: Required for hunting, licences for fishing. Available from park headquarters and other DOC offices.

Facilities: Park headquarters and information centre at St Arnaud. Park campgrounds at Rotoiti (St Arnaud) and Rotoroa. Huts, bridges and track network throughout the park, lake jetties. Accommodation, restaurant and shop at St Arnaud, luxury lodge at Rotoroa. Guided walks, fishing and rafting (nearby).

Watching wildlife: South Island Bush Parrot, Mountain Parrot, Yellow-crowned Parakeet, New Zealand Falcon, South Island Robin, Blue Duck, tui and bellbird.

Landscapes: Lakes, mountains, river valleys, beech forest, waterfalls and alpine tarns.

Visitor activities: Tramping, short walks, climbing, skiing, ski touring, fishing, boating. Rafting just outside the park.

Precautions: Insect repellent for sandflies is advisable. Wasps can be a problem from February to April.

chorus'. At about 900 metres (3000 feet) above sea level, the beech forests become stunted, then give way to a wonderful diversity of natural ecosystems that encompass tussock fields, rock and scree slopes, tarns and wetlands and meadows filled with alpine flowers, herbs and grasses. These mountain tops are also the domain of ground-hopping pipits (pīhoihoi), tiny Rock Wren and the kākā's cheeky alpine relation, the Mountain Parrot (kea).

On a good day in summer these are wonderful places for trampers to wander; but in winter they are covered with snow and ice and can be slippery and treacherous. The mountains should be left to those trampers who have specialist climbing expertise.

Above: *Lake Rotoiti is a product of colossal glacial forces. About two million years ago, glaciers scoured out the valleys which then filled with water as the ice retreated.*

Right: *Daybreak on the misty heights of Robert Ridge. Safe walking on the open mountain tops is very weather dependent.*

Legend behind the lakes

The lakes of the park are of special significance to the local Māori people, who have their own way of describing the glacial sculpting of the land. According to legend, Rotoiti and Rotoroa were the first of all the great lakes throughout the South Island to have been created by an ancestral chief named Rākaihautū, who used his digging stick (*kō*) to dig massive hollows in the ground as he travelled southwards through the inland.

Rākaihautū filled these holes with water and food (fish and waterfowl) which later became an important food source for Māori travellers as they passed by on their way to the greenstone supplies of the West Coast. While the lakes and valleys of Nelson Lakes provided routes for early Māori travellers and European explorers, apart from a brief period of farming in some of the lower valleys, this remote mountainous region has been left largely undisturbed by humans.

Outdoor Recreation

Protection of the natural values here has been ensured since the national park was created in 1956. Since that time it has become a popular holiday and outdoor recreation playground.

The park's long river valleys are linked by alpine passes which provide great natural tramping routes that, in good summertime weather, are negotiable by most trampers. Most popular is the two- to four-day

***Below:** Vegetable Sheep, a peculiar, endemic alpine plant so named for its woolly texture, belongs to the daisy family.*

***Overleaf:** New Zealand has one of the richest collections of lichens in the world. This Foliose Lichen, which resembles leaves, grows in Travers Valley.*

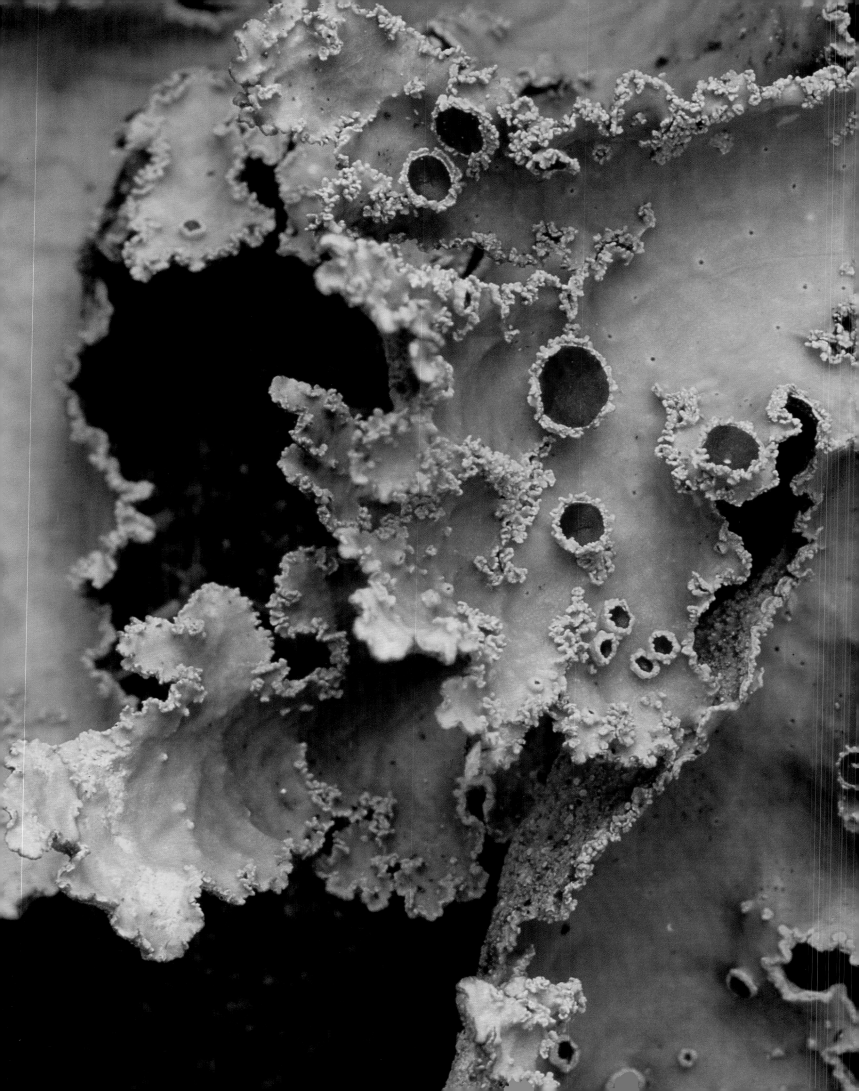

Above: *High in the mountains above the beech forests, cheeky Mountain Parrots (kea) make themselves known to visitors.*

Though it flows outside the park, mention should be made of the wild Buller, or Kawatari River a favourite spot for rafting, kayaking and fishing. Because so much of its catchment is protected, the Buller is the largest, substantially unmodified river in New Zealand.

Revive Rotoiti

One of the South Island's successful conservation stories is occurring in an area of beech forest beside Lake Rotoiti. 'Revive Rotoiti' is one of the first 'mainland island' projects in the country, where the surrounding community and school have thrown their weight behind DOC's goal to restore the region's 'honeydew' beech forests by ridding them of introduced wasps, possums and stoats. The sweet honeydew that gives these forests their distinctive character is produced by small, sap-sucking insects that live in the beech tree trunks. Traditionally this provides food for native birds, insects and lizards, but in recent years has been monopolized by an invasion of introduced wasps. However, the Revive Rotoiti project has quickly made an impact. Within its first two years, wasp numbers have been reduced by 90 per cent and possum numbers cut to nearly zero. Early results include record breeding seasons of the Bush Parrot and increased numbers of South Island Robin. One of the reasons for selecting Rotoiti as a 'mainland island' was its easy access, making it an ideal site to showcase and share the conservation success. New walking tracks, including one suitable for wheelchairs, are sure to entice more visitors to Nelson Lakes than the 90,000 wildlife enthusiasts that it currently attracts a year.

Travers/Sabine circuit. This encompasses open river flats, beech forest, wetlands, waterfalls and tarns, alpine meadows and flowers, and birdlife.

Winter pursuits in the park include mountaineering, skiing and ski touring. The Mount Robert skifield has rope tows and is accessible by a two hour uphill walk or, on weekends only, a helicopter shuttle. At both Rotoiti and Rotoroa, visitors can enjoy recreational boating and sailing, short forest walks and park camping areas.

Right: *Kayaking is a popular and environment-friendly pastime in the park.*

ABEL TASMAN NATIONAL PARK

Golden Sands, Blue Waters

Sweeping golden sands, lagoons, estuaries and sculptured granite headlands, lapped by the sea-blue waters of Tasman Bay, epitomize this very popular coastal park. Each year, thousands of trampers (hikers) follow the gentle forest tracks, cross the estuaries and wander the beaches of the Abel Tasman Coastal Walk, New Zealand's most popular Great Walk. Sea kayakers, sometimes accompanied by seals and dolphins, paddle into inlets, lagoons and on through the waters of Tonga Island Marine Reserve, and camp in remote bays accessible only by sea.

Away from the coast, the park's lesser known uplands are rugged hills covered with beech forest and the dramatic, almost surreal marble karst landscape of Canaan Downs.

Abel Tasman is the smallest of New Zealand's parks and, despite its stunning coastline, arguably the most modified. For several hundred years, Māori people lived along the coast in seasonal fishing and gardening villages. From the mid-1800s European settlers logged forests, quarried granite and burned the hillsides to create pasture. Farming, never a viable option on the harsh granite soils, was short-lived. During the early 1900s

Top right: Despite being the smallest national park in the country, stunning golden beaches and clear waters make Abel Tasman one of the most popular.

people from the Nelson region, attracted by the charms of the coastline, established holiday homes in the bays and inlets. Their concern over logging operations, spearheaded by local conservationist Perrine Moncrieff, inspired a successful campaign, which led to the creation of a national park.

The park, established in 1942, was named after Dutch explorer Abel Tasman, the first European to visit New Zealand. His short stay was marred by a fatal skirmish with Māori people along the coastline, resulting in the death of four of his ship's crew members.

Today, the coastal hills are covered with regenerating manuka and kanuka (tea tree species) forests, mixed with some Black Beech. In the more fertile, damp coastal gullies where regeneration is faster, a richer variety of broadleaf shrubs, tree ferns, vines and kiekie (a climbing plant of the Pandanus family, with long leaves prized by Māori for weaving) thrives. Tui, bellbirds (korimako), fantails (pīwakawaka) and Wood Pigeon (kererū) are the main forest birds; riflemen (tītitipounamu), Bush Parrots (kākā), Mountain Parrots (kea), Yellow-crowned Parakeets (kākāriki) and South Island Robins (kakaruai) are also present.

The most well known area is the park's coastline. Weathering and wave action of the granite, which forms the bedrock of the park, has sculpted diverse and distinctive landforms: islands, reefs, rock stacks, wave-cut platforms, rounded boulders and rocky headlands.

Location: Northern coast of the South Island.

Climate: High sunshine hours, hot summers, mild winters. Rain year-round. Slightly colder on the upland areas.

When to go: Anytime. Summer is particularly popular.

Access: Several access points by road. Regular bus services run to Marahau, Wainui and Totaranui and water taxis are available along the park's eastern coastline.

Permits/Reservations: Hut bookings are required for the Abel Tasman Coastal Walk during summer. Bookings also required for the Totaranui campground between December 20 and January 31.

Facilities: Tracks (trails), huts, camping areas, a visitor centre at Totaranui (staffed during summer) and serviced camping ground with boat ramp and water-ski lane. Takaka and Motueka are the nearest towns, with shops, restaurants, motels, hotels and DOC visitor centres. Sea kayaking guides and equipment, coastal cruises and guided walks are available.

Wildlife: New Zealand Fur Seals, Little Blue Penguins, Common and Bottlenose Dolphins, sea birds, wading birds and forest birds.

Landscapes: Golden beaches, granite headlands and rock forms, islands, estuaries, lagoons, sandspits, coastal forest, beech forest, marble karst (sinkholes, fluted rock, caves).

Visitor activities: Tramping, short walks, sea kayaking, sailing, swimming, snorkelling, diving, seal viewing, coastal cruises, camping.

Right: The park is blessed with beautiful bush-lined bays such as Te Pukatea Bay, The Anchorage and Torrent Bay.

The park's famous golden beaches have been formed of sparkling weathered particles of quartz, mica and golden feldspar, minerals eroded from granite and carried to the sea by streams, then swept along the coast by currents and tides. The 4-metre (13 feet) tidal range here is one of the highest in the country. The park's characteristic crescent bays were eroded from basins of less resistant rock between ridges of harder rocks. The overall result is an intricate variety of sand-spits and bars such as those at Torrent Bay and Bark Bay, shallow estuaries like Awaroa, and a golden procession of crescent-shaped beaches, such as Totaranui, Tonga Bay and Anchorage.

No other place in New Zealand contains the plant and animal communities of the park's sheltered coastline. Barnacles, periwinkles, tubeworms and sea-weeds occupy tidal bands, underwater seaweeds are grazed by sea urchins and cat's eye univalves, while underwater reefs support bryzoans – coral-like colonies of tiny, tentacled animals which are important habitats for fish.

Estuaries contain salt marsh vegetation such as rushes, sea primroses and dense mats of the Red-tipped Glasswort plant. These sandy places are home to many fish, snails, worms and crabs, which are food for wading birds such as Oystercatchers, Pied Stilts, White Faced Herons plus threatened bitterns, Banded Rail and Reef Herons (matuku moana). Woodhen (weka) and fernbirds (mātā) also frequent the wetland areas. Sea birds such as Caspian and White-fronted

Below: A Blue Cod rests in the clear waters off Tonga Island Marine Reserve, propped characteristically on its pelvic and caudal fins.

Terns (tara), gulls, shags (kōau), fluttering shearwaters and Australasian Gannets dive offshore for fish.

The park's rivers and streams, which are mostly tea-coloured from tannins leached from the soil, are an important habitat for kōkopu (an adult form of galaxiid, or whitebait) and other native freshwater fish. Introduced trout, which prey on and compete with these native fish, prefer clear water and are rarely seen in the park's waterways.

Tonga Island Marine Reserve

In 1993 a marine reserve was created adjacent to the park. Tonga Island Marine Reserve protects a marine area of nearly 2000 hectares (4942 acres) which encompasses islands, reefs, estuaries and 12 kilometres (7.8 miles) of coastline. Now that all fishing has stopped, populations of more common inshore fish such as wrasse, Blue Cod, snapper, Tarakihi and Moki, are expected to increase.

Within the reserve, Tonga Island provides a refuge for New Zealand Fur Seals (kekeno) and Little Blue Penguins (kororā), and native plants that are becoming rare on the mainland, such as the large-leafed whau and taupata, one of New Zealand's divaricated coprosma shrub species.

Above: The less used northern circuit of the park's coastal track offers more beautiful bays and golden beaches but without the crowds of the southern section.

Left: Sea kayakers take a breather on Onetahuti Beach in Tonga Island Marine Reserve.

A Strange Karst Landscape

While much of the focus of Abel Tasman centres on the coast, the inland high country also contains significant natural features and dramatic landforms.

Canaan Downs sits at the northern end of a thick belt of ancient marble rock that extends through neighbouring Kahurangi National Park. The associated karst landscape, created by the dissolving action of water on the rock, contains strange and striking landforms – fluted rock, sinkholes, caves, vanishing streams and a complex subterranean drainage system.

A park road winds to the heart of Canaan Downs and a short track leads to Harwoods Hole, a 176 metre (577 feet) sinkhole which is the deepest vertical drop in the country. Although it is impossible to see far into this chasm, adventurous cavers relish the challenge of abseiling into its dark depths. A lookout nearby compensates with excellent views across fluted marble outcrops. The park's Inland Track penetrates the forested uplands of the park. This two- to three-day track is rougher and

steeper than the Coastal Walk, but rewards trampers with constantly changing forest types and excellent lookout points. A feature of this walk is Moa Park, a small enclave of Red Tussock, alpine herbs and flowers that is the only subalpine area in the park.

FAREWELL SPIT NATURE RESERVE AND PUPONGA

Sand, Wind and Wading birds

This narrow, windswept sandspit, which stretches nearly 30 kilometres (19 miles) away from the northern tip of the South Island, is an internationally recognized bird sanctuary. Over 90 species of birds have been recorded here, including an estimated one-third of all the hundreds of thousands of migratory birds that fly to New Zealand each year to escape the Northern Hemisphere winter. The reserve has been officially acknowledged by the United Nations' Nature Resources Ramsar Convention (which aims to recognize and protect wetlands of international importance) as a wetland of worldwide significance.

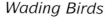

Puponga Farm Park, at the base of Farewell Spit, is known for its dune lakes, swamps, spectacular coastal formations and superb short walks.

Farewell Spit/Onetahua

Farewell Spit, appropriately named Onetahua ('heap of sand') by the Māori people, is the largest sandspit in the country. At high tide it extends for nearly 30 kilometres (19 miles) and is about 1 kilometre (half a mile) wide, but as the tide recedes it expands tenfold. At low tide a vast 9000 hectares (22,240 acres) of beach and sandflats are uncovered, over a width of up to 10 kilometres (6 miles).

The sand of the spit has its origins in mountains well to the south. Eroded granites, schists and other rocks are ground to small particles, carried by rivers to the sea

Above right: Farewell Spit, New Zealand's largest sandspit, is the summertime home of hundreds of thousands of migrant birds.

and swept north by strong Westland currents. Then the winds take over, sweeping sand along and across the spit, both building and destroying dunes in an ever-changing landscape. This process, which began some 14,000 years ago after the end of the last ice age still continues, with an estimated 3000 to 4000 cubic metres (141,260 cubic feet) of new sand deposited on the spit each year.

Wading Birds

The sandy beaches, low dunes, tidal flats, shellbanks and saltmarsh of the spit are prime habitats for wading birds; the crabs, worms, molluscs, sand hoppers and myriad other tiny life they contain provide a veritable 'buffet' for the birds.

Of all the bird species on the spit, the summer migrants create the most fascination. Generally up to 100,000 Bar-tailed Godwits (kūaka) and 70,000 Red Knots (huahou) spend their summer in New Zealand. Of these, around 15,000 Godwits and 9000 Red Knots settle along Farewell Spit, joined by 1000 Ruddy Turnstones and 600 Banded Dotterels. Rarer migrant waders include wrybills, Mongolian Dotterels, Eastern Curlews, Wimbrels and Grey-tailed Tattlers.

Each year, these waders depart from their Northern Hemisphere summer breeding grounds in the Alaskan and Siberian tundras and embark on one of the most amazing migrations ever known. Catching tail winds, using inborn navigation systems and flying in energy-saving V-formations at speeds of 80 kilometres per hour (50 miles per hour) at altitudes of 5000 metres (16,400 feet), the birds complete a journey of 12,000 kilometres (7450 miles). These birds cannot land on the sea, so they fly up to 4000 kilometres (2500 miles) at a

Above: *On the beach at Fossil Point, Puponga, blocks of mudstone that have fallen off sea cliffs are filled with fossilized shells.*

pare for their return journey with mass practice flights and feeding frenzies, 'stocking up' for the arduous journey ahead. (During one March, a Red Knot was observed eating 1000 small shellfish and snails in a single day.) A small number of migratory birds stay behind, wintering over with other species who live and breed on the spit.

New Zealand Migrants and Waders

Southern Black-backed Gulls have established two colonies in the sand dunes on the spit. Caspian Terns, the biggest terns in the Southern Hemisphere, and the smaller White-fronted Terns (tara) nest on shell-banks at the far end of the windswept spit alongside a recently established colony of Australasian Gannets. Gannet numbers have increased dramatically in New Zealand in the last 50 years. The new sea-level gannet colony at the spit differs from that of the rock stack and headland terrain normally preferred by gannets, and was almost wiped out during a cyclone in 1997. Only 50 chicks survived the storm, but by the year 2000 nearly 2000 pairs were recorded at the colony.

Farewell Spit is also an important feeding ground for New Zealand Waders. Variable Oystercatchers establish territories in pairs along the outer beach. Banded

time and rest at stopping-off points throughout Asia. In New Zealand they are protected birds and often live in wildlife sanctuaries. However, during their migratory journey, they negotiate a gauntlet of unprotected and threatened habitats. Once on Farewell Spit, the birds feed on the intertidal zones at low tides and roost in the dunes at high tides. When March approaches, they pre-

Dotterels, South Island Pied Oystercatchers and Pied Stilts, which breed in the braided rivers and wetlands of the South Island, prefer to spend winter in the milder climes of the spit.

A Trap for Whales

Farewell Spit has historically proven a disastrous trap for migratory whales, possibly because their sonar systems cannot detect the low-lying sandspit. In 1991, 325 Pilot Whales beached themselves near the base of the spit. This incident became one of the most successful whale rescues in the world when, after prolonged vigilance, DOC staff and volunteers were able to refloat 312 of the stranded mammals.

Ships have also experienced difficulties negotiating the low-lying spit. Following a series of 10 shipwrecks in 40 years, a lighthouse was erected in 1870 near the end of the spit. Lighthouse keepers and their families lived on-site in what was one of New Zealand's most isolated communities. This changed only in 1984 when operation of the light became fully automatic. A mail service started for the lighthouse families in 1946 has since evolved into an ecotour safari service. Today the area is a DOC-protected nature reserve, falling into its strictest category of conservation protection and access is firmly restricted to licensed tourist trip operators, fishermen who hold permits and approved scientific groups.

Puponga Farm Park

The 470-hectare (1160 acres) Puponga Farm Park provides a link between Farewell Spit Nature Reserve and the adjoining Kahurangi National Park. The park has several great walking tracks – some run across cliff tops with panoramic views over Farewell Spit and Golden Bay, others to the dramatic rock arches and seascapes of Wharariki Beach and Fossil Point, and across the base of the spit itself.

Remnant coastal forest located within the park contains colonies of rare Powelliphanta Land Snails, while birds such as Marsh Crake, Bitterns and Fernbirds (mātā) live in the swamps and wetlands. Sea birds, Little Blue Penguins (kororā) and New Zealand Fur Seals (kekeno) live on the beaches of Wharariki and Fossil Point.

Extensive middens ('rubbish heaps' of shell and bone) and other archaeological evidence at Puponga Farm Park tell of long periods of occupancy by early Māori people. The region was popular for its strategic location and plentiful food sources.

Bottom left: *Appropriately named Onetahu (heap of sand) by the Māori people, Farewell Spit is made up of eroded rock from the mountains further south, which is swept to sea by rivers and along the coast by ocean currents.*

Bottom centre: *Faultlines and constant wave erosion create caves along the coastal cliffs of Puponga Farm Park.*

Bottom right: *Each summer, tens of thousands of wading birds fly to Farewell Spit from their Northern Hemisphere breeding grounds, resting on the way at stopping points throughout Asia.*

KAHURANGI NATIONAL PARK

Marble Mountains

Kahurangi, New Zealand's second largest national park, contains some of the most outstanding natural landforms, habitats, and plant and animal communities of any of New Zealand's protected conservation areas.

Visitors are attracted to the park by its special landscapes and vast wilderness. The park covers much of the northwest corner of the South Island and extends all the way from alpine tops and tablelands through valleys, lakes and forests to the remote and rugged west coast. Tramping options range from the historic Heaphy Track, one of New Zealand's Great Walks, to remote wilderness routes. Caving, day walks, fishing (for introduced trout) and river rafting are other activities for which the park is popular.

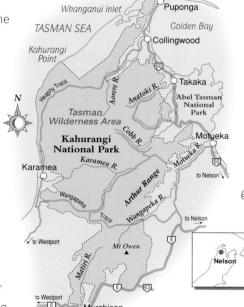

Sculpted Landforms

Kahurangi's geology is fascinating and complex. Within the park are New Zealand's oldest rocks, fossils and landforms. Also evident are the finest marble karst landscapes

Opposite: The Oparapara limestone arch is one of Kahurangi's many distinctive and dramatic karst landscape formations.

Above right: The habitat range of Kahurangi National Park provides sanctuary for 18 species of native birds, including the New Zealand Pigeon, which has become threatened in other areas.

and the longest, deepest and oldest cave systems. Three basic rock types – sedimentary, metamorphic and igneous – are present, as are the influences of glaciation and tectonic movement.

Marble mountains and associated karst landscapes are a distinctive feature, characterized by fascinating landforms: curiously fluted rock, arches, sinkholes, shafts, caves and disappearing and reappearing streams. The magnificent Mount Owen massif and more readily accessible Mount Arthur are considered outstanding examples of glaciated marble landforms. Mount Owen (1875 metres, or 6154 feet) is the highest peak in the park, though Kahurangi's mountains are not high compared with mountains of the main divide, further south.

Mounts Owen and Arthur are also known as the 'mountains with plumbing'. Underground, water has slowly dissolved the marble to create extensive underground drainage systems that contain their own, special ecosystems and have become a mecca for international speleologists, or cavers. The Nettlebed passages under Mount Arthur reach a depth of 889 metres (2918 feet), which is the deepest cave system in the Southern Hemisphere. The longest is the Bulmer system beneath Mount Owen, where over 40 kilometres (25 miles) of passages have been surveyed, with plenty yet to explore.

Further west the Honeycomb Caves in Oparara Valley, near Karamea, contain a 'treasure chest' of sub-fossil bird remains, dating back 20,000 years and including bones of several species which are now extinct,

Location: In the northwest of the South Island.

Climate: Milder than more southern parks. Snow can fall throughout the year and the highest levels are snowbound in winter. Inland, heavy frosts are frequent. Heavy rainfall.

When to go: Anytime. However, some tramping routes may be snowbound in winter.

Access: Nelson, the nearest city, is served by daily road and air services. From Nelson drive west on SH60 or southwest on SH6 to the park region. Roads lead to the park from Motueka, Takaka, Murchison and Karamea (some are steep, unsealed and subject to flooding or snow). Small operators offer air services to Motueka, Takaka and Karamea.

Permits/Reservations: Permits required for hunting, licences for fishing of introduced trout

Facilities: There are DOC visitor centres and a full range of accommodation services in Nelson and in the towns surrounding the park. The park offers camping and picnic areas, huts, shelters and walking tracks. Guided tramping, walking, rafting, fishing, hunting and caving tours are available. Air and road shuttle services operate for the Heaphy and Wangapeka Tracks.

Wildlife: Great Spotted Kiwi (roa), Mountain and Bush Parrots plus common forest birds, sea birds, land snails, Giant Weta.

Landscapes: Marble karst formations, glaciated landforms, alpine tops, tablelands and downs. Beech and podocarp forests, coastal rainforests. Alpine tarns, lakes, wetlands, coastline of beaches and bluffs, river valleys, vistas of great mountainous expanse.

Visitor activities: Tramping, day walks and short walks, caving, rafting/kayaking, fishing and hunting.

Above left to right:

Kahurangi has an incredible diversity of plants, with over 1200 different native species: Mountain Daisy (Celmisia traversii); a flowering coastal shrub (Hebe Elliptica); and a subalpine hebe are just some of the plants that flourish here.

such as the moa (one of the tallest birds that ever lived). Above ground, spectacular marble arches are within easy walking distance from the nearest road end.

There are more geological curiosities. The Mount Arthur tablelands, Gouland Downs (on the Heaphy Track), Gunner Downs and Matiri Plateaux are remnants of ancient peneplains, the oldest landforms in New Zealand. Granites of the park are similar to those in Fiordland, 450 kilometres (280 miles) to the south, because some 25 million years ago the two regions

were contiguous before lateral earth movement along the South Island's Alpine Fault shifted Fiordland southwards. Glacier-formed landscapes are also a feature of Kahurangi, particularly in the Cobb Valley, which offers fine examples of cirque lakes, U-shaped valleys and moraines.

Floral Diversity

This geological complexity is the basis of the park's huge range of natural ecosystems, and plantlife is incredibly diverse. Growing within Kahurangi are more than half

Left: *Marble karst formations on Kahurangi's Mount Owen massif.*

of New Zealand's 2500 native plant species, over 80 per cent of all alpine species, of which 67 species are found nowhere else and 50 species are considered rare or endangered.

The park's greatest plant diversity is found on the alpine tops. Because this region largely escaped New Zealand's most recent period of glaciation, it was a major refuge for many plants and creatures destroyed by great ice sheets in other areas.

Many of New Zealand's forest types grow in Kahurangi. Beech (tawai) forests cover the drier inland valley slopes, lofty podocarps with luxuriant understoreys fill western valleys, and forests of an almost subtropical nature, featuring nikau palms, tree ferns and the climbing plant kiekie, flourish along much of the coast. At higher altitudes are subalpine forests of distinctive *Dracophyllum traversii* (neinei) and Mountain Cedar (kaikawaka).

Wildlife Wonders

Similarly, the great habitat range provides sanctuary for an abundance of animal species, many unique to this region. There are 18 species of native birds, including several threatened species. The park is one of three remaining strongholds in New Zealand of the Great Spotted Kiwi (roa). The large size of the park means it is well suited to birds that range widely, such as the South Island Bush Parrot (kākā), Mountain Parrot (kea) and New Zealand Falcon (kārearea). Yellow-crowned Parakeet (kākāriki) live among the mid-altitude beech forests, rare Blue Duck (kōwhiowhio) frequent remote,

swift-flowing rivers, Rock Wren inhabit rocky outcrops above the bush line while fernbirds (mātā) and ground-foraging weka dwell in western wetland regions known as pakihi. Visitors are most likely to encounter a number of the more common birds that live in the park, for example, the songster bellbirds (korimako) and tui, and sociable South Island Robins (kakaruai).

Kahurangi is also a stronghold for half of New Zealand's 40 species of native land snails. These ancient, carnivorous creatures from the *Powelliphanta* genus have evolved over 80 million years and have adapted to various environments. They shelter from prey during the day and feed at night, on worms that grow up to a metre

Left: *Kahurangi is one of only three remaining strongholds in New Zealand for the Great Spotted Kiwi (roa).*

Opposite bottom: *Cobb Valley, one of the park's classic glacier-shaped landscapes. A road leads to the valley's reservoir, which features camping areas and the start of several tramping trails in the park.*

(3 feet) in length. There is a host of other wildlife in the park, including Long- and Short-tailed Bats, four species of gecko, Giant Weta and 12 native fish species. Many of the park's rivers have remained free from introduced trout, an unusual situation in mainland New Zealand today and therefore of special ecological value. New Zealand Fur Seals (kekeno), Little Blue Penguins (kororā) and other sea birds live along the park's remote coastline.

Living underground, in Kahurangi's extensive cave systems, are more rarities – tiny, blind and colourless invertebrates known as troglobites and New Zealand's largest spider, the Kahurangi Cave Spider. This spider, which is also one of the world's rarest, has a leg span of up to 12 centimetres (4.7 inches).

Tramping in the Park

Previous grazing and mining, together with hydroelectric power development, have had some impacts on peripheral areas of Kahurangi. However, many visitors are attracted to the park by its vast wilderness. Most of Kahurangi's near half a million hectares (1.2 million acres) remains nature's own territory. In the heart of the park is the Tasman Wilderness Area, an 87,000-hectare (215,000 acres) expanse of remote valleys, lakes, gorges and mountains where special protection decrees no development of any kind – not even tramping huts or tracks. In other areas, where huts and tracks are allowed, wilderness is still a feature. Some tracks are marked only by occasional poles and good navigation skills are necessary.

Right: *Lower Grid-Iron Rock shelter in Takaka Valley is designed and built by the hand of nature, albeit with some modifications. This shelter is used by trampers.*

Nevertheless, this huge park is also blessed with several high-standard walking tracks, huts, shelters and, at major access points, interpretive information.

The Heaphy Track is one of New Zealand's oldest and most popular tramping trips. Local Māori people followed this route to the coast for hundreds of years; gold prospectors developed it further in the late 1800s and the first Heaphy Hut was built in 1907. Today, some 4000 people walk the 78-kilometre (49 miles) track each year, traversing forests, tussocked downs, river valleys and beaches.

Other popular places with good road access for short walks and tramping routes are Mount Arthur, Cobb Valley, Wangapeka Valley and Karamea.

Above: Trident Hut, one of the 62 park huts in Kahurangi, nestles beside Adelaide Tarn high on the Douglas range.

Left: The Kahurangi Caves support unique animal life, such as this Cave Spider, one of the world's rarest and most ancient spider species. It is also the biggest native spider in New Zealand.

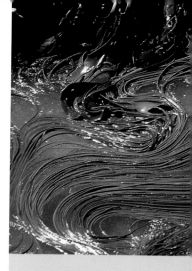

KAIKŌURA

Marine Mammal Haven

There are few places with such a huge diversity of marine life so readily accessible to people and existing in such a spectacular natural setting, as Kaikōura.

Here, visitors can catch a glimpse of a giant whale as it frolicks in the sea, swim with dolphins, or simply wander the rocky peninsula coastline where seals sleep, gambol or swim and sea birds nest in their thousands against an impressive mountain backdrop.

Whales are the primary drawcard. Sperm Whales (paraoa) browse closer to shore at Kaikōura than anywhere else in the world while Humpbacks (paikea), Pilot Whales and Orca call to feed during seasonal migrations. Dusky, Common, Hector's and sometimes Bottlenose Dolphins inhabit these waters. New Zealand Fur Seal (kekeno) colonies line the coast. Gulls, shags (kōau) and terns (tara) congregate in coastal colonies, rafts of Hutton's Shearwaters (tītī) can be seen throughout summer, while Australasian Gannets (takapu) and Royal Albatross (toroa) from as far away as the Subantarctic Islands feed offshore. Kaikōura boasts this incredible abundance of wildlife because of its unique marine environment.

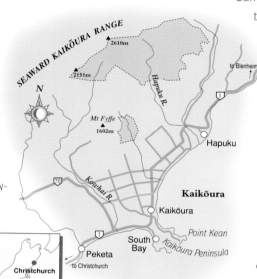

Opposite: A Sperm Whale dives to the ocean depths while the Seaward Kaikōura Ranges reach skywards. Kaikōura is one of the few places where Sperm Whales come so close to shore.

Top right: Underwater forests of Giant Bull Kelp provide shelter for the fish that live around the coast of Kaikōura Peninsula.

Sea Canyons and Currents

One kilometre (half a mile) offshore, the seabed plunges into deep canyons known as the Hikurangi Trench, part of a marine ravine system that extends from Kaikōura to Samoa in the South Pacific. Living in these canyons are deep-water fish and giant squid, favoured food of the Sperm Whale.

Just offshore sea currents meet – warm, subtropical currents that mingle with cold, nutrient-rich waters from southern climes and are energized by the sun. This sets in motion a complex food chain that supports the diverse marine life. Starting with microscopic phytoplankton, the tiniest of living organisms, the chain moves along to zooplankton (crabs, worms and krill), then small fish, sea birds, seals and larger fish, to sharks, dolphins and, eventually, the whales.

From Killing to Conserving

When Kaikōura was established in the mid-1800s, killing whales was the economic mainstay of the township. At the same time, seal populations along this and other New Zealand coastlines were hunted almost to extinction for their skins. The Māori name, Kaikōura, refers to the eating of yet another local sea creature, the rock lobster (kōura).

Fortunately, the tide has turned. Since 1978, all marine mammals have been legally protected in New Zealand and strict quota restrictions have been imposed on commercial fishing. Kaikōura has once again become a safe and attractive feeding ground for marine life, and whale and seal populations are still increasing.

Location: On the east coast of the South Island.

Climate: Mild but prone to cool sea breezes.

When to go: Year-round. Summer is preferable for swimming with seals and dolphins. In winter the mountain backdrop will usually be snow-covered. Sperm Whales can be seen throughout the year, Humpback Whales are most active in June and Orca visit year-round, but mostly October to December.

Access: By road, SH1, 2.5 hours' drive from Christchurch, 2 hours' drive from Picton. Daily rail and bus services. By air, daily flights from Christchurch via Whale Watch Air.

Permits: None required, but fishing and shell fishing limits apply.

Facilities: Kaikōura township has a full range of services – restaurants, shops and accommodation. The visitor centre provides interpretative audio-visual presentations and displays. Natural heritage tours – whale watching, swimming with dolphins and seals, shark diving, fishing tours, etc.

Landscapes: Seascapes framed by a backdrop of snow-capped mountains. Rocky coastline, wave-cut tidal platforms, limestone formations, coastal forest.

Watching wildlife: Sperm Whales and possible Pilot Whales, Humpbacks and Orca. Dusky, Common, and Hector's Dolphins, New Zealand Fur Seals, rock lobster, sea birds, occasional Yellow-eyed Penguins.

Visitor activities: Whale watching and dolphin watching, swimming with dolphins and seals, sea bird watching, short walks, surfing, snorkelling, and scuba diving.

Below: *Dolphin watch cruising – visitors to Kaikōura may also swim with dolphins provided they follow strict guidelines not to disturb them.*

Bottom: *Tidal platforms on the Peninsula Walkway.*

Now, people come to see and appreciate the marine mammals, not kill them. Ecotourism, along with farming and fishing, has become the backbone of Kaikōura's economy. A plethora of whale watching cruises and flights, dolphin 'encounters', 'swimming with seals', and bird-watching tours – all carefully monitored by DOC to ensure the marine mammal life is not disturbed – attract thousands of visitors each year from around the globe.

In conjunction with this tourism development, intensive research has been undertaken to ensure commercial whale and dolphin watching ventures do not jeopardize the ecosystem that sustains them and keeps them close to Kaikōura. Research on Kaikōura's unique marine environment – in particular the marine canyons, whales and giant squid – has been undertaken by international agencies, including National Geographic and the Smithsonian Institute.

The company Whale Watch Kaikōura, which has won international tourism awards, is owned by the Ngai Tahu tribe. Ngai Tahu people have lived around Kaikōura for several hundred years, utilizing the rich natural food sources and developing a legacy of colourful history and legendary ancestors. Over recent years, development of the whale watching venture has provided employment for young tribal members and played a major part in revitalizing Kaikōura township. And

what's more, the company promises a 95 per cent chance of seeing a whale – while no whale sightings incur a generous refund.

Peninsula Walkway

Near the township, the Peninsula Walkway is a great place to observe marine wildlife. Here, as nutrient-rich ocean waters nourish reef systems and rock pools, forests of giant Bull Kelp (rimurapa) shelter reef fish and shellfish. A colony of New Zealand Fur Seals (kekeno) lives on the tidal platforms and huge colonies of sea birds, in particular Red Billed Gulls (tarapunga) and White-fronted Terns (tara), cover the promontories and cliffs.

The peninsula was once an island, but has been joined to the mainland by debris eroded from the mountains behind it. Over thousands of years the peninsula's limestone sediments have been twisted, uplifted, and exposed, while softer sandstones have been washed by the sea, leaving dramatic landforms of bluffs, promontories, and wave-cut tidal platforms.

Inland

The Kaikōura Ranges dominate the coastline. Travelling the highway which runs the narrow gauntlet between wild, rocky coastline and these steep, often snow-covered mountains is a spectacular experience.

Isolated from the main alpine fault that built the Southern Alps/Kā Tiritiri o te Moana, the Kaikōura ranges are young, unstable and undergoing the fastest uplift of any New Zealand mountains. They provide habitat for many endemic species, including the Marlborough Rock Daisy, the rare Black-eyed Gecko and several species of weta. Hutton's Shearwater (tītī) feed at sea but nest in burrows high in these often snowy mountains. The other five shearwater species found in New Zealand live on offshore islands and nest close to the coast.

The Seaward and Inland Kaikōura ranges present a range of opportunities for walking, tramping, and climbing. Close to the township, several DOC walks pass through coastal forest, while superb views are the reward after the walk to the Mount Fyffe summit (1602 metres; 5258 feet).

The Inland Kaikōura Range presents more challenging and remote tramping and climbing, suitable only for those with experience. Further north is Molesworth Station, New Zealand's largest farm which, with its extensive, high country setting, also contains large areas of significant conservation value.

VICTORIA FOREST PARK

A Geological Jigsaw

Victoria is New Zealand's largest forest park and protects a huge expanse of granite mountains, beech (tawai) forest and special ecological features in addition to a rich cultural history.

The park is dominated by the Victoria and Brunner Ranges, bounded by the Buller, Inangahua, Grey and Maruia rivers, and blanketed with some of New Zealand's finest beech forest. Mineralization within the park has led to a heritage of gold and coal mining, and the region has been the cornerstone of national conservation battles to protect native beech forests from logging.

Ironically, Victoria also rates as one of the country's least well known parks, possibly due to the fact that major tourist flows are directed towards the region's national parks. Yet the park is encircled by major highways, from which a network of old mining roads and tracks now serve as excellent walking, mountain biking and four-wheel-driving opportunities. Whitewater rafting, kayaking and fishing, for introduced trout, are popular activities on the park's rivers.

While the park's fringes have been affected by intensive mining activity and associated forest clearance, the Victoria Range is largely untracked and unmodified. Thrust upwards by movements of the earth's crust, then gouged and shaped by glaciation, these mountains are

not high by general South Island standards. The highest peaks average about 1500 to 1600 metres (4920 to 5250 feet) and have no permanent snowfields. They are nevertheless steep, rugged and covered with forest for all but the upper few hundred metres where subalpine shrublands and herb fields give way to open granite tops.

Rahu Scenic Reserve, which lines SH7 as it passes through the park, is the starting point for the few tramping tracks that lead onto the southern Victoria Range. A steep day climb to the distinctive, pyramid-shaped Mount Haast (1587 metres; 5209 feet) is popular and rewarding, though suitable only for experienced trampers. Tramping aside, the drive through Rahu Scenic Reserve, where the road is lined with magnificent Red and Silver Beech trees, is a great scenic experience.

A Geological Medley

There are few places in New Zealand where so many different kinds and ages of rocks and mineral deposits are found in such close proximity as in this park.

The South Island Alpine Fault cuts across the southeastern corner of the park. The resulting difference in base rock brings about a distinctive landscape change. On the eastern side of the fault clear, blue-green-coloured rivers flow over shingle beds of greywacke and schist. However, most of the park lies on the western side of the fault, where brown-coloured rivers, often described as 'tea-stained', flow over bouldery beds of ancient granite.

Top right: *Many species of summer-flowering gentians grow in New Zealand's alpine regions.*

Location: South Island, partly in West Coast and Nelson.

Climate: Dry (in the rainshadow of Paparoa Range), hot and fine in summer, frosts and fogs are likely in winter.

When to go: Anytime.

Access: By road on SH7 (3 hours' drive from Christchurch), SH6 (3 hours' drive from Blenheim and Nelson or SH69 (1 hour's drive from Westport). Regular bus services run to Reefton.

Permits/Reservations: Licences required for fishing (for introduced trout), permits for hunting (introduced Red Deer). Gold panning is restricted to recreational gold panning areas.

Facilities: Range of accommodation at Reefton and Murchison (DOC camping areas, motels, home stays and backpackers' lodges), several cafes and restaurants, shops, petrol and visitor centres. Facilities in the park include tracks, huts, Waiuta Lodge and historic displays.

Watching wildlife: South Island Bush Parrots, South Island Robins plus common native forest birds.

Landscapes: Beech forest, mountain ranges, regenerating forest, rivers, Lake Christabel.

Visitor activities: Short walks, tramping, historic appreciation, fishing (for introduced trout), whitewater rafting, kayaking, gold panning, scenic drives.

Precautions: Be wary of dangerous mine shafts in old mining areas. Historic sites and relics are protected by the Historic Places Act.

This hard, crystalline rock, composed of quartz, feldspar and mica conglomerates, and the mineralized solutions of gold-bearing quartz veins, has brought about significant impact on the region. In the 1870s Reefton and nearby areas were brought to life by a quartz mining mania that lasted 60 years and produced some of the richest takings in New Zealand's gold mining history. Mining of alluvial gold in the park's rivers, particularly the Inangahua and Upper Grey catchments, has also continued spasmodically since the 1880s.

Below: Landlocked Lake Christabel nestles within a pristine forested catchment area in Victoria Forest Park.

Today old miners' tracks, mining relics and ghost towns, often marked by stands of exotic trees that contrast with surrounding native forest, tell of the frenetic activity that once centred on the Reefton goldfields. Interpretative displays and restored mining equipment at the former settlements of Murray Creek, Kirwans Creek, Big River, Waiuta (once a town of 600 people) and, just north of the park, Lyell (where the population peaked at 2000) provide a thorough insight into the mining history. Blacks Point Museum, at Murrays Creek, is well worth a visit. Two popular tramping trips follow the Big River and Kirwans Tracks through former gold mining regions.

The forests disturbed by the gold mining era have since regenerated, but further devastation of the region's forests began in the 1950s, when milling of indigenous trees became a major industry. In the 1960s, a move to restrict intensive cutting rates (albeit to sustain the milling industry) escalated into a full-scale conservation battle that gripped the imagination of the nation. In 1977 the Maruia Declaration – the first petition of its kind in this country – received an unprecedented 341,000 signatures and helped thwart the milling of beech forest in Maruia valley.

Beech Haven

Beech forests are a significant feature of the park: all species of beech occurring in New Zealand grow here. Examples of Red, Silver, Hard, Black and the sub species Mountain Beech can be found within 5 kilometres (3

miles) of Reefton. This presents great opportunities for amateur botanizing, for observing the ecological niches each species prefers and identifying individual species. But be warned – only Silver Beech is easily distinguishable! If in doubt, it may be more rewarding to simply admire a well known feature of beech forests, the special dappled light that filters through the open foliage, whatever species the trees may be.

While beech dominates the park, lofty podocarps, particularly Red Pine (rimu), miro and White Pine (kahikatea), share some of the lower valley regions, along with kāmahi and southern rātā. At about 1400 metres (4600 feet), the forests give way to tussocks, grasses and alpine herbs such as Mountain Daisies (tikumu), celmisias, gentians and ourisias.

Visitors to the park are likely to see a variety of birds including friendly South Island Robins (kakaruai), the songster tui and bellbirds (korimako), tiny riflemen (tītītipounamu), Yellow-crowned Parakeets (kākāriki) and the Bush Parrot (South Island kākā). Great Spotted Kiwi (roa) calls may be heard at night.

Lake Christabel

A beautiful feature of this park is Lake Christabel. Walking tracks lead into the lake, which lies within an unmodified forested catchment and was formed when a

massive slip blocked the Blue Grey River valley. As the lake is completely landlocked, native fish have had to adapt in order to migrate to the sea. Kōaro, a species of galaxiid (whose juvenile form is known as whitebait) have adapted to live solely within the lake and its tributary streams. Long Finned Eels continue to migrate by moving over the ground to the Blue Grey River, then negotiating a series of cascades further downstream.

Above: Relics of a prosperous though short-lived gold mining era lie rusting in the park's forests. Others are restored, in historic displays.

Left: Rahu River tumbles its boulder-strewn course through overhanging beech forest, on the southeastern corner of Victoria Park.

PAPAROA NATIONAL PARK

Limestone Landscape

Diversity and dramatic limestone landforms are features of Paparoa, a park wedged between the ancient, weathered crest of the Paparoa Range and the sculpted cliffs and coves of the coastline. Linking the mountains and sea is a low-lying, forested limestone basin, filled with peculiar karst landforms of canyons, caves, fluted rock, sinkholes and disappearing streams.

Paparoa is one of New Zealand's newest national parks, created in 1987 after a major logging proposal for the West Coast forests initiated a vigorous conservation campaign. Park boundaries were carefully chosen to safeguard a range of ecosystems, from the mountain tops to the coast.

Varied forest types, micro-climates, altitudinal range and high-fertility limestone ecosystems have created a huge diversity of natural habitats. Both the park's forests and coastline support the highest concentration of native birds recorded in New Zealand and, in the limestone basin alone, botanists have identified at least 25 distinct forest communities.

The best-known and most visited features of Paparoa are the coastal 'pancake rocks' and blowholes at Punakaiki, where westerly sea swells surge against

Opposite: Limestone sculptures and the work of water are the special features of Paparoa, seen here in this selection of rocks existing in different areas of the national park.

Top right: The seed sac of a Nikau Palm. These subtropical palms thrive in the coastal park's moist, temperate climate.

extraordinary layered limestone stacks and erupt in geyser-like explosions from chasms and collapsed sea caverns. The wheelchair-standard track to these rocks and blowholes, enhanced with stylish interpretative signs, is possibly the most visited short walk in all of New Zealand's national parks.

Paparoa's coastline is a visual treat for travellers on the scenic West Coast highway. It is an even greater spectacle for those venturing on short tracks such as Truman, at Te Miko. Here, the sea- and weather-blasted limestone and sandstone coast is typified by the cliffs, caverns, a blowhole and a waterfall which plunges to the rock-strewn beach. Early Māori travellers negotiated the Te Miko cliffs via ladders made of rata vine and flax.

Inland is the limestone basin where, over time, continued effects of water have dissolved the soft, soluble limestone and created the peculiar landscape known as karst.

Of Karst and Caves

Rivers in the park have sculpted the limestone into deep chasms and canyons, a spectacle easily viewed via a short walk from the Punakaiki coast into the Pororari valley. Other karst features are disappearing streams, sinkholes and dry streambeds, all indicators of an elaborate subterranean system of shafts, passages and caves.

The Fox River Cave, with its 200-metre (656 feet) passage and stunning calcite formations, is a historic tourist attraction. The upper cave is safe to visit. The Fox River also showcases some of the park's finest limestone

Location: South Island West Coast.

Climate: Mild and wet, with some periods of settled weather.

When to go: Anytime (the most settled weather is from January to April, and in mid-winter).

Access: By road via SH6. There are airports at Westport and Hokitika. Daily bus services.

Permits/Reservations: Required for hunting (introduced goats and deer).

Facilities: In the park – walking tracks and campsites. At Punakaiki there is a park visitor centre, café/store, craft shop, camping ground (with cabins), tavern, motels and backpacker lodges. Also canoes for hire, guided canoeing trips, Westland black petrel tours, Fox River Cave tours (torches are necessary for exploring caves).

Wildlife: Westland Black Petrel and the Great Spotted Kiwi (sometimes heard at night) sea birds and forest birds, New Zealand Fur Seals, Hector's Dolphins.

Landscapes: Limestone karst formations (caves, river canyons, overhangs, sinkholes, disappearing streams), coastal cliffs, caverns, 'pancake rocks' and blowholes, craggy mountain ranges, subtropical coastal forest, lowland

Visitor activities: Short walks, day walks, tramping, camping, bird watching, canoeing, caving and scenic driving.

Precautions: The limestone country is filled with hidden potholes and shafts. Keep to the tracks. Inland tramping tracks involve river crossings and streambed travel. Choose fording spots carefully and on coastal tracks, be wary of cliff edges and sudden tidal changes.

formations – canyons, sculptured rock pools and disappearing streams. About three hours' walk up the riverbed is a massive limestone overhang known as the Ballroom, a well-known, sheltered campsite.

Another easily visited cave is the Punakaiki Cavern, beside the main highway, with its 130 metres (427 feet) of passages and occasional stalactites and glow worms. It is recommended that visitors take a torch!

Visiting other caves in the park requires the expertise of experienced speleologists, or cavers. Organized caving groups have explored caves throughout the park's limestone basin. Many of these are storehouses for important fossil material of birds, reptiles and even mammals. The Xanadu system – New Zealand's best example of an 'epiphreatic maze cave', a cave with multiple passages and constantly changing water levels – is also known for its impressive stalactites and stalagmites.

Below: A large limestone overhang creates this natural shelter, called the Ballroom, which is a popular campsite.

Ancient Rock

On the eastern side of the park, limestone gives way to old granite and gneiss rock in the Paparoa Range. These mountains, which reach a height of 1500 metres (4920 feet) above sea level, are made of the most ancient rocks known in New Zealand. The rocks bear close resemblance to Fiordland because they were once aligned with the Fiordland mountains, before being separated by the Alpine Fault within the last 10 million years. The untracked jumble of craggy peaks and pinnacles and glaciated hanging valleys are often covered in dense cloud. They present a formidable challenge to trampers attempting to traverse their tops.

The park's only tramping track is the gently graded Inland Pack Track, initially formed in 1867 when gold strikes at the Fox River brought a short-lived flurry of activity to the region. This track, which follows the naturally gentle grade of a limestone depression (syncline) and passes through pristine lowland forest and impressive limestone formations, was the main transport route until the coast road was completed in 1927. There are no huts or bridges along the route and heavy rain and rising river levels can prevent travel. However, there are delightful campsites (such as the Ballroom Overhang) and two coastal track links that provide shorter walks.

Subtropical Rainforest

Paparoa's moist and temperate coastal climate has produced a luxuriant covering of subtropical lowland rainforest. The limestone basin is covered with dense forest

Left: Late spring flowers of the hardy, distinctive cabbage tree.

of podocarps, Red Beech (tawai), broadleaf (kāpuka) and tree ferns. On the coast, nikau palms and northern rātā thrive, near the southern limits of their distribution, among entanglements of kiekie and other climbing vines. Dense windshorn shrublands of flax (harakeke) and cabbage trees (ti rākau) manage to survive against salt-laden wind and waves.

In the wetter, cooler montane climate of the Paparoa Range, Silver Beech forest merges with subalpine shrubs of dracophyllum, Pink Pine and Mountain Flax (wharariki). Higher still, daisies (tīkumu) and gentians survive among Golden Snow Tussock and Olearia shrubs. In the north of the park, wetlands known as 'pakihi' on old terraces of the Tiropahi River add yet more floral diversity to the area.

Left: Each year thousands of visitors come to admire the spectacle of the Pancake Rock blowholes at Dolomite Point, Punakaiki.

Special Bird Species

One of the noteworthy birds in the park is the Great Spotted Kiwi (roroa). Paparoa is one of only two areas where numbers are known to be relatively high. However, sightings of these nocturnal birds are rare.

The endemic Westland Black Petrel (tītī) breeds only on the Punakaiki coast and is one of the few mainland petrel colonies to have survived since the introduction of rats, cats and stoats. These petrels live at sea except for during their winter breeding season, when couples raise their chicks in burrows on coastal terraces, and take off for their daily feeding flights from exposed rocks or trees. Watching thousands of petrels fly in at dusk is a memorable sight.

LAKE SUMNER FOREST PARK AND LEWIS PASS NATIONAL RESERVE

Highway Mountains and Hot Springs

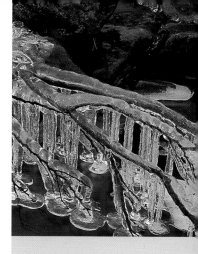

These adjoining areas lie in the midst of a vast wilderness region of mountains, lakes, rivers and beech forests, surrounded by other national and forest parks. Lewis Pass National Reserve was created in 1985 with the aim of protecting the area's outstanding natural and ecological values. But for its smaller size, it would have qualified for national park status. Lake Sumner Forest Park was established in 1940, when pastoral grazing leases held in the main valleys expired.

The two areas contain several recreation features. The 67-kilometre (42 miles) St James Walkway passes through the national reserve, forest park and high country farmland. Other tramping routes cross the South Island main divide over low alpine passes. Hot pools are found throughout the two areas.

The national reserve is traversed by the Lewis Pass highway, a very scenic drive that crosses the lowest pass over the South Island's main divide. The highway, which

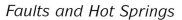

follows the Maruia River, is lined with pristine beech forest and delightful short walks, day walks as well as riverside camping. Picnic spots are dotted along the way. The forest park is not as easily accessible, however, and 'walks' are longer tramping trips of several days' duration, following routes and old pack tracks.

Faults and Hot Springs

As with other parks along the South Island main divide, fault movement and glaciation have played major roles in creating the landform of these two areas. The lakes, such as Sumner, are glacial-gouged troughs. The crest of the Southern Alps/Kā Tiritiri o te Moana dominates the western border of the forest park, while other subsidiary ranges extend throughout the park and national reserve. The highest peak in the region is Mount Crossley (1987 metres; 6521 feet) on the Dampier Range.

Hot springs, issuing from faultline fractures in the region's bedrock, have long been a drawcard. There are several in the forest park, though not all deep enough for bathing. On Lewis Pass highway there are small springs near Sylvia Flat camping area and further north is the popular Maruia Springs Thermal Resort.

While sedimentary greywacke and slate-like argillite are the main base rocks of the region, an outcrop of older marble occurs in the area west of Lake Daniells. Rare fossil corals, tiny sea animal imprints (graptolites) and sea lilies (crinoids) – estimated to be more than 200 million years old – have been discovered in this marble.

Opposite: Frosted Mountain Beech trees create a fairy tale scene in Lewis Pass National Reserve.

Top right: Trees and a mountain stream caught in the icy grip of winter in Lake Sumner Forest Park.

Location: South Island, in North Canterbury and Westland.

Climate: Generally hot summers, cold winters, drier towards the east. Winter snow usually covers alpine passes and much of St James Walkway. Avalanches are a threat in spring.

When to go: Anytime for short walks. Summer for tramping.

Access: By road, two hours from Christchurch and 2.5 hours from Nelson. Daily bus services travel SH7, which traverses the region. St James Walkway and Lewis Pass National Reserve tracks leave from SH7. Main Forest Park entry points are Windy Point (on SH7) and the Lake Sumner Road from SH7 to Lake Taylor (has several fords).

Permits/Reservations: Permits are required for hunting and licences for fishing. Four-wheel-drive access to Lock Katrine requires lock combination number from DOC.

Facilities: Huts, bridges and tracks in the national reserve and park. Informal camping areas along SH7 and at Lake Taylor. Springs Junction has a store, petrol, café and motels. Maruia Springs has a hotel, hot springs and camping. Tramper transport available for St James Walkway.

Wildlife: Prolific native forest birds and waterfowl.

Landscapes: Beech forests, river valleys, lakes, mountain ranges, subalpine meadows, lakes.

Visitor activities: Tramping, day walks, short walks, camping, canoeing, hot springs, fishing (introduced Brown and Rainbow Trout).

Precautions: Winter tramping requires snow climbing expertise.

Right: A five-minute walk from the highway leads to this alpine tarn.

Below: A curious Paradise Shelduck chick. Adult birds live in pairs along high country rivers. Their loud honking calls alert visitors to their presence.

Beech Forests and Birdlife

The lower mountain slopes throughout the park and reserve are covered with magnificent stands of Red, Silver and Mountain Beech (tawai) forest. In the park, forests of the Hurunui Valley are particularly impressive for the high numbers of threatened native bird species they support. Here one finds threatened Yellowhead (mohua) and the only sizable population remaining of Orange-fronted Parakeet (kākāriki), along with South Island Bush Parrot (kākā), New Zealand Falcon (kārearea), Mountain Parrot (kea), Great Spotted Kiwi (roroa), Long-tailed Cuckoo (koekoeā) and Shining Cuckoo (pīpīwharauroa).

One of DOC's 'mainland island' projects, which aims to protect and enhance habitats by controlling introduced pests such as possums and stoats, is based in the two branches of the Hurunui.

Historic Passes and Valley Routes

At the head of the north branch of the Hurunui, Harper Pass leads across the main divide to the Taramakau River, in Arthur's Pass National Park. This low-level pass (963 metres; 3161 feet) was once a major highway for Māori travelling to the west coast greenstone (pounamu) fields. Later European explorers, gold prospectors and runholders driving sheep to the west coast also used the route, and for a time during the 1860s, small stores and liquor stores were set up along the way to serve the numerous travellers.

Passes further north – namely Hope Pass saddling the Hope and Tutaekuri Rivers, and Amuri Pass at the

Below: Nina Valley blanketed in a winter snow-storm. The region's tramping routes are generally covered with snow in winter.

head of Doubtful River – were also popular routes. However, in the late 1800s, when goldfields further north became more prosperous and the road across Arthur's Pass, to the south, was completed, these valleys became deserted. Now they are used only by trampers.

Tussocks, grasses and prickly native matagouri shrubs cover the valleys' river flats, in places competing with weeds introduced by previous grazing of stock. Paradise Shelduck (pūtakitaki) and introduced Canada Geese are two of the more common species found on the extensive wetlands, rivers and lakes throughout the forest park and national reserve. Grey Ducks (pārera) and Black Shags (kōau) are also present in Lake Sumner, along with visiting White Heron (kōtuku) and Southern Crested Grebe (kāmana).

The region's major rivers are the Hurunui, Hope, Boyle and Maruia. The Hurunui flows into Lake Sumner, on the park boundary, which is accessible only by a walking track via the Hope and Kiwi valleys, or by a restricted four-wheel-drive road that leads past neighbouring Loch Katrine and Lake Taylor. Outside the park, these adjacent lakes and surrounding areas are nevertheless popular holiday spots for campers, anglers, kayakers and mountain bikers.

One of the most popular and scenic walks in the region is the walk into Lake Daniells, in the Lake Lewis reserve. This features prolific native birdlife, magnificent Red Beech forest and the beautiful Maruia River gorge. Here, the clear blue-green water that cuts through marble rock is a feature of the three-hour walk to the lake. A longer (three to four days) well-known walk near Lewis Pass, the St James Walkway, traverses mountains, beech forests and subalpine meadows.

ARTHUR'S PASS NATIONAL PARK

An Accessible Alpine Park

The essence of Arthur's Pass National Park is its mountains, eastern beech forests, western rainforests and transport history that allows easy access to the heart of this alpine park.

As the park straddles the South Island main divide, the contrasting east–west climates and altitudes result in distinctive physical differences and a huge variety of natural habitats. On the western side, where moist, westerly weather systems prevail, deeply gorged rivers flow through dense rainforests. On the rain-shadowed eastern side of the Southern Alps/Kā Tiritiri o te Moana wide, shingle-filled riverbeds are flanked by vast beech forests. In the mountains between these east and west regions is an alpine wonderland of snow-covered peaks, remnant glaciers, and huge scree (small rocks, or shingle, that cover mountain slopes). Within easy walking distance from the main highway are alpine meadows filled with flowers, tussock (clumpy grasslike subalpine vegetation) fields and tarns (small mountain lakes).

The historic, spectacular highway that cuts through the park and crosses the main divide via Arthur's Pass is the highest of the few passes over the Southern Alps/Kā Tiritiri o te Moana. Several notable engineering feats mark the building of this road through the steep, erosion-prone mountains, not least its initial completion back in

Map showing Arthur's Pass National Park, with features including Taramakau R., Otehake Wilderness Area, Otira R., Deception R., Mt Franklin, Mt Rolleston, Mingha R., Poulter R., Haardon R., Waimakariri R., Mt Murchison, Arthur's Pass Visitor Centre, and routes to Greymouth and Christchurch. Inset map of South Island showing Christchurch.

1866. Construction of the Otira Tunnel in 1923 united the east and west coasts and, as recently as 1999, a large viaduct was built to reduce the hazards of floods and slips.

Visitors can thus penetrate the heart of the park in comfort, by car or train. There is no need for an extended tramping exertion to witness the splendour of the mountain peaks, the power of waterfalls and rock slides, the delicacy of the many alpine flowers, or the cheeky Mountain Parrots (kea).

As the highway climbs then descends the pass, the distinctive vegetation transitions of the park all unfold within one hour's driving. Tall beech forest in the lower, drier eastern valleys becomes stunted as the road gains altitude, then the trees give way to subalpine shrublands and tussock-filled valleys that are flanked by towering mountain walls. Descending to the west coast rainforest, the trees grow tall again. Some of New Zealand's biggest species, podocarps and rātā, emerge above the common canopy tree, kāmahi, and a tangled profusion of smaller trees, shrubs and ferns.

High quality, short walking tracks from the Arthur's Pass highway showcase these scenic and natural features: delights such as the Punchbowl Falls at Arthur's Pass Village, the meadows of Dobson Nature Walk and Otira Valley, as well as the luxuriant, summer-flowering rātā forest of the Cockayne Nature Walk, at Kellys Creek.

Leonard Cockayne, one of New Zealand's most eminent ecologists, helped generate awareness of the region's natural values in the early 1900s, when he

Top right: The Otira Viaduct, built to reduce the hazards of floods and slips on the spectacular alpine road traversing the park.

Location: Central South Island.

Climate: Sudden weather changes. Temperatures range from 20°C (68° F) in summer to below zero in winter. Heavy rainfall occurs on the western side of the park. Heavy snowfalls likely in winter.

When to go: Summer for tramping and alpine flowers. Winter is best for skiing and climbing.

Access: By road, SH73, 153km (95 miles) from Christchurch and 98km (60 miles) from Greymouth. Daily bus and train services.

Permits: Required for hunting (introduced Red Deer and Chamois). Licences required for trout fishing.

Facilities: Arthur's Pass Village offers accommodation, some restaurants, shops and a park visitor centre. Lodge and hotel accommodation is available in nearby towns and high country farms. The park features tracks, huts, bridges, basic camping and picnic areas. There are several skifields in the region. Christchurch-based companies offer guided climbing, tramping and scenic tour services. Ski equipment is available for hire at skifields.

Watching wildlife: Mountain Parrot Bush Parrot, alpine flowers (buttercups, gentians, daisies, eyebrights), best in January. Southern Rātā flower, best December-January.

Landscapes: Snowy mountains, beech forests, wide, open river valleys, podocarp forests, waterfalls, scree slopes.

Visitor activities: Walks, tramping, climbing, skiing, camping, scenic drives, hunting, fishing.

lived at Kelly's Creek, studied botany and encouraged the government to legally protect the forests. Two reserves were set aside in 1901 and, in 1929, Arthur's Pass became the first national park in the South Island.

The park's variety of protected habitats support a wide range of native wildlife species, including a particularly diverse invertebrate fauna population. Mischievous Mountain Parrots are regular roadside entertainers. Their bush 'cousins', the South Island Bush Parrots (kākā), make their presence known by screeching loudly from high above the treetops. Blue Duck (kōwhiowhio) live in remote mountain streams and along the many channels of open, wide 'braided' rivers, while the eastern side of the park provides nesting grounds for migrant birds such as the Wrybill and Black-fronted Tern. Great Spotted Kiwi (roroa) live on both sides of the main divide. Common forest birds in the park include the bellbird (korimako), fantail (pīwakawaka), South Island Robin, South Island Tit (miromiro) and the Grey Warbler (riroriro). Less common are the Yellow-crowned Parakeet (kākāriki) and the threatened Yellowhead (mohua).

Back-country Recreation

There is far more to the national park than that seen from the highway and both trampers and dedicated climbers will find challenging trails to explore. The eastern valleys of the park provide natural routes, some of which lead to passes where main divide crossings are feasible for summertime trampers.

One such example, the (normally) two-day Mingha–Deception valley trip over Goat Pass, forms the running section of a well known triathlon event ('Coast to Coast'). This attracts hundreds of competitors who cross the width of the South Island in one or two days. In the north of the park, the Harpers Pass route that connects with Lake Sumner Forest Park was travelled by early Māori people seeking West Coast pounamu (greenstone), and years later by prospectors in pursuit of West Coast gold.

Despite its other attractions, the park is essentially an alpine area. Some tramping routes and alpine passes are suitable only for well-equipped people with solid mountaineering experience. A number of the 16 2000-metre-plus (over 6500 feet) mountains in the park, in particular, Rolleston (2275m, or 7466ft), Murchison (2408m, or 7900ft) and Franklin (2145m, or 7000ft) are popular winter snow-climbing challenges, although avalanches are a constant threat.

Skiing has been a traditional pursuit in these mountains for years, particularly with Christchurch enthusiasts who have been able to travel there easily by road or rail. There are several skifields in the region, including the Temple Basin field in the park, two fields in neighbouring Craigieburn Forest Park and a further three fields in nearby ranges.

Uplift and Erosion

As with most other South Island national parks, the landforms of Arthur's Pass have been shaped over the past two million years by the three powerful natural forces: tectonic uplift, glaciation and erosion. The mountains have been forced upwards by the collision of two of the earth's crustal plates, glaciers have carved out U-shaped valleys and the brittle, greywacke rock, a very common sedimentary-type of rock in the park, has been severely eroded over time by water.

Ten small glaciers remain high in the park's mountains. They are but tiny remnants of earlier giants that used to extend west, almost to the coast, and eastwards, as far as the Canterbury Plains.

The ongoing process of erosion can be a dramatic affair. Massive rock avalanches are a feature of the park's landscape and one example can be seen from the road at the head of Otira Gorge.

Falling Mountain, the biggest in the park, fills an awesome 3 kilometres (2 miles) of riverbed in the remote, upper Otehake River. This avalanche occurred as a result of a major earthquake in 1929, testimony to the presence here of the great Alpine Fault. Evidence of erosion – steep scree slopes, crumbling ridges and shingle-filled rivers – is found throughout the park. As it flows across the park boundary, the Waimakariri River is estimated to have a gravel bed some 300 metres (900 feet) deep.

This is formidable country, crafted by nature's powerful, ongoing forces. Awe-inspiring and potentially dangerous to today's well-equipped recreational visitors, it was no doubt even more challenging for those earlier travellers; Maori in pursuit of greenstone, prospectors searching for West Coast gold and surveyors. Arthur's Pass itself was named after the British surveyor Arthur Dobson, the first European to 'discover' this route through the mountains.

Opposite top: One of the less visited tramping areas is the Taipo River headwaters, on the west side of the divide.

Opposite bottom: The park is essentially an alpine region where hardy, low growing tussocks, shrubs and alpine herbs survive the harsh environment.

Below left: Recreation in the park ranges from gentle walks to challenging climbs, such as this popular Temple Buttress rock climb.

Below right: Beech forests give way to subalpine shrubs and tussocks in the park's upper alpine valleys.

Westland/Tai Poutini National Park

Where Glaciers Meet Rainforest

There are few places in the world where natural wilderness remains intact from mountain tops through to the sea, and where glaciers meet with rainforest. Westland/Tai Poutini is a park of superlatives, and one of four adjoining parks which make up the 2.6-million-hectare (6.4 million acres) Te Wahipounamu/South-West New Zealand stretch of land that is classified as a World Heritage Area.

Westland/Tai Poutini encompasses New Zealand's highest mountains and fastest moving glaciers. The park also offers a stunning combination of permanent snowfields, temperate rainforests, rivers, lakes, lagoons and coastline. The mountains rise abruptly from the coastal lowlands, and within a mere 20 kilometres (12 miles) from its shared boundary with Aoraki/Mount Cook National Park, on the South Island's main divide, the park plunges from an altitude of over 3000 thousand metres (9800 feet) to sea level.

Opposite top: Guided walkers on Fox Glacier/Te Moeka o Tuawe. There are few places in the world where glaciers are as accessible as in Westland/Tai Poutini.

Opposite bottom, left and right: The glacier is an ever-changing jumble of cracks and crevices; an ice river grinds its way down from snowfields in New Zealand's highest mountains.

Top right: Drivers; beware of kiwi!

Magnificent Mountains

New Zealand's Southern Alps/Kā Tiritiri o te Moana have been thrust upwards by the collision of the earth's crustal plates along the Alpine Fault. In Westland that uplift has occurred rapidly (in a geological sense), hence the dramatically steep rise of the mountains from the lowland plains.

The biggest peaks, all over 3000 metres (9800 feet), are Mounts Tasman, Douglas, Sefton, Elie de Beaumont and The Minarets. These are popular climbing challenges, though stormy weather, impassable river gorges and vast snowfields with hidden crevasses make climbing from the west side of the alps a difficult proposition. New Zealand's highest mountain, Aoraki/Mount Cook, stands beyond the park boundary but is nevertheless prominent on the Westland skyline.

Countering the ongoing uplift process have been the eroding forces of ice, water and wind. Westland receives one of the heaviest rainfalls in the world. The mountains stand in the path of prevailing moist westerly winds, which sweep across the Tasman Sea and cool rapidly as they are forced upwards against the bulk of the mountain chain. Heavy rain on the coast turns to huge snowfalls at higher altitudes, and land above 2500 metres (8200 feet) is covered with permanent snow. These snowfields accumulate in large basins, or neves, and as the weight of new snow forces air from the underlying snow, compressed snow crystals turn to blue glacial ice. Gravity forces the glacial ice downhill, and so the glaciers begin their powerful journey.

Location: South Island west coast.

Climate: Mild temperatures, heavy rainfall and heavy snowfalls in the mountains. Storms occur at any time of the year, spring and early summer are particularly wet.

When to go: Anytime.

Access: By road via SH6 (the Haast Highway). Daily bus services.

Permits/Reservations: A permit is required to enter Waitangiroto Nature Reserve at Okarito Lagoon. Permits required for hunting (for introduced deer).

Facilities: Franz Josef/Waiau and Fox Glacier villages each have a shop, petrol sales, restaurants and varying accommodation (hotels, motels, youth hostel and camping grounds). A park visitor centre offers information, audio-visual presentations, publication sales and a summer visitor programme at Franz Josef/Waiau. Glacier and, alpine guides, scenic flights, river and lagoon kayaking, White Heron nature reserve tours available.

Wildlife: White Heron, Royal Spoonbills, migratory waders, South Island Bush Parrot, Mountain Parrot.

Landscapes: New Zealand's highest snow-covered mountains, glaciers, temperate rainforest, kahikatea-fringed lakes and lagoons, beaches, wide braided rivers, hot springs.

Visitor activities: Walks to glaciers, rain forest, lakes, beaches and lagoons, tramping, climbing (for experienced and equipped climbers), bird watching, lagoon kayaking, nature heritage tours.

Precautions: Ice collapse and rock-falls can occur anytime at the terminal face of the glaciers. Keep behind rope barriers. If crossing rivers on the beach, beware of quicksand and fast tidal flows.

Two Great Glaciers

There are over 60 glaciers in Westland/Tai Poutini; these ice rivers scour their way down the park's valleys, breaking into a jumble of crevasses and grinding the bedrock into powder as they move, eventually melting in the warmer temperatures of lower altitudes, just 12 kilometres (7 miles) from the sea.

Two glaciers are dominating features of the park. Franz Josef (Kā Roimata o Hine Hukatere) and Fox (Te Moeka o Tuawe) are two of the fastest moving and most accessible glaciers in the world, and are the only glaciers to exist at such temperate latitudes. Their spectacular presence attracts thousands of tourists each year, and their retreating paths have played a major hand in shaping the character of park landscapes, leaving a legacy of lakes and glacial deposits.

The two glaciers are fed from particularly huge snowfields, which cram into steep and narrow valleys. They move fast – an average of 3 to 4 metres (10 to 13 feet) each day. By comparison, the Tasman Glacier in Aoraki/Mount Cook National Park moves at 650 millimetres (25 inches) a day.

Above: *A Royal Spoonbill, a self-introduced wader from Australia, breeds in the Okarito Lagoon.*

Below: *Tourists landing on Fox Glacier/Te Moeka o Tuawe.*

Remarkable Rainforests

Dense rainforests that extend across the lowlands from the glaciers to the sea thrive in mild temperatures and heavy rainfall. Glacial moraines and old river terraces are covered with majestic Red Pine (rimu); the Okarito and Waikukupa forests within the park support the highest densities of rimu forest in the country. New Zealand's tallest tree, White Pine (kahikatea), dominates the wetter alluvial plains and lake margins. Within these forests flourish a tangled and usually sodden profusion of smaller trees, shrubs, vines, ferns, mosses and epiphytes. While the podocarps flourish, the park is distinctive for its lack of beech (tawai) forest. Beech is dominant in many South Island parks but has never recovered from being wiped out by glaciation in Westland.

The lower mountain slopes and valleys are filled with Southern Rātā and kāmahi trees. Close to the glacier terminals, tiny but hardy lichens and mosses begin the slow process of plant colonization and provide visual contrast among the stark landscape of ice and rock.

Bird Watcher's Paradise

Many of New Zealand's native bird species, including seasonal migrants, are present in the park, along with a significant array of aquatic fauna, lizards, snails and bats.

The lowland rainforests are laced with lakes, lagoons and deep, slow-flowing waterways which provide outstanding natural habits, unrivalled elsewhere in New Zealand. These places support 17 species of native fresh water fish, plus many species of waterfowl, including one of New Zealand's rarest water birds, the Southern Crested Grebe (kāmana).

Coastal, White Pine-fringed lagoons, which occupy troughs of former glacial tongues, are peaceful refuges in contrast with the bouldery beaches, constantly hammered by westerly ocean swells that enclose them. On the park's northern margins is Okarito Lagoon, the largest remaining natural estuary in New Zealand and a bird watcher's paradise. This lagoon supports thousands of native and migratory birds and is the main feeding ground of Royal Spoonbills and White Herons (kōtuku). The kōtuku breed nearby in kahikatea trees, alongside the Waitangoroto River – coincidentally at the same time of year as the annual migration in the river of whitebait, their favoured food.

The park's Okarito forest is home to a small and endemic population of Okarito Brown Kiwi. These birds number less than 200 and DOC staff are carrying out research and management work to ensure their long-term survival. Visitors to the Park are likely to come across kea, the cheeky Mountain Parrot, while they visit the glaciers, or hear the raucous screech of kākā, the kea's Bush Parrot relative, high above the trees during the course of a lowland forest walk.

They are less likely to spot the tiny but hardy Rock Wren, which lives high above the tree line, or the Blue Duck (kōwhiowhio), which frequents remote mountain streams. Other fauna in the park, such as the Long-tailed Bats, Westland Skinks and carnivorous land snails, are even harder to find.

Opposite right: Glaciers described as 'God's great ploughs' leave their powerful mark on the rock-face landscape.

Below: Nearing Marcel Col on Heemskirk Glacier. Climbing is pariculary challenging in the park.

People

Westland/Tai Poutini has never been a heavily populated region. Early Māori lived in a few coastal settlements and passed through in search of greenstone (pounamu). Sealers stayed briefly to exploit the coast of its seal populations and, in the 1860s, the discovery of gold brought a short-lived period of boom, then bust. There has been some farm development on the lowlands in the region of the park.

The glaciers, lakes and rainforest have long been popular drawcards; from the early 1900s, guiding and accommodation services have been established to cater for growing numbers of tourists. Tourism is now the economic mainstay of the region with a host of accommodation, guiding, kayaking and scenic flight services operating from Franz Josef/Waiau and Fox Glacier villages.

Natural wilderness continues well beyond the southern park boundary, much of it a protected scenic reserve. There can be few places in the world that match this area in its singular beauty. It is not often that one can drive for hours on a main highway through primeval rainforest, with snow-covered mountains on one side and remote surf beaches on the other as one does on the West Coast's Haast Highway.

AORAKI/MOUNT COOK NATIONAL PARK

Highest Mountain, Longest Glacier

This is New Zealand's true alpine park – a World Heritage Site which includes the highest mountains, longest glacier and the most extensive permanent snow- and icefields.

The park, which is part of the Te Wahipounamu/South-West New Zealand World Heritage Area, lies on the eastern side of the Southern Alps/Kā Tiritiri o te Moana and is bordered along its main dividing ridge with Westland/Tai Poutini National Park.

Aoraki/Mount Cook is an extremely popular national park. Sight-seeing tourists arrive by coach or plane, while dedicated climbers visit to explore the challenges of what is regarded as one of the best climbing regions in all of New Zealand and Australia.

Between these two extremes, many more visitors explore the short walks and admire the varied park features – alpine tarns, flowers, the mountains and glacier views. Walking, climbing or simply being encircled and dwarfed by 3000-metre-high (9800 feet) mountains, is an awe-inspiring experience.

Left: Two great glacial rivers, the Hooker (foreground) and Tasman, flow from the park; their milky colour a result of the glacial debris they carry.

Top right: The giant Mountain Buttercup (Ranunculus lyalli), often misnomered as the Mount Cook Lily, has become almost as symbolic of the park as Aoraki/Mount Cook itself.

The park gets its name from its highest mountain – Aoraki/Mount Cook – also the highest in New Zealand. The Māori people of the South Island, Ngai Tahu, regard Aoraki as a god. In Ngai Tahu mythology, Aoraki was the son of the sky father Raki, and the South Island landmass is his upturned canoe. When the canoe capsized, Aoraki and his crew climbed to the high side of the wreck and became the great mountains of the Southern Alps/Kā Tiritiri o te Moana. This special relationship between the mountains and Ngai Tahu was officially acknowledged in 1997, when the park was given the dual name of Aoraki/Mount Cook. The name Cook comes from James Cook, the first English explorer to visit New Zealand.

Aoraki/Mount Cook (3754 metres, or 12,315 feet) is surrounded in the park by more than 20 other mountain peaks which are over 3000 metres (9800 feet) high and have permanent snow- and icefields. These mountains have been pushed upwards by two of the earth's tectonic plates as they collided along the South Island's Alpine Fault. However, this powerful mountain-building process has been countered by constant erosion, as the sedimentary rocks that make up the mountains are being worn down by the mighty forces of water, wind, and ice.

Climbing these challenging mountains has been a tradition in the park since the 1880s. Aoraki/Mount Cook was first climbed in 1894 and the European con-

Location: Central Southern Alps/Kā Tiritiri o te Moana.

Climate: Subject to sudden and dramatic change, with heavy rainfall, snow and gales. Also long settled periods of fine weather. Can be very hot in summer. In winter, frosts and snow are likely at low levels.

When to go: Anytime. Spring and summer for alpine flowers. Spring and summer for climbing, but dependent on snow and ice conditions. Winter climbing is an extreme sport. Winter and spring for glacier and cross-country skiing.

Access: By road via SH8 from Timaru to Lake Pukaki, then SH80 to Aoraki/Mt Cook Village. About three hours' drive from Timaru, five from Christchurch. There are daily flights from Christchurch and Queenstown.

Permits: Not required for climbing, but trip intention forms must be completed at the park visitor centre if entering the park overnight or for longer periods.

Facilities: At Aoraki/Mount Cook Village accommodation (four-star hotel, motels, youth hostel and camping area). Also a store, restaurants, self-serve petrol, alpine guide agency and park visitor centre. Walking tracks and park huts. Climbing gear and ski hire available.

Viewing wildlife: Alpine flowers, Mountain Parrot (kea).

Landscapes: Mountains, glaciers, snowfields, glacial lakes and glacier-fed rivers, waterfalls, avalanches

Visitor activities: Walking, tramping, climbing, ski-mountaineering, cross- country and glacier skiing, scenic flights and glacier landings, glacier lake cruises, four-wheel-drive tours. Guides available for climbing, walking and glacier skiing.

cept of mountain guiding, which developed in the park in those pioneering times, continues today. Climbing the peak will always be the premier challenge, but adjacent mountains – such as Tasman, Sefton, Malte Brun, La Perouse and Elie de Beaumont – are also spectacular climbs and offer a formidable challenge. The park has proved to be a fine training ground for some of New Zealand's great Himalayan climbers, including Sir Edmund Hillary and the late Rob Hall and Gary Ball. Several high altitude huts and bivouacs, some perched on breathtaking, even precarious, mountainside sites, provide shelter for climbers from the sudden and severe storms that frequently and often unpredictably lash this environment.

Glacial Landscapes

Glaciation is an awe-inspiring feature of the park's land-scape. Over a third of the 70,000-hectare (173,000 acres) park is covered with glacial ice. Five major and many smaller glaciers slowly carve the valley floors, transporting huge loads of sedimentary rubble from the mountains and depositing them at the glacier terminals in rubble piles called moraines. As the ice gradually melts, milky coloured lakes, filled with rock that has been ground by the ice to a fine, flour-like substance, have formed at the glacier terminals.

The constantly changing landscapes created by the glaciers are both a pleasure and problem for park

visitors. In some places, growing moraine walls, huge piles of debris carried down by the glaciers, cause difficulties for climbers seeking access into the park's upper valleys. Conversely, boat trips across the murky Tasman glacial lakes to the glacier's ice terminal provide a fascinating option for less energetically inclined tourists.

Today's glaciers are but tiny remnants of the immense glaciers of the ice ages which, most recently as 40,000 years ago, extended well beyond the park and carved the huge basins of three nearby glacial lakes, Tekapo, Pukaki and Ohau. Nevertheless, at 29 kilometre (18 miles) in length, Tasman Glacier is one of the longest in the temperate regions of the world. While it slowly but powerfully continues its natural landscaping work, the Tasman also presents a range of recreation and sightseeing options for park visitors. These include scenic flights in small ski planes and helicopters, glacier landings and glacier skiing.

Tramping in the Park

The ice, snow and rock of the mountains and glaciers might seem to present a barren, inhospitable environment for plantlife, yet the park contains a huge diversity of alpine vegetation. Grasslands, alpine shrublands, tussock fields, rock gardens, scree (shingle) slopes and very small remnants of beech forest provide environments for a prolific range of plantlife, including several species endemic to the park. Most notable are the alpine flowers; in particular the Giant Mountain Buttercup (*Ranunculus lyalli*). This is commonly misnomered the Mount Cook Lily and has become almost as symbolic of the park as Aoraki/Mount Cook itself.

Several native birds survive in the harsh alpine environment, species such as the tiny Rock Wren, New Zealand Pipit (pīhoihoi), New Zealand Falcon (kārearea) and the kea, an oft-precocious mountain parrot.

Climbing expertise may be a requirement to explore the high peaks and passes of the park. However, less adventurous visitors can explore a surprising range of alpine environments and view points on top quality trails within just an hour's walk from the park village.

Unlike in many other, more heavily forested parks, where several hours' climb is necessary just to reach the forest edge, Aoraki/Mount Cook's alpine shrublands and mountain flowers are easily accessible. The most popular tracks lead to various scenic spots – mountain tarns on Mount Sebastapol, alpine flowers and glacial land-

Left: *The tiny but resilient Rock Wren lives in the high mountains and survives harsh winters by sheltering in small rock crevices beneath the snow.*

scapes of the Hooker Valley and superb views of the Mueller Glacier and Mount Sefton from Kea Point. Longer tramping opportunities in the park are limited, as one cannot travel far before requiring technical climbing expertise and equipment. However, the journey to Mueller Hut is a popular summer trip that takes three to four hours.

Some hardy adventurers opt for mountaineering and winter cross-country skiing in basins and valleys away from the ski planes of the Tasman Glacier.

An integral part of Aoraki/Mount Cook's history and tradition centres on the tourist hotel, the Mount Cook Hermitage, which has accommodated climbers and nature-loving tourists from all around the world since 1884. The present hotel is the third in this area as ravages of flood and fire have destroyed its predecessors.

Left: *Looking across Lake Pukaki to Aoraki/Mount Cook. Glaciers once extended far from the mountains, and carved the beds of huge lakes such as Pukaki.*

MOUNT ASPIRING NATIONAL PARK

Mountain Wilderness

This park is one of the greatest areas of mountain wilderness in New Zealand. Mount Aspiring is the country's third largest national park, second in size only to the marbled mountains of Kahurangi and the massive expanse of Fiordland, on its south-western border.

The park's mountains, glaciers, snowfields, valleys and forests straddle the South Island main divide and sprawl across the southern end of the Southern Alps/Kā Tiritiri o te Moana. Dominating the landscape is Mount Aspiring/Tititea (3027 metres, or 9935 feet), the highest and most glaciated mountain in New Zealand outside the Aoraki/Mount Cook region. Named Tititea ('glistening peak') by the Māori people, Mount Aspiring soars skyward in the classical alpine horn shape reminiscent of Switzerland's famous Matterhorn.

Since the park's establishment in 1964, significant additions have drawn more complete and representative ecosystems under the umbrella of national park protection. The park is now nearly double its original size and is a major part of the 2.6-million-hectare (6.4 million acres) Te Wahipounamu/South-West New Zealand World

Opposite: *Lake Harris fills a glacier-shaped hollow high on the mountainous border between Mount Aspiring and Fiordland national parks. One of New Zealand's premier walks, the Routeburn Track, passes by the lake.*

Top right: *Damselflies are among the fastest flying insects and have eyes with all-round vision that help them catch prey.*

Heritage Area, along with neighbouring parks Westland/Tai Poutini, Aoraki/Mount Cook and Fiordland.

The park encompasses three major regions of recreational use, plus a massive area of untracked wilderness consisting of glaciers, mountains, valleys and wildlife habitats that require days of foot travel to reach. One-quarter of the park (over 80,000 hectares, or 198,000 acres) is designated as the Olivine Wilderness, where no huts, tracks or aircraft landings are permitted. This serves to ensure that the 60 kilometres (37 miles) of the main divide, with its icy mountains, remote valleys and unruly rivers, are visited only on nature's terms.

Historically, the park region was devoid of human footprints but for journeys by Māori, who visited seasonal hunting camps and crossed mountain passes to reach the West Coast greenstone (pounamu) fields, and thereafter, European explorers.

Mount Aspiring/Tititea was first climbed in 1909; then climbers turned to other alpine peaks emanating from the Aspiring massif for new challenges. For many years trampers have explored the natural valley routes that are linked by mountain passes, some more easily negotiable than others. There is a huge choice; grassy river flats, hemmed by towering mountains with beech forest covering their lower flanks, which lead to subalpine meadows, rocky cirques, waterfalls and glacial lakes.

Popular valley routes are the Dart, Rees, West Matukituki, Wilkin, Siberia and Young, while the well-known Routeburn Track – a New Zealand Great Walk – crosses from the park's Routeburn Valley into Fiordland.

Location: Southwestern South Island.

Climate: Changeable. Usually settled in late summer. High rainfall, particularly on the western side. Summers mild, winters cold and frosty, with snow to low levels. Permanent snow above 2000m (6500 ft).

When to go: Anytime for short walks and scenic flights. Summer for tramping and climbing, winter for ski mountaineering.

Access: Main entrance points are Haast highway (SH6), Glenorchy and Matukituki Valley. Daily bus services.

Permits/Reservations: Bookings are required for the Routeburn Track from late October to May. Permits required for hunting, licences for fishing.

Facilities: In the park – huts, tracks camping areas, airstrips. DOC visitor centres at Haast, Makarora, Glenorchy, Wanaka and Queenstown. A range of accommodation and basic services at Haast, Makarora and Glenorchy. Full services at Queenstown and Wanaka. Tramper transport provided by bus, jet boat and aircraft.

Wildlife: Prolific birdlife.

Landscapes: Mountains, glaciers, Olivine Ice Plateau, Red Hills, vast river valleys, beech forests, subalpine meadows, river gorges and big, clear rock pools.

Visitor activities: Climbing, tramping, short walks, ski mountaineering, jet boating, river kayaking, scenic drives, scenic flights, hunting and fishing (for introduced deer and trout).

Precautions: Avalanche risk can make some tramping routes dangerous or impassable in winter.

Some of these routes are seasonal, as many passes in winter are suited only for individuals with snow climbing expertise. In more recent years, park staff have developed many short walks that enable a greater range of visitors, including those in wheelchairs, to explore delightful landscape features around the park fringes. Completion of the Haast Pass/Tioripatea highway in 1960 opened a window on the park's northern splendour. Now, tourists ride in coaches and campervans through forested river gorges and over Haast Pass/ Tioripatea, where previously Māori travellers and explorers crossed the tortuous route by foot. Long before them, some 10,000 to 200,000 years ago, a massive glacier scoured its way across the rocky ridgeline to shape this ice-smoothed pass.

Ice-sculpted Landscapes

Today the park's high-altitude snowfields are dominated by the large Olivine Ice Plateau and the Volta and Bonar glaciers. However, these and a hundred other glaciers throughout the park are but tiny remnants of the massive ice sheets which once covered the region.

The emphatic imprint of ice is seen in several landscapes – from the glacier-honed, spear-shaped summit of Mount Aspiring/Tititea, through the lakes, cirque basins, hanging valleys, moraines, U-Shaped valleys to the east of the park, the deep, glacier-gouged troughs of Lakes Wakatipu and Wanaka in the east of the park. The ice has carved its handiwork in the brittle schist rock, made up of shining mica, quartz and feldspars. As the rock is easily eroded by wind and water, the ice-sculpted landscapes are characterized by huge scree slopes.

(kākāriki) and a significant population of Haast Kiwi, a variety of the Southern Tokoeka species. The Mount Aspiring and Fiordland beech forests are the only places where endangered Yellowhead (mohua) survive in reasonable numbers, and research into predator control to sustain these populations is currently being undertaken in the Red Beech forests of the park's Dart Valley.

On the western side of the main divide, where the rainfall is nearly four times greater than the rainshadowed eastern side, lowland Silver Beech forests are mixed with podocarps such as Red Pine (rimu), matai, miro and White Pine (kahikatea), and are filled with a jungle-like profusion of dense understorey shrubs, ferns and vines.

The park's subalpine 'gardens' rate among the country's most prolific and diverse. These communities flourish in the valley heads above the tree line, on rock outcrops, snow banks and in alpine bogs, while some hardy lichens survive even above the permanent snowline. The park contains huge expanses of varying tussocks, shrublands and herb fields where the world's largest Mountain Buttercup (*Ranunculus lyallii*), Celmisia daisies and gentians are some of the flowering

Above: Trampers return to the Routeburn Track after a climb to Conical Hill, north of Harris Saddle.

Opposite top: Beech species dominate the park's forests.

Opposite far right: In the Red Hills, the reddish tinge of 'ultramafic' rock caused by its high mineral content, contrasts with grey schists in the rest of the park.

Opposite bottom: New Zealand's well-known Routeburn Track follows alongside the forest-lined Routeburn River, before climbing over the Humboldt mountains into Fiordland National Park.

Curious Red Hills

A geological curiosity is the Red Hills region, in the southwestern corner of the park. These hills are made of 'ultramafic' rocks, with high mineral contents of magnesium, iron and serpentine. The presence of similar Red Hills near Nelson – 500 kilometres (310 miles) to the north – is a geological phenomenon attributed to lateral displacement of the Alpine Fault. The striking Red Hills are also notable for their barrenness; their oxide soils are too toxic for all but the hardiest plants.

The dramatic contrast between schist and ultramafic rock is clearly shown in the park at Simonin Pass, where the Livingston Fault draws a sharp line between barren, red-coloured scree and schist slopes that are covered with Silver Beech forest.

Birds above the Bush Line

Beech (tawai) forests dominate the park. Silver Beech is most common in northern areas, while Red Beech grows to the south, particularly in the Routeburn and Dart valleys. These extensive forests provide habitats for a huge variety of native birds, including the rifleman (tĩti-tipounamu), Brown Creeper, Yellow-crowned Parakeet

delights. These alpine regions are also the domain of New Zealand's Mountain Parrot (kea), and the tiny, resilient Rock Wren, the only remaining species of the ancient New Zealand wren genus. This bird manages to survive the harsh alpine winter by sheltering in small rock crevices beneath the snow.

FIORDLAND NATIONAL PARK

Ice-sculpted Grandeur

To those who know Fiordland, the very mention of the name exudes an air of majesty and awe. For Fiordland is one of the great natural areas of the world – a massive 1.2-million-hectare (3 million acres) expanse of glaciated mountain landforms, remote fiord-indented coastline, lakes, rivers and the largest continuous tract of native forest in New Zealand. The range of ecosystems and habitats in the park, which takes up the entire south-western corner of the South Island, supports a huge abundance of animals and plants. Some of these areas are so remote that one bird species, the flightless Takahe, existing only in New Zealand and once believed to be extinct, has actually since been 're-discovered'.

Fiordland National Park is the largest in New Zealand, the fifth largest in the world, and comprises a major part of the Te Wahipounamu/South-West New Zealand World Heritage Area. Within the park are several world-renowned tourist destinations, Milford Sound/Piopiotahi, Doubtful Sound/Patea and the Milford, Routeburn, Kepler and Hollyford tracks.

Opposite: *Mountains of water in the Merrie Range, Southern Fiordland. Moist westerly winds prevail throughout the park, and rain falls over 200 days each year.*

Top right: *The delicate harebell (*Wahlenbergia pygmaea*), a perennial herb that flowers from November to February.*

Although much of Fiordland is remote wilderness, a well-established tourism infrastructure enables people of all ages and fitness levels to experience special parts of the park. Each year, thousands of international tourists partake in scenic cruises on the lakes and fiords, coach tours along the dramatic mountain-lined Milford highway, flights, ecotours, short walks, guided walks and wilderness fishing. For the more adventurous, Fiordland presents a challenging menu of tramping (hiking), climbing, hunting, kayaking and diving.

An Ancient Landscape

Three key factors have shaped Fiordland's distinctive land form: tectonic uplift, glaciation and the hard, ancient rock of its mountains. Unlike in other, erosion-prone South Island mountains, the hard crystalline and metamorphic rocks of Fiordland have resisted erosion. The landscape is thus little changed since great glaciers shaped the fiords, lakes and U-shaped valleys so characteristic of the park.

Fiords (erroneously called sounds) are found in only a few places around the world. In Fiordland, glaciers flowing west from the mountains gouged deep trenches that have since been flooded by the sea and formed the fiords that give the park its name. Over 1000 kilometres (620 miles) of remote coastline are indented by 14 fiords. They penetrate deep into the mountains, 30 to 40 kilometres (18 to 25 miles) in length, up to 500 metres (1640 feet) deep and bounded by sheer walls that reach up to a staggering 1.5 kilometres (0.9 miles) in height. Reportedly the world's highest sea cliff is Mitre

Location: Southwest South Island.

Climate: Mild summers and cold winters. Snow in winter and heavy rain throughout the year.

When to go: Summer for tramping and alpine flowers, winter for climbing, anytime for other activities. Avalanche danger sometimes closes Milford Highway in winter and spring.

Access: By road, SH6 from Queenstown or Invercargill, then SH94 to Te Anau. By air, daily flights to Manapouri.

Permits: Required for hunting (Red Deer and Elk). Fishing licences for fishing of introduced trout.

Facilities: Park visitor centre at Te Anau. A vast network of walking tracks, bridges, huts, camping and picnic areas. Te Anau has a full range of accommodation and services. Accommodation is also available at Manapouri, Te Anau Downs and Milford. Numerous transport and other tourist services.

Watching wildlife: Fiordland Crested Penguins, Little Blue Penguins, New Zealand Fur Seals, Bottlenose Dolphins, Yellowhead, South Island Robins, Bush and Mountain Parrot, Sandflies.

Landscapes: Mountains, fiords, native forests, lakes, river, waterfalls, wetlands, alpine meadows.

Visitor activities: Short walks, tramping, climbing (snow and rock), diving, sea and lake kayaking, mountain biking, hunting, fishing, camping, scenic flights (helicopter, fixed wing and float plane options), scenic drives, lake and fiord cruises, guided walks, natural heritage tours

Precautions: In Spring, be wary of avalanche danger on the Milford Road, near the Homer Tunnel, and on the Milford Track.

Opposite top: Loch Maree, in the Seaforth valley along the Dusky track.

Opposite bottom: Fiordland Crested Penguins, among the world's rarest, nest in caves and undergrowth on the remote coastal islands.

Peak, which rises 1700 metres (5580 feet) sheer from the water of Milford Sound/Piopiotahi. These fiords support a unique marine environment, including the world's biggest and shallowest population of Black Coral. Two marine reserves protect small portions of this environment and an underwater observatory in Milford Sound/Piopiotahi offers public viewing of just some of this amazing underwater world.

Still in the fiords, more special inhabitants live above the surface, such as one of the world's rarest penguins, the endemic Fiordland Crested Penguin (tawaki). However, this timid penguin is rarely seen; visitors cruising the fiords are more likely to come across dolphins, such as the pod of Bottlenose Dolphins that live in Doubtful Sound/Patea, Fur Seals or some of the myriad sea birds that thrive in this remote, coastal environment.

Water-dominated Domain

Water dominates Fiordland – be it rain, snow or ice – the lakes, fiords, rivers and waterfalls are constantly and dramatically replenished by one of the wettest climates found anywhere in the world. This is not necessarily a deterrent to park visitors, though floods, avalanches and snowfalls can sometimes interrupt travel in the park. From a safe distance, the awe-inspiring

spectacle of massive volumes of water cascading down sheer mountain walls is a true Fiordland experience, and one not to be missed.

East-flowing glaciers chiselled the basins filled now by lakes. Of these, Te Anau is the biggest, Manapouri arguably the most beautiful, Hauroko the deepest and Poteriteri the most remote. All look magnificent. These lakes form the eastern boundary to the park and are the major access points to the vast forests and mountains that line their western shores. Lake Manapouri has a special place in New Zealand's conservation history. In the 1970s, a plan to raise the lake's level for hydro-electricity generation was thwarted by a concerted conservation campaign, the first of its kind in this country.

Special Plants and Animals

Fiordland's primeval rainforests thrive in this moist climate. Most dominant is beech forest, the dark tree trunks often wreathed with lichens, mosses and filmy ferns. But the great podocarps are also present and, as one would expect in such a vast wilderness area, there is a staggering diversity of vegetation types that includes wetlands, estuaries, coastal dunes, subalpine shrublands, tussock fields and alpine herb fields. There are few places in the temperate world where glaciers and alpine herb fields are found just 5 kilometres (3 miles) away

from densely-forested coastlines, as is the case in the mountains near the mouth of Milford Sound/Piopiotahi.

Fiordland is also home to large numbers of endemic and threatened plants and animals. Some 30 plant species exist only in Fiordland, 300 of the park's incredible 3000 insect species are endemic and there are also significant populations of endemic snails, lizards and skinks. Visitors to Fiordland are bound to come across namu, the pesky sandfly!

One of the most special of all the native species remaining in Fiordland is the endangered Large Flightless Rail (takahē) thought to be extinct until it was 'rediscovered' in a remote tussock valley in 1948. Numbers of the takahē have today increased to around 120, while others have been relocated to island sanctuaries to improve the bird's chances of survival.

Several bird species now rarely seen in other areas of New Zealand have survived in bigger populations in the great Fiordland wilderness. Observant park visitors may chance sightings of yellowhead (mohua), Yellow-crowned Parakeet (kākāriki), New Zealand Falcon (kārearea) and South Island Robin. Brown Teal (pateke) and Blue Duck (kōwhiowhio) live in the park's rivers and streams, while Tokoeka, the South Island subspecies of Brown Kiwi, are reasonably common and the Mountain Parrot, kea, is likely to make its cheeky presence known.

Above: Waterfalls are a feature of the park. Fiordland's heavy rainfall can quickly turn gentle falls into raging torrents.

Right: Looking into remote Dusky Sound and Southern Fiordland from Pigeon Island.

Opposite: Frequently photographed, Mitre Peak in Milford Sound/Piopiotahi, is one of New Zealand's most popular tourist destinations.

Fiordland's Māori History

The very physical nature of rugged, remote Fiordland has thankfully thwarted large-scale human settlement. Nevertheless, Māori stories and place names for features throughout the park (though not all acknowledged on present-day maps) tell of these people's strong association with the region. Archaeological evidence points to pre–1800 Māori dwellings in southern coastline areas. Further north, the present-day Milford Track was a common route travelled by Māori to reach the valuable greenstone jade (pounamu) of Milford Sound/Piopiotahi.

According to Māori, the great fiords were created by their legendary ancestor, Tū Te Rakiwhānoa, who carved them from the hard mountain rock with his bare hands. He started in the south, leaving ragged coastlines and many islands. As he moved north his technique improved, so by the time he reached Piopiotahi he carved the perfect, steep-sided fiord. But Tū Te Rakiwhānoa decided his work was too perfect and, for balance, he introduced namu, the sandfly. The first European arrivals included British explorer Captain James Cook, then sealers, whalers, surveyors and prospectors brought a busy but short-lived flurry of activity around the Fiordland coast.

Tourism

The scenic grandeur of Fiordland has long been a draw-card for international tourists. For over 100 years the Milford Track has linked Lake Te Anau with Milford Sound/Piopiotahi via two glacial-shaped valleys and an alpine pass. The Milford, Routeburn and Kepler tracks are 'Great Walks' and the Hollyford Track is also extremely popular. There are a host of other, equally impressive tramping options (a network encompassing numerous tracks and some 60 huts) plus a host of shorter scenic walks that explore the forests, glacial lakes, waterfalls and alpine tarns of Fiordland.

In the north of the park, the Darran Mountains, challenging rock-climbing routes and Fiordland's highest mountain, Tutoko (2746 metres, or 9012 feet), attract

adventurous, wilderness-seeking climbers. However, many of Fiordland's visitors experience the might of Fiordland without stepping onto a forest track. The Milford Road, which carves through some of the park's highest mountains via the Homer Tunnel, is regarded as one of the most stunning scenic drives in the world.

A frenetic scenic flight schedule makes the small Milford airstrip the busiest airfield in the country, while thousands more tourists opt for launch cruises on mountain-flanked lakes and fiords.

Conservation and tourism have happily co-existed since the Fiordland National Park was established in 1952. Half a million people now visit the park each year, yet there must remain some remote parts of this vast wilderness where no human foot has ever stepped.

OTAGO PENINSULA

Wildlife Treasure Trove

One of the world's largest sea birds and possibly the rarest penguin, the Northern Royal Albatross and the Yellow-eyed Penguin, are the stars of the incredibly diverse wildlife population based on Otago Peninsula, less than an hour's drive from Dunedin.

Nowhere else does the ocean-going Northern Royal Albatross (toroa) nest so close to human settlement. These majestic fliers circumnavigate the Southern Ocean, live at sea for years at a time and breed mostly on the remote, windswept Chatham Islands. For some inexplicable reason, they have also chosen to nest on Otago Peninsula's Taiaroa Head, within the boundary of Dunedin City, easily accessible by road.

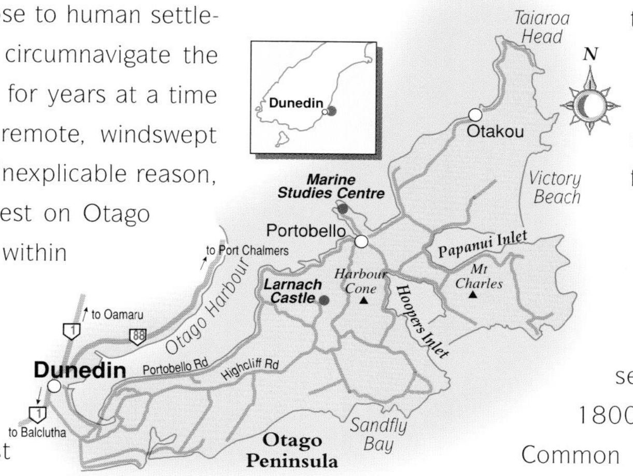

Yellow-eyed Penguins (hoiho) are the third largest and arguably the rarest of the world's 18 penguin species. The Peninsula's coastal margins have become a major stronghold for these birds, which breed only on the Subantarctic Islands, Stewart Island and the southeast coast of the South Island.

Sharing the Otago Peninsula is a host of other wildlife. Three species of shags (kōau) – Spotted Shags, Little Shags and rare Stewart Island Shags – nest around Taiaroa Head. Little Blue Penguins (kororā), New Zealand Fur Seals (kekeno), and Southern Elephant Seals (ihupuku) share the coastal zones. Gulls and terns (tara) fill the daytime sky, and Sooty Shearwaters (tītī) fly home to their burrows at night.

The world's rarest sea lion, New Zealand Sea Lion (rāpoka), hauls out onto the Peninsula's beaches. Most are young males, stragglers from their breeding colonies of the Auckland Islands, 460 kilometres (286 miles) to the south. However, in 1993, one female produced the first sea lion birth that has been recorded on the mainland since the sea lion population was decimated by the skin-seeking sealing gangs of the 1800s. Dusky, Bottlenose and Common Dolphins and Southern Right Whale (tohorā) sometimes enter the harbour.

The presence of handy food sources explains why abundant wildlife lives on the peninsula's beaches, inlets and rocky headlands. Close to shore the sea's continental shelf falls into deep, submarine canyons, providing convenient access to a veritable 'supermarket' of marine food.

The Royals

Northern Royal Albatross began breeding on Taiaroa Head, the windswept promontory that guards the entrance to Otago Harbour, in the early 1900s. Since then the slowly expanding colony has been monitored closely by ornithologists and scientists. A critical factor in safeguarding the birds, their eggs and chicks from the dangers of such proximity to human 'civilization' has been constant vigilance from threats such as stoats, cats, dogs, and ferrets, not forgetting overly curious

Map labels: Taiaroa Head, N, Dunedin, Otakou, Marine Studies Centre, Victory Beach, Portobello, to Port Chalmers, Papanui Inlet, Mt Charles, Larnach Castle, Harbour Cone, to Oamaru, Otago Harbour, Hoopers Inlet, Dunedin, Portobello Rd, Highcliff Rd, to Balclutha, Sandfly Bay, Otago Peninsula

Opposite: Rakiriri, meaning 'angry sky', was the Otago Māori name for the ancient Dunedin volcano which formed Otago harbour and peninsula. This sunrise aptly mirrors the name.

Top right: A dedicated conservation effort has helped increase numbers of the Yellow-eyed Penguin, a very rare species.

Location: Southeast coast of the South Island, within Dunedin City.

Climate: Mild summers, cold winters with frosts and occasional snow.

When to go: Any time of the year. Albatross viewing is restricted during spring when the birds are breeding. The visitor centre and displays are open daily throughout the year; the colony is closed from about mid-November to 26 November each year.

Access: Daily services to Dunedin by air, bus and train. From Dunedin City several roads lead to the peninsula, which starts 4km (2.5 miles) from the city centre. Chartered coach tours and harbour wildlife cruises are available.

Facilities: Royal Albatross Centre at Taiaroa Head (guided tours, interpretative displays). Peninsula villages have shops, petrol, craft, cafes and accommodation, including farm stays, backpackers lodges, motels, and camping grounds. Full range of services in Dunedin City, including visitor information centre.

Permits: Not required, but access to the albatross colony is only permitted through the visitor centre.

Visitor activities: Wildlife watching, harbour cruises, short walks, swimming, surfing, picnics.

Landscapes: Eroded and farmed rolling hills, volcanic cones, sea cliffs and basalt formations, sand dunes, beaches, tidal inlets.

Watching wildlife: Northern Royal Albatross, Yellow-eyed Penguins, New Zealand Fur Seals, Stewart Island Shags, Spotted Shags, Little Shags, Little Blue Penguins, Leopard Seals, New Zealand Sea Lions, several species of gulls, terns and wading birds.

Right: Nowhere does the ocean-flying Northern Royal Albatross nest so close to human settlement as on Taiaroa Head, Otago Peninsula.

Opposite left: Victory Beach, one of the peninsula's favourite haul-out spot for New Zealand Sea Lions.

Below: The colony of Stewart Island Shags on Taiaroa Head is the largest on the mainland.

humans. Today about 100 Northern Royal Albatross are based at Taiaroa Head. The colony is fenced and managed by DOC as a Nature Reserve. The Royal Albatross Centre, run by the Otago Peninsula Trust, provides comprehensive displays and audiovisuals, a viewing observatory and guided tours.

From the observatory, visitors can watch the birds' behaviour, which varies throughout the breeding cycle. If it's windy, there will be the incredible flying techniques to admire. Those huge, three-metre (10 feet) wing spans have finely tuned aerodynamic features that enable albatross to soar effortlessly and to fly hundreds of kilometres at a time, at speeds of up to 100 kilometres (60 miles) per hour.

Protection of the Hoiho

Meanwhile, down on the peninsula's beaches, visitors can witness a significant conservation success story: the resurgence in numbers of the rare and endangered Yellow-eyed Penguin (hoiho).

Unlike other penguin species, the hoiho is a shy bird which nests in the shelter of coastal shrubland, sometimes several hundred metres from the sea. After fishing at sea all day, the penguins return to their nests at night. However they frighten easily and will stay at sea, even if they have chicks to feed, if they see threatening animals or humans between the sea and their nests.

Hoiho numbers on the peninsula became threatened when their habitat was decimated by farm development and the birds were disturbed by introduced animal predators. As the population reached crisis point a very public campaign to save the bird was spearheaded by the Yellow-eyed Penguin Trust. Since 1987 the Trust has co-ordinated conservation organizations in its efforts to safeguard penguin habitats.

Some peninsula farmers with colonies on their land have initiated their own conservation measures, such as predator control, revegetation work, building nesting boxes, and installing tunnels and hides so birds can come ashore and nest in private while humans watch without disturbance. The benefits are twofold – effective penguin protection and the development of very successful ecotourism ventures.

In other areas, such as at Sandfly Bay Wildlife Reserve, colonies are managed by DOC and have public viewing hides. The department manages several nature reserves, wildlife refuges and recreation reserves on the peninsula and is responsible for the general welfare of protected species under the Wildlife Act. Hooper's Inlet Wildlife

In contrast, the golden-coloured sand dunes of Sandfly Bay reach an astonishing 300 metres (980 feet) in height. The sand, schist material from the heart of Central Otago, is carried to sea by the Clutha River, then swept north by sea currents.

Peninsula wildlife has lived alongside human settlements for hundreds of years. For generations, Māori subtribes of Kati Mamoe and Ngai Tahu lived around the settlement of Otakou (Otago) and utilized nearby Pukekura (Taiaroa Head) as a defensive retreat. Otakou Marae remains an important centre for the Peninsula subtribe, Ngai Te Paki.

After the mid-1800s, British immigrants made a significant mark on the peninsula landscape by clearing forest, developing farms and building intricate stone walls. Intriguing features of Otago Peninsula's human heritage include Larnach Castle and Glenfalloch Gardens, where a huge old podocarp mataī tree is testament to the forest that once covered the peninsula.

Today much of peninsula land is farmed and a number of the people who live here commute to work in Dunedin City. But with the establishment of tourism award-winning natural heritage tours, and as awareness of the peninsula's special wildlife inhabitants grows, the future of the majestic sea birds, endangered penguins, and other marine life has hopefully become assured.

Above: The peninsula is a stronghold for the rare, shrub-dwelling Jewelled Gecko.

Below: Taiaroa Head guards the entrance to Otago Harbour.

Sanctuary, a vast wetland indenting the seaward side of the Otago Peninsula, is alive with water birds, among them terns (tara), gulls, herons, stilts, plovers, and oystercatchers.

On the harbour side, at Portobello, the University of Otago manages the New Zealand Marine Studies Centre. Interpretative displays, an aquarium and laboratory are open to the public.

Diverse Landscapes

Wildlife watching on Otago Peninsula involves a tour of interesting natural landscapes. Several walking tracks lead to towering sea cliffs, collapsed sea caverns and wave-worn stacks of columnar basalt that contrast sharply with the green pastureland of peninsula farms.

The Dunedin area is volcanic in origin: with the main volcano at Otago Harbour, and associated vents, cones, domes, and lava flows easily discernible along the length of the peninsula. Red volcanic rocks exposed on the cliffs of Taiaroa Head explain the Māori name, Pukekura, meaning 'red hill', for this significant headland.

THE CATLINS

Wild and Windswept

A forest park, several scientific and scenic reserves and a dramatically rugged and beautiful coastline that teems with marine life make up the area known as The Catlins.

For many, this remote, southeastern corner of the South Island is an unknown, or forgotten, part of New Zealand. But for those who appreciate the beauty of the natural world, the Catlins represents an outstanding example of primeval New Zealand. Sea lions, seals and penguins share this spectacular coastline; rare Hector's Dolphins cavort in the offshore surf; and further inland, waterfalls are framed by lush rainforest that resounds with native birdsong. The Catlins and South Westland are the only two areas where tall, majestic podocarp forest grows over sand dunes beside the beach.

In recent years several ecotourism ventures have been developed to cater for the increasing number of people becoming aware of the Catlins region. A key attraction is that most of the special features can be reached easily by short walks – few more than 30 minutes in duration.

Opposite: Nugget Point, scenic spectacle and wildlife wonder, is home to sea lions, seals, penguins, shags and a host of other sea birds.

Top Right: An ancient tree stump, estimated to be 160 million years old, at a fossilized forest site in Curio Bay.

Precious Forest Remnants

As with much of New Zealand, pioneer farmers and timber millers have made a significant impact on the Catlins forests. Sawmills have operated throughout the region since the 1860s, with timber extracted by rivers, a railway, and later by road. However, just one mill still remains operational today, the railway has closed and more than 54,000 hectares (133,000 acres) of forest is now legally protected in reserves or forest park.

Although farming remains an economic mainstay for this sparsely populated region, the presence of rough pastures and blackened tree stumps throughout the area are testimony to the formidable adversary nature has presented to those intent on 'breaking in' this land.

Local people now show a strong commitment to retaining the natural values of the Catlins, with the development of an ecotourism industry and community initiatives such as the Papatowai Forest Heritage Trust, formed to protect regenerating bush.

The Catlins contain many contrasting features – forest types found nowhere else, marine wildlife that lives only in this part of New Zealand or on the Subantartic Islands and just about every conceivable coastal landform there is. Probably the best way to describe such contrasts is to embark on a written 'Catlins' tour.

Tokata – Nugget Point

This small, steep headland is both a dramatic spectacle and a scientific reserve. Historically, the headland was an important seafood gathering place for early Māori, who called it Tokata. The name 'nugget' refers to the

Location: Southeast corner of the South Island.

Climate: Mild throughout the year. High rainfall.

When to go: Any time of the year.

Access: By road, SH92 traverses the Catlins coast from Balclutha to Invercargill. Tourist coach tours are available from Invercargill and Dunedin.

Permits: Not required.

Facilities: Shops and petrol at Owaka and Papatowai. Camping, motels, and home stay accommodation throughout the region. Eco-tours and cruises available. Visitor information centres at Owaka, Invercargill and Dunedin. DOC tracks, bridges, and information panels.

Watching wildlife: Yellow-eyed Penguins, New Zealand Sea Lions, New Zealand Fur Seals, Southern Elephant Seals, Hector's Dolphins.

Landscapes: Coastal – beaches, estuaries, sea cliffs, caves, blowholes, rock stacks. Vegetation – coastal podocarp forest, Silver Beech forest, rāta/kāmahi forest, dune lakes, waterfalls, fossil forest. Native flowers – Southern Rāta, fuchsia, kāmahi flowers, Catlins Coast Daisy.

Visitor activities: Short walks, natural heritage tours, sea kayaking, wildlife watching, dolphin cruises.

Precautions: Take care not to disturb Yellow-eyed Penguins – they will be reluctant to come ashore to their nests if people are visible. Be wary of seals and sea lions; do not approach them or block their path to the sea.

wave-eroded rock stacks off the point of the headland which apparently resemble gold nuggets.

Just offshore, productive feeding grounds attract a diversity of marine life to the headland. Nugget Point is the only place in the country where New Zealand Fur Seals (kekeno), New Zealand Sea Lions (rāpoka) and Southern Elephant Seals (ihupuku) co-exist. Colonies of Yellow-eyed Penguins (hoiho), Little Blue Penguins (kororā), Spotted Shags, Sooty Shearwaters (tītī), Australasian Gannets and Royal Spoonbills occupy the beaches, cliffs, and rock stacks. DOC has installed a public viewing hide at Roaring Bay, near the start of the headland, so visitors can watch shy Yellow-eyed Penguins moving between the sea and their nests, which are based on land.

Native vegetation, much of it thoroughly wind-shorn, needs to be hardy and salt-tolerant to survive on this wild, windswept promontory. Nevertheless, two flowering native plants – clematis and the endemic Catlins Coast Daisy – cover the headland with bold splashes of white during spring and summer. In the sea itself, huge underwater forests of kelp – 15-metre-tall (50 feet) Bladder Kelp and hardy Bull Kelp (rimurapa) – swirl wildly in the often raging seas. And on the steep walls of the offshore rock stacks lives an underwater community of colourful corals, sponges, sea squirts, sea urchins and jewel anemones.

The Nugget Point lighthouse, now fully automatic, has shone for coastal shipping since 1870. Although a remote region today, the Catlins coast was once a busy shipping route for traders working between Dunedin and Australia, and the notoriously violent seas here have claimed the lives of many ships.

Surat Bay

This sandy beach and river estuary is a favoured haulout spot for New Zealand Sea Lions (rāpoka). These massive animals (adult males can weigh over 400 kilograms, or 880 pounds) mostly breed in the Subantartic Islands. After being hunted for their food and skins during the 1800s, their numbers are again thriving around the southern South Island coast.

Catlins River

Pure stands of Silver Beech forest (tawai), the southernmost in New Zealand, grow along the middle and upper reaches of the Catlins River. This forest is home to the few remaining flocks of Yellowhead (mohua), now a threatened species.

Purakaunui and Other Waterfalls

Purakaunui Falls have become the scenic icon of the Catlins; images of the cascades falling delicately across

Below: *One of the growing population of New Zealand Fur Seals that live along the Catlins Coast.*

Bottom right: *An easy walk leads to Lake Wilkie, a dune lake. This is a stunning example of natural revegetation, a process evolving from small wetland species to young forest and mature podocarp trees.*

three wide terraces have graced many a scenic book and calendar. They are one of three Catlins waterfalls that are easily reached by short walking tracks which lead through distinctive forest features. At Purakaunui there is a diverse mix of Silver Beech, Red Pine (rimu), kāmahi, and broadleaf trees (kāpuka). Silver Beech and impressively lush tree ferns line the walk to McLean Falls, on the remarkably pristine Tautuku River and, at Mataī Falls, summer-flowering fuchsia (kōtukutuku) attracts large numbers of New Zealand's melodious honey eaters, tui and bellbirds (korimako).

Tahakopa River and Papatowai

At the Tahakopa River mouth, its northern bank is lined with magnificent coastal podocarp forest. Towering Red Pine (rimu) overlook the beach; this is classic Catlins forest. Only in this region and in remote South Westland do the giant podocarps grow on sand dunes so close to the coast. The Tahakopa forest is one of the few remaining coastal podocarp stands that survived the Catlins milling era, and is now protected as a reserve.

Across the Tahakopa estuary is the small settlement of Papatowai, where holiday homes, a delightful camping ground, ecotourism ventures and the only shop in the central Catlins entice visitors. A 20-minute walk here encompasses sandy beach, rocky shoreline, dense rain-

forest and a possible encounter with some of the marine wildlife that frequents the Catlins coast.

Above: A rare Hector's Dolphin frolics in the offshore surf at the Catlins.

Tautuku Bay and Lake Wilkie

Tautuku is where the term 'primeval New Zealand' is aptly applied. A broad bay lined with sandy beach and luxuriant coastal podocarp forest, a sprawling estuary, an unmodified forest-filled river catchment, a dune lake hidden in the forest, and a wildlife sanctuary on offshore rockstacks; they are all here.

Several short walks highlight Tautuku's features. A boardwalk penetrates the swampy jointed rushes of the estuary, a favoured habitat of the threatened fernbird (mātā). An easy walk leads through the coastal podocarp forest to the beach, and, nearby, another short walk reveals one of the precious gems of the Catlins, Lake Wilkie.

Apart from its scenic beauty, the forest surrounding this dune lake is a magnificent example of forest succession — where clearly defined zones show how the forests here evolved. In summer, red-flowering Rātā is an added bonus for visitors.

Curio Bay

Exposed on tidal platforms at Curio Bay is a geological fascination — a well-preserved fossil forest that dates back 160 million years. Volcanic ash and mud flows buried this forest of Jurassic-aged conifer trees, in a time before even birds or flowering plants had evolved.

Just around the corner from Curio Bay is Porpoise Bay, the home of a pod of the world's smallest and rarest dolphin, Hector's Dolphin. Porpoise Bay is the only known place where these dolphins live permanently so close to shore. These dolphins can be seen from land, or from a dolphin cruise, although visitors are reminded that it is illegal to disturb or harass any marine mammal.

STEWART ISLAND/ RAKIURA

Isolated Island Habitat

Stewart Island is perhaps one of the largest, unspoilt forested islands in the world. Set apart geographically, in the wild Roaring Forties latitudes on the subantarctic edge of New Zealand, the island has been left largely to nature's devices and is a treasure chest of unmodified ecosystems and habitats – and a haven for rare plants and endangered wildlife.

The island is New Zealand's third largest – nearly 2000 square kilometres (772 square miles) in size and yet barely 400 people live there. The population centres on the only town, Oban. The rest of the island is a natural wilderness of dense coastal rainforests, freshwater wetlands, vast sand dunes, granite mountains and tundra-like alpine vegetation. Nearly 200 smaller islands and rocky islets surround the coastline. Some of these are the last refuges for New Zealand's rarest birds, such as the heavyweight of the parrot world, the kākāpō.

For visitors, Stewart Island provides a rare chance to experience primeval New Zealand. The Rakiura Track, north of Paterson Inlet/Whaka a Te Wera, is one of New Zealand's Great Walks. Another track completes an eight- to ten-day northwest circuit of the island, the longest back-country walk in New Zealand. Day walks explore forests and coastline near Oban, including the Ulva Island wildlife sanctuary. Sea kayaking and natural heritage tours and cruises are other options – nature tourism is a major part of the livelihood of Stewart Island residents. Also popular is hunting of the island's introduced White-tail Deer herd, an activity encouraged to control these forest-eating animals.

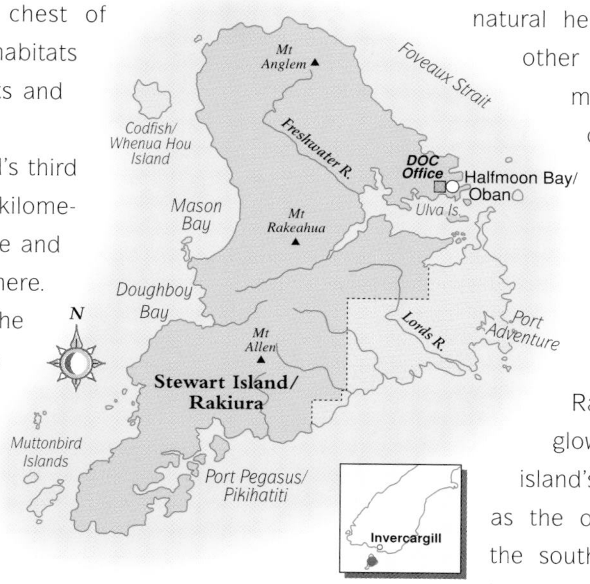

The island's Māori name, Rakiura, means 'land of the glowing skies'. It refers to the island's magnificent sunsets, as well as the often spectacular displays of the southern lights, *aurora australis*. Māori people lived around the island's coast for hundreds of years and still maintain traditional harvesting rights of Muttonbird or Sooty Shearwater (tītī) on the Rakiura Māori-owned Tītī Islands, surrounding Stewart Island.

Outstanding Ecosystems

The dense rainforests that cover much of the island are the southernmost podocarp forests in the world. Nine podocarp species grow here, mixed with kāmahi and Southern Rātā. A distinctive feature is the lack of several forest species which are common in the North and South Islands, for example beech (tawai), kōwhai and mahoe. These forests resound with native birdsong. Along with more common tuī, bellbirds (korimako), fan-

Opposite top: *Tramping in a tunnel of manuka forest.*

Opposite bottom: *This rare, dune-creeping herb* Gunnera Hamiltonii *grows only on Stewart Island.*

Top right: *Stunted rātā trees covered in moss.*

Location: Southernmost of New Zealand's three main islands, 30km (19 miles) south of the South Island.

Climate: Warm summers, cool winters, with few frosts or snowfalls. Cloudy, windy and wet – most days see some rainfall.`

When to go: Anytime. In summer there are exceptionally long daylight hours; the reverse applies in winter.

Access: Daily flights from Invercargill and ferry services from Bluff.

Permits/Reservations: Permits required for hunting.

Facilities: Tracks, huts, campsites. In Oban – visitor centre, accommodation (luxury lodge, home stays, hotels, motel, backpacker hostel and campground), restaurant and takeaways, store, craft shop, range of natural heritage tours and cruises, helicopter, launch and yacht charters, water and road taxis, guided walks and sea kayaking tours.

Wildlife: Great range of forest and sea birds, including kiwi, Red-crowned Parakeet, South Island kākā, New Zealand Dotterel, Yellow-eyed Penguin and Fiordland Crested Penguin, New Zealand Sea Lion and Fur Seals. Kākāpō live on Whenua Hou/Codfish Island, a nature reserve closed to the public.

Landscapes: Dense, podocarp rainforests, sheltered inlets, wetlands. High-rise sand dunes and sprawling beaches, granite mountain domes, alpine herb fields and shrublands, forest-covered islets and rock stacks.

Visitor activities: Tramping, bird watching, short walks, sea kayaking, hunting, fishing,

Precautions: When visiting Ulva Island ensure boats and bags are checked to prevent accidental reintroduction of mice, rats, or other pests.

Map labels: Mt Anglem, Foveaux Strait, Codfish/Whenua Hou Island, Freshwater R., DOC Office, Halfmoon Bay/Oban, Mason Bay, Mt Rakeahua, Ulva Is., Doughboy Bay, N, Lords R., Port Adventure, Mt Allen, Stewart Island/Rakiura, Muttonbird Islands, Port Pegasus/Pikihatiti, Invercargill

Right: Mason Bay, a long,
remote stretch of beach and
dunes on Stewart Island's
exposed and windswept
west coast.

tails (pīwakawaka), Grey Warblers (riroriro), tomtits (miromiro) and Brown Creepers are several species which are endemic or threatened (or both). Red-crowned Parakeets (kākāriki) are more conspicuous than their yellow-crowned cousins, a reversal of the norm in South Island forests.

The island is also a stronghold for threatened Bush Parrots (South Island kākā), Stewart Island Weka, Stewart Island Robin. One of the island's most special residents, Southern Kiwi (tokoeka) is also prolific. Southern Kiwi are also found in Fiordland, but unlike their northern cousins, the Stewart Island Kiwi boldly feed during daylight hours. For this reason, Stewart Island is known as one of the most likely places to see kiwi in the wild.

In coastal fringes, Muttonbird Scrub (tētēaweka) is the local term used to describe a hardy band of wind- and salt-resistant tree daisies that form dense cover for weka, three species of penguin, kiwi, fernbird (mātā), and Banded Rail.

One of the reasons for the island's rich birdlife is the absence of mustelids – introduced ferrets and stoats – which have seriously affected the bird populations.

Freshwater Estuaries and the Tin Range

On the island's exposed west coast, windswept beaches are backed by sand dunes of staggering proportions. Behind the 15-kilometre-long (9 miles) expanse of sandy beach at Mason Bay, the 'Big Sandhill' climbs an incredible 156 metres (511 feet)), bound together by native dune plants such as the golden-coloured Pingao. Further north, beaches with telling names of Smoky, Ruggedy and Hellfire

Below: The subalpine-dwelling Harlequin Gecko is one of the five lizard species that lives only on remote Stewart Island.

face the prevailing westerlies which, over hundreds of years, have blown sand up to 20 kilometres (12 miles) inland.

In contrast the lee, eastern side of the island is punctuated with several sheltered inlets – drowned river valleys now surrounded with mature native forests that grow right to the water's edge. The largest is Paterson Inlet/Whaka a Te Wera, which cuts a swathe deep into the centre of the island and rates as one of the largest and least modified estuaries in the country. At the head of the inlet, Freshwater Valley follows a fault-bounded trough westwards into the heart of Stewart Island's rugged interior.

Freshwater habitats are among the island's most complete natural ecosystems. They support 15 species of freshwater fish, including large numbers of giant kōkopu, the largest of all galaxiids which are now rare in mainland waterways. Unlike in most New Zealand waterways, the island is free of introduced trout, which threaten native fish.

The highest place in Stewart Island is Mount Anglem/Hananui (980 metres; 3216 feet), an imposing 9-kilometre-long (6 miles) massif of igneous diorite rock that dominates the northern interior and hosts a rich alpine plantlife. Many of the herbs, dwarf shrubs and speargrasses here grow nowhere else; 21 of the island's 23 endemic plants grow in the alpine zone. Flowering herbs, Bog Lily, Mountain Daisies and Mountain Buttercups also flourish on Mount Anglem/Hananui.

The granite domes of the Tin Range, which dominate the southern Stewart Island skyline, are unique in New Zealand. These weathered knobs are more akin to landscapes in Rio de Janeiro, or California's Yosemite Valley.

Bottom left: *A fern-frond curtain hangs over the bank of a tannin-stained creek at Doughboy Bay.*

Bottom centre: *Trampers wander through knee-high tussock in one of the alpine zones on the Island.*

Their names, Gog and Magog, are Celtic. Intriguingly, alpine shrublands high on the Tin Range are home to a colony of coastal wading birds, one of New Zealand's most endangered species, the New Zealand Dotterel. Unlike its northern cousins, who breed and feed on coastal sands, this southern subspecies travels from mountain top to coast to feed. In 1999, after five years of intensive feral cat control on the range, the population had risen from 65 birds to 144.

The Tin Range was also the last mainland location of the world's largest and only flightless parrot, the kākāpō. During the mid-1980s, conservation staff caught the last 40 of these highly endangered birds and to save them from the threat of feral cats, relocated them to offshore island refuges.

Island Wildlife Habitats

One such refuge is Whenua Hou/Codfish Island, a 1400-hectare (3460 acres) nature reserve, which lies 4 kilometres (2.5 miles) off the northwestern Stewart Island coast. Fernbirds (mātā) and Short-tailed Bats also live here.

Ulva Island, in Paterson Inlet/Whaka a Te Wera, is a rat-free open sanctuary where tourists who follow strict quarantine measures are allowed to visit the island and observe several species of native birds now uncommon in mainland forests.

At the time of writing, the New Zealand government was considering a proposal to establish a Stewart Island/Rakiura National Park. Encompassing 163,000 hectare (403,000 acres), this could become New Zealand's fifth largest national park.

Below: *The aptly named Ruggedy Mountains rise steeply on the island's mountainous northwestern corner.*

SUBANTARCTIC ISLANDS

Rugged, Remote and Rare

Location: Southern Ocean (New Zealand territory), between latitudes 47 to 42 degrees south.

Climate: Windswept (gale-force westerly winds), constant rainfall (rain falls an average of 300 days of the year), low sunshine hours.

When to go: Nature heritage cruises visit in summer.

Access: Only by approved cruise companies. Tourism is strictly controlled and no compromise of natural values or protection management is tolerated.

Permits/Reservations: To protect the fragile and rare island ecosystems, all tourist visits are governed by strict regulations and quarantine procedures. All tourists require a permit, are allowed to land only on a few designated places, and are accompanied by a DOC representative.

Facilities: Boardwalks (to direct visitors and avoid trampling of vegetation). Note: in the Southland Museum, Invercargill, a special gallery is devoted to the Subantarctic Islands.

Wildlife: New Zealand Sea Lions, New Zealand Fur Seals, several species of albatross, penguins, cormorants, petrels, shearwaters. Huge numbers of sea birds and seals.

Landscapes: Steep sea cliffs, windswept tussock-covered moors, guano-covered rock platforms, rocky coastline, seascapes, mega herb gardens, Southern rāta forests.

Visitor activities: Wildlife watching, botanizing.

Precautions: Be careful to follow quarantine procedures to avoid the accidental introduction of animal pests (especially rodents).

Millions of sea birds, thousands of marine mammals and some of the world's southernmost forests are found on the windswept, remote Subantarctic Islands that lie 200 to 820 kilometres (124 to 500 miles) southeast of New Zealand. These five island groups, the Snares, Bounty, Auckland, Campbell and Antipodes, comprise 800 islands. They are New Zealand's most remote protected natural areas and, as a unique nature reserve, the islands enjoy the highest level of protection available under New Zealand legislation. They have been accorded World Heritage Status for their natural values and have also been designated a world centre of floristic diversity by the World Conservation Union.

These are true oceanic islands. Geological isolation over a long period has resulted in the evolution of distinctive plants, birds, seals and invertebrate animals, with numerous rare or endemic elements.

No people live on the bleak Subantarctic Islands. The only visitors are conservation scientists and tourists from natural heritage cruises. Yet life is in abundance. It manifests itself in teeming populations of penguins, petrels, shearwaters, shags and albatrosses, and crowded breeding grounds of seals and Sea Lions.

The islands support such huge populations because of the high productivity of the surrounding seas; this region of the Southern Ocean is a nutrient-rich cocktail

of currents. And because there is nothing else in this vast ocean but these scattered pockets of land, they are the only places on which sea birds and seals can breed.

Two of the island groups, Snares and Bounty, are remnants of an ancient land mass and built of hard granite and metamorphic rock. The remaining three are volcanic islands, as evidenced by their landforms of old craters, lava cliffs and rock stacks. The climate is exceptionally bleak. Westerly gales are constant and rain falls almost daily. The islands lie within the Roaring Forties and Furious Fifties – windswept latitudes which were crossed regularly throughout the 1800s by mariners on sailing ships plying the great circle route from Australia to Britain.

The Impact of Humans

These seamen brought brief but significant human impact. First there was the sealing era, when sealers ruthlessly exploited stocks of New Zealand Fur Seals (kekeno) and New Zealand Sea Lions (rāpoka). Seal populations have since recovered, and these marine mammals now enjoy full protection.

An era of shipwrecks followed, marked by incredible stories of survivors' hardship and heartbreak. After several shipwrecks, the New Zealand government established castaway provisions on the Auckland and Antipodes groups, which included the release of rabbits and goats. A later but brief farming era on Auckland Island saw sheep and cattle added to the introduced animal population. In recent years the removal of these animals, which seriously affected the islands' natural ecosystems, has been a priority for conservation staff.

Top left: A Salvin's Mollymawk chick perches on its nest, composed of mud and feathers.

Several islands in the five groups which remained unaffected rate among the last substantial areas in the world to be unmodified by humans or introduced animals.

Sea Bird Communities

The Subantarctic Islands support the most diverse sea bird community in the Southern Ocean. More than 120 species have been recorded here, including 40 which breed on the islands, representing 11 per cent of all sea bird species in the world.

Ten of the world's 24 albatross species breed here, including five endemic species. Campbell Island is the main breeding ground for the Southern Royal Albatross, the world's largest sea bird, and for the Campbell Island Mollymawk, also endemic. In total, six species of albatross breed on Campbell Island. The other endemic albatrosses are the slightly smaller Gibson's Albatross, whose breeding range is limited to the Auckland Islands, the Antipodean Albatross, which breeds mainly in the Antipodes, and the White-capped Mollymawk.

Crowded penguin colonies are a feature of the islands, in places their concentrated mass kills off groves of trees and tussocks, which recover as the colonies move on. Two of the four species present are endemic to the islands. On the Snares group, an estimated 20,000 endemic Snares Crested Penguin (pokotiwha) pairs breed in over 100 colonies. The Antipodes and Bounty islands are the main breeding grounds for some 5700 pairs of the endemic erect Crested Penguin and the Campbell Islands are the main breeding ground for one of the world's rarest penguins, Yellow-eyed Penguin (hoiho). The latter has been subject to a vociferous conservation campaign focusing on its mainland habitats of Otago Peninsula and the Catlins coast.

Three endemic cormorant species which nest on cliff-edge colonies include the world's rarest cormorant, the Bounty Island Shag. A population of about 500 lives on the Bounty Islands, which are reputed to be among the more visually dramatic examples of the subantarctic wildlife 'cities'. The small islands have no vegetation; they are covered instead by hundreds of shags, penguins, mollymawks, Cape Pigeons and an estimated 20,000 seals, all competing for space.

However, for sheer volumes of birds, the Snares are the most outstanding. These islands support nearly three million pairs of Sooty Shearwaters (tītī), up to 100,000 pairs of diving petrels and 20,000 Snares Crested Penguins. Visitors to the Snares talk of black

Left: A Yellow-eyed Penguin seeks refuge on one of the Campbell Island penguin colonies.

Below: The bleak landscape of the Antipodes Islands. Covered in grasslands and tussocks, the area is a popular breeding ground for thousands of sea birds.

clouds of these birds filling the skies at dusk as they return from their offshore feeding grounds.

The list of rare and endemic species continues with the teal, snipe, parakeet, rail, pipit, dotterel and other land birds living on the five island groups. Just 25 pairs of the flightless Campbell Island Teal — one of the world's most endangered ducks — survive on tiny, 20-hectare (49 acres) Dent Island. As recently as 1997, a previously unknown species of snipe was discovered on a tiny island of the Campbell group.

Marine Mammal Sanctuary

Nearly 200 years after being hunted almost to extinction, the subantarctic populations of New Zealand Fur Seals and New Zealand Sea Lions have recovered well. Leopard Seals and Southern Elephant Seals (ihupuku) also breed here.

New Zealand Sea Lions — reportedly the rarest of the world's five sea lion species — breed almost solely on the Auckland Islands. The vulnerability of this small population (numbering an estimated 14,000) and the deaths of up to 100 sea lions each year by drowning in the nets of foreign squid trawlers, led in 1993 to the establishment

of the Auckland Island Marine Mammal Sanctuary. All commercial fishing is now prohibited within 12 nautical miles (22 kilometres) of the island group.

The Southern Ocean Whale Sanctuary, which was established in 1994 by the International Whaling Commission and covers a vast 11,000-square-kilometre (4000 square miles) expanse of ocean, also provides protection for another marine mammal, the Southern Right Whale (tohorā). As with the seals, this whale species is starting to recover from severe hunting pressure in the 1800s. The Subantarctic Islands are on the migratory path of several other species of these magnificent mammals, including Sei, Fin, Blue and Sperm (parāora) Whales and Orca.

Mega Herbs and Rata Forests

Vividly coloured gardens of 'mega' herbs are a feature of the flora of the Subantarctic Islands. While the alpine flowers of the South Island mountains delight with their delicate, pale colours, the large leaves and vibrant shades of these more southern herbs are a dramatic contrast. Colours range from vivid blue in the forget-me-nots, bright purple and pink in gentians and mauve in the carrot relatives. The plants' large foliage is a likely adaptation to the cloudy, moist and cool conditions.

A number of plant species reach the limit of their ecological tolerance in the subantarctic region. The southernmost forests in the southwest Pacific Ocean, dominated by dwarf forests of Southern rātā, grow on the Auckland Islands. The Tree Daisy (*Olearia lyalli*), dominates the forest of the Snares, while giant tussock grasses, herbs and stunted woody shrubs cover much of Campbell and the Antipodes.

Below: The higher alpine areas of Campbell Island, the southernmost subantarctic island, are dominated by meadows of Bulbinella Rossi, a member of the lily family.

SUMMARY OF CONSERVATION AREAS

Eight million hectares (almost 20 million acres), one-third of all New Zealand, is protected as conservation land and managed by the Department of Conservation. There are 13 national parks, 20 forest or conservation parks and about 3500 reserves which are protected for their natural, scenic, recreational, historic, scientific or wildlife qualities. Another 1.1 million hectares (2.2 million acres) are protected in one marine park and 13 marine reserves.

Regional councils in New Zealand's major cities also manage parks for conservation and recreation purposes.

Major conservation areas:

Abel Tasman National Park (22,530 hectares/55,672 acres). Small coastal park. Golden beaches, estuaries. Popular sea kayaking and coastal walking. Forested interior with marble karst landscapes. Adjacent Tonga Island Marine Reserve.

Aoraki/Mount Cook National Park (70,728 hectares/174,769 acres). New Zealand's highest mountain and longest glacier. Focus for mountaineering, glacier skiing, walks and scenic flights. World Heritage Area.

Aorangi Forest Park (19,373 hectares/47,871 acres). Forested ranges on the North Island's south coast.

Arthur's Pass National Park (114,394 hectares/282,667 acres). Glaciated mountains, contrasting forest types. Arthur's Pass historic highway and railway provides easy access to subalpine regions.

Bay of Islands (reserves over an area of 1000 square kilometres/386 square miles). Islands, tidal inlets, mangroves, coastal forests. Rich marine life. History and water-based recreation.

Cape Kidnappers Nature Reserve (15 hectares/37 acres). Largest mainland colony of Australasian Gannets, spectacular geological formations.

Catlins Forest Park (58,131 hectares/143,642 acres). Lowland podocarp forest growing on coastal dunelands. Waterfalls. Adjoining spectacular coastline and marine mammal habitats.

Chatham Islands. Remote group of islands 850 kilometres (528 miles) east of New Zealand. High wildlife values – habitat for some of the world's rarest birds: Black Robin, Magenta Petrel and Chatham Islands Pigeon. Significant endemism of flora and fauna, due to the islands' remoteness and long period of geographical isolation.

Coromandel Forest Park (74,961 hectares/185,230 acres). Spectacular old volcanic mountain ranges with kauri forest. Adjacent to farm parks, recreation reserves, Mount Moehau Ecological Area and Te Whanganui a Hei Marine Reserve.

Craigieburn Forest Park (44,000 hectares/108,724 acres). Eastern boundary of Arthur's Pass National Park. Mountains, beech forest, ski fields.

Farewell Spit Nature Reserve (11,423 hectares/28,226 acres). Huge sandspit at the northwestern tip of the South Island. Outstanding habitat for migratory wading birds. Adjacent to Puponga Farm Park (470 hectares/ 1161 acres).

Fiordland National Park (1,257,000 hectares/3,106,047 acres). New Zealand's largest national park, in southwestern corner of the South Island. A huge wilderness of glaciated fiords, lakes, mountains and river valleys. Diverse forests, island wildlife sanctuaries, two marine reserves, huge diversity of wildlife habitats. World Heritage Area.

Hanmer Forest Park (16,852 hectares/41,641 acres). Native and exotic forests by thermal springs, just north of Christchurch.

Hauraki Gulf Marine Park (encompasses four marine reserves and over 50 islands, including wildlife sanctuaries and nature reserves). Outstanding wildlife habitats, marine ecosystems, water-based and island-based recreation and history.

Kahurangi National Park (451,494 hectares/1,115,642 acres). Second largest national park in New Zealand, vast wilderness of geological and biological diversity. Mountains, marble karst landscape, cave systems, forests, river valleys, remote coastline.

Kaimai-Mamaku Forest Park (37,141 hectares/91,775 acres). Forested ranges between Waikato and Bay of Plenty.

Kaimanawa Forest Park (76,700 hectares/189,526 acres). Mountains, beech forests, tussock valleys in the central North Island.

Kapiti Island Nature Reserve (1960 hectares/4843 acres). Premier island wildlife refuge near Wellington. Free of predators and home to many rare native birds.

Karori Wildlife Sanctuary (250 hectares/618 acres). Ground-breaking private conservation project within Wellington City. Regenerating forest and a sanctuary for endangered native species, encircled by a fence that prevents predators from entering.

Kaweka Forest Park (67,145 hectares/165,915 acres). Mountains, beech forests, big rivers. Adjoining Kaimanawa Forest Park.

Kermadec Islands Nature Reserve (3279 hectares/8100 acres). Remote volcanic islands 1000 kilometres (620 miles) northeast of New Zealand. Great variety of endemic flora and fauna. Surrounded by Kermadec Islands Marine Reserve; large (by world standards) and regarded as an outstanding marine habitat.

Lake Sumner Forest Park (73,968 hectares/182,775 acres). Mountains, rivers, lakes and low alpine tramping passes across the South Island main divide.

Lewis Pass National Reserve (13,845 hectares/34,211 acres). Hot springs, mountains, rivers, beech forests, subalpine tussock fields.

Marlborough Sounds (protected areas total 50,000 hectares/ 123,550 acres). A vast area of waterways, island nature reserves, scenic reserves and a marine reserve at the northern tip of the South Island.

Mount Aspiring National Park (355,518 hectares/878,485 acres). Wilderness of mountains, glaciers, snowfields, river valleys and beech forests. Focal point is horn-shaped Mount Aspiring. World Heritage Area.

Mount Bruce National Wildlife Centre. A centre for research, education and captive breeding programmes of endangered native wildlife. Opportunity to see some of New Zealand's most threatened wildlife.

Mount Richmond Forest Park (184,000 hectares/454,664 acres). Mountain ranges, beech forest, rivers, geological and botanical interest.

Nelson Lakes National Park (101,753 hectares/251,432 acres). Alpine park with beech forests, glacial lakes, river valleys and alpine tops.

Northland Forest Park (several reserves totalling 80,000 hectares/ 197,680 acres). Subtropical rainforest dominated by kauri, New Zealand's largest trees.

Otago Goldfields Park (several small reserves in Central Otago). Historic goldmining sites in tussock valleys and rocky tors.

Otago Peninsula. Several reserves and wildlife habitats by Dunedin City. Main features are Northern Royal Albatross, rare Yellow-eyed Penguins and spectacular seascapes.

Paparoa National Park (30,560 hectares/755,137 acres). West coast park with dramatic karst landscapes featuring Pancake Rocks at Punakaiki, cave systems and river canyons. Coastal rainforest and mountain backdrop (Paparoa Ranges).

Pirongia Forest Park (16,738 hectares/41,360 acres). Based on three extinct volcanoes of Mount Pirongia, 30 kilometres/19 miles from Hamilton City. Heavily forested.

Poor Knights Islands Nature Reserve (267 hectares/660 acres) and Marine Reserve (extends for 800 metres/half a mile around islands). Volcanic islands off east coast of the North Island. Millions of seabirds. Endemic plants. World-class diving.

Pureora Forest Park (80,344 hectares/198,530 acres). Ranges west of Lake Taupo with magnificent podocarp forest.

Raukumara Forest Park (115,100 hectares/284,412 acres). Remote and rugged forest-covered ranges on the North Island's east coast. Motu River (wilderness rafting) and Mount Hikurangi (first place to see the sun).

Rimutaka Forest Park (19,670 hectares/48,605 acres). Small forested park, 45 kilometres/28 miles from Wellington City.

Ruahine Forest Park (94,000 hectares/232,274 acres). Based on Ruahine and subsidiary ranges. Podocarp, beech and leatherwood forests, tussock tops.

Stewart Island/Rakiura (proposed national park of 163,000 hectares/ 402,773 acres). One of largest areas of natural wilderness in New Zealand. Coastal rainforests, wetlands, sand dunes, granite mountains and tundra-like alpine vegetation. Nearby islands provide refuges for some of New Zealand's rarest birds, such as the kākāpō.

Subantarctic Islands Five island groups in New Zealand's subantarctic territory classified as Nature Reserves (total area of 75,464 hectares/ 186,472 acres). A huge diversity and abundance of seabirds and marine mammals. A World Conservation Union 'world centre' of floristic diversity and a World Heritage Site.

Taranaki-Egmont National Park (33,534 hectares/82,863 acres). Based around the volcanic cone of Mount Taranaki. Lowland forests to alpine plants.

Tararua Forest Park (116,627 hectares/288,185 acres). Based on Tararua Ranges, close to Wellington City. Mountains, forests, river gorges.

Te Paki Reserves (several scientific, recreation and island nature reserves and farm park totalling 23,000 hectares/56 833 acres). Dunelands at the northernmost end of the North Island.

Te Urewera National Park (217,000 hectares/536,207 acres). Largest national park in the North Island. Vast expanse of forest-covered ranges, lakes and river valleys.

Tongariro National Park (79,596 hectares/196,682 acres). Alpine park based around three active volcanoes. Snowfields, lakes, forests. World Heritage Area.

Victoria Forest Park (209,237 hectares/517,025 acres). Largest forest park in New Zealand. Mountains, beech forests, Lake Christabel and goldmining history.

Westhaven (Te Tai Tapu) Marine Reserve (536 hectares/1324 acres) and adjoining Westhaven (Whanganui Inlet) Wildlife Management Reserve (2112 ha/5219 acres). One of the largest and least modified estuaries in New Zealand, fringed with rainforest. Outstanding marine and wildlife habitat.

Westland/Tai Poutini National Park (117,547 hectares/290,458 acres). New Zealand's highest mountains and the world's only glaciers in a temperate region. Unbroken natural wilderness extending from mountaintops to the sea. Snowfields, rainforest, lakes and lagoons. World Heritage Area.

Whanganui National Park (74,231 hectares/183,424 acres). Based around the Whanganui River, a major scenic and historic waterway. Large tract of lowland forest.

Whirinaki Forest Park (60,900 hectares/150,483 acres). South of Rotorua. Magnificent podocarp forests.

GLOSSARY

alluvial – adjective describing materials deposited from rivers.

Alpine Fault – geological faultline along the South Island main divide.

Aotearoa – Māori name for New Zealand.

beech forest – Nothofagus (southern beech) covers over half the area of New Zealand's native forests. There are four New Zealand species: red, hard, black and silver beech and a sub species, mountain beech.

Blue Duck – rare species of duck found only in remote, swift-flowing mountain rivers and one of only four species of torrent duck in the world. It has two Māori names – whio (in the North Island and northern part of the South Island) and kowhiowhio (in the rest of the South Island).

braided river – river with channels that branch, and then rejoin, like the strands of a braid.

broadleaf – plants or shrubs with broad leaves, as distinctive from smaller leaves of beech and podocarp species.

DOC – Department of Conservation, the government department which manages conservation land.

endemic – plants or animals unique to a particular region, or country.

epiphyte – a plant which lives on another plant or tree.

exotic – plant or animal introduced from another country.

fishing licence – required to fish for introduced trout in any New Zealand waterway. Available in most sports shops and some visitor centres. Fish and Game licences cover all New Zealand except for Taupo, where a Taupo Fisheries Management Area licence is required.

Gondwana – ancient supercontinent that existed in the Southern Hemisphere in Triassic-Jurassic geological time.

granite – hard igneous rock, rich in quartz, feldspars and micas.

greywacke – grey-coloured, hardened sedimentary rock.

hunting permit – required for hunting of introduced animals (deer, goats, pigs, chamois, thar). Available from DOC offices.

introduced plant or animal – plant or animal introduced from another country, not native to New Zealand (and often with disastrous results to the balance of nature).

iwi – Maori tribal group.

kākāriki – Maori name for small parrots, also the Maori word for green.

kererū/kūpapa – Maori name for New Zealand pigeon. Kūpapa is the name used in northern New Zealand.

Kiwi – New Zealand's national symbol and one of the country's most endangered species, this flightless bird is a member of the ratite family.